FORUM (NON) CONVENIENS IN ENGLAND

The *forum (non) conveniens* doctrine provides the basis for the discretionary exercise of jurisdiction by English courts in private international law disputes. London's pre-eminence as a centre for international commercial litigation has led to the frequent deployment of this doctrine in proceedings where parties disagree over where the case should be heard. The doctrine's significance is not limited to England but extends to many Commonwealth jurisdictions which have embraced it. This is the first book-length study devoted entirely to examining the *forum (non) conveniens* doctrine's past, present, and future from the perspective of the law in England. By offering a meticulous and critical analysis of relevant historical and contemporary sources in England and elsewhere, it seeks to fill gaps in relevant knowledge of the English *forum (non) conveniens* doctrine, and to challenge certain views concerning its operation that have come to be regarded as representing the orthodoxy. In this respect, the book attempts to refine our understanding of the doctrine's historical development, evaluate its application in the years following its formal recognition in England, and examine the case for revising it, given the changing nature of international commercial litigation in recent decades. The book's ultimate objective is to act as an authoritative and a comprehensive reference point for those with an interest in the *forum (non) conveniens* doctrine, more specifically, and cross-border private litigation, more generally.

Volume 21 in the series Studies in Private International Law

Studies in Private International Law

Recent titles in the series

Forum (Non) Conveniens in England

Past, Present, and Future

Ardavan Arzandeh

·HART·

OXFORD · LONDON · NEW YORK · NEW DELHI · SYDNEY

HART PUBLISHING

Bloomsbury Publishing Plc

Kemp House, Chawley Park, Cumnor Hill, Oxford, OX2 9PH, UK

HART PUBLISHING, the Hart/Stag logo, BLOOMSBURY and the Diana logo are
trademarks of Bloomsbury Publishing Plc

First published in Great Britain 2019

First published in hardback, 2019
Paperback edition, 2020

A catalogue record for this book is available from the British Library.

Library of Congress Cataloging-in-Publication Data

Names: Arzandeh, Ardavan.

Title: Forum (non) conveniens in England : past, present, and future / Ardavan Arzandeh.

Description: Oxford, UK ; Portland, Oregon : Hart, an imprint of Bloomsbury, 2019. | Includes
bibliographical references and index.

Identifiers: LCCN 2018030887 | ISBN 9781782256403 (hardback)

Subjects: LCSH: Forum non conveniens—England.

Classification: LCC KD681.J87 A79 2018 | DDC 346.42—dc23

LC record available at https://lccn.loc.gov/2018030887

ISBN: HB: 978-1-78225-640-3
PB: 978-1-50994-502-3
ePDF: 978-1-50992-577-3
ePub: 978-1-50992-578-0

Typeset by Compuscript Ltd, Shannon

SERIES EDITOR'S PREFACE

This is the first monograph devoted to *forum non conveniens* in England. It does not attempt to set out in detail the English case law on this plea. Instead it endeavours to give the reader an understanding of how the modern plea established by the House of Lords in *Spiliada* in 1986 came about in England and Wales, how it has influenced the development of the law in Scotland and in some other Commonwealth countries and to make suggestions for how the judges could reform the second limb of the plea concerning justice.

The writer skilfully uses a modern legal historical approach to analyse the non-linear development of the English law on what are the circumstances in which a court which has jurisdiction (either as of right or because service out is provided for by a head of jurisdiction) can exercise a discretion to decline or not take jurisdiction from the 1880's through to *Spiliada*. He carefully shows the influence of Scots law on this development both in ways that are well understood (eg from Lord Goff's speech in *Spiliada*) and much less well understood (eg in the moderate English case law of the early part of the twentieth century). The writer also shows how this branch of English law has developed by a mixture of comparative law borrowing from Scotland and creative common law development of the earlier English case law by some great judges (notably Lords Reid, Wilberforce, Diplock and Goff). Furthermore Dr Ardavan Arzandeh makes a convincing case that the judicial creativity was helped by the published work of some of the leading academic writers in the field (notably Adrian Briggs, Rhona Schuz and David McClean).

Dr Arzandeh's proposals for law reform are underpinned by a blend of theoretical and pragmatic justifications. He highlights several English cases in which the second limb of *Spiliada* was the main focus. He notes problems with the length and cost of those proceedings and that at least some of the rulings might be regarded as examples of judicial chauvinism. In order to ensure that *forum non conveniens* will work more efficiently and to reduce the risk of judicial chauvinism, Dr Arzandeh advocates a human rights solution for the second limb of the *Spiliada* approach to *forum non conveniens*.

As a series editor it is good to be able to note another contribution mixing pragmatism with human rights in order to produce private international law rules that work efficiently and fairly (see the earlier contribution of Lara Walker, *Maintenance and Child Support in Private International Law*). As a Scots private international lawyer it is interesting to see that Lord Goff's main innovation in *Spiliada*, compared to the Scottish doctrine of *forum non conveniens* (to separate out the second limb on "justice" from the first limb on "appropriateness" to create a two stage test rather than a single test), may not be the most successful part of his judgment. Both Scotland and England might benefit from carefully considering Dr Arzandeh's interesting proposal to restrict the second limb to situations where sending the case away from England or Scotland would be a violation of Article 6 of the ECHR (as defined in expulsion cases).

Paul Beaumont (University of Aberdeen)

PREFACE

This book examines the *forum (non) conveniens* doctrine's past, present, and future from the perspective of the law in England. The doctrine provides the basis for the discretionary exercise of jurisdiction by English courts in private international law disputes. London's attractiveness as a centre for the litigation of international commercial disputes means that the doctrine has been routinely in contention before its courts, particularly where parties disagree over the venue in which the case should be heard. These occasions arise both in cases where courts are asked to stay the proceedings brought before them as of right (based on the *forum non conveniens* doctrine), and in cases in which permission is sought to serve claim forms on defendants outside England (through the operation of the *forum conveniens* doctrine).

The book's chief objective is to refine our understanding of the *forum (non) conveniens* doctrine's historical development, evaluate its application in the years following its formal recognition in England, and assess the case for revising it, given the changing nature of international commercial litigation in recent decades. Ultimately, the book sets out to provide an authoritative and comprehensive reference point for those with an interest in the *forum (non) conveniens* doctrine, in particular, and cross-border private litigation, in general.

I would like to express my gratitude to those whose input has made it possible for me to write this book. I am especially grateful to Professor Jonathan Hill, who first taught me conflict of laws as a postgraduate student (in 2006), and, subsequently, supervised my doctorate (2007–2011) at the University of Bristol. I would not have been able to produce this book without having had the benefit of his insightful and considered supervision during those years. I am also grateful to Professor Harry McVea, for very kindly taking the time to read and comment on the draft manuscript. His encouragement, good humour, and wisdom were instrumental in helping me pull through the marathon that writing a book is.

I would like to thank the publishers and editors of the *Journal of Private International Law* who have given me permission to reproduce an updated version of an earlier journal article, entitled 'Should the *Spiliada* test be revised' (2014) 10 *Journal of Private International Law* 89 (available online at https://doi.org/10.5235/17441048.10.1.89), in Chapter 5 of this book. I am also grateful to Professor Paul Beaumont, the General Editor of Hart Publishing's *Studies in Private International Law* for including this book in this series. Finally, thanks are owed to Sinead Moloney and her team at Hart Publishing for all their efforts in making it possible to bring this work to completion.

On a personal level, I am grateful to my family – my parents, sister, and wife – for their love, encouragement, and patience. It is to them that this book is dedicated.

As far as possible, I have tried to state the law as on 1 April 2018.

Ardavan Arzandeh
April 2018

CONTENTS

TABLE OF CASES

US Courts

TABLE OF LEGISLATION

International

United Kingdom

A. Statutes

B. Statutory Instruments and Rules

1

Introduction

I. The English *Forum (Non) Conveniens* Doctrine[1]

More than three decades ago, the English House of Lords handed down its landmark ruling in *Spiliada Maritime Corporation v Cansulex Ltd*.[2] For two main reasons, the decision in *Spiliada* can be legitimately regarded as one of the most important judicial pronouncements in English conflict of laws in the twentieth century.

In the first place, it was in Lord Goff of Chieveley's influential speech in *Spiliada* that the doctrine of *forum non conveniens* was finally recognised as the basis for granting stays of proceedings brought during the defendant's presence in England.[3] The journey towards this recognition had begun in earnest in 1973 in *The Atlantic Star*.[4] In that case, the House of Lords was invited to discard the 'vexatious-and-oppressive' test,[5] which provided the basis for the English courts' practice of discretionary staying of proceedings at that time, and, in its place, adopt the Scottish doctrine of *forum non conveniens*. The court declined that invitation, though it was persuaded to employ a 'liberal' reading of the vexatious-and-oppressive test.[6] Some four years later, in *MacShannon v Rockware Glass Ltd*,[7] the House of Lords took a more decisive step in the direction of embracing the doctrine when it replaced the liberalised vexatious-and-oppressive test with a new formulation. The transformation in the English courts' approach in staying of as-of-right proceedings in England was completed in *Spiliada* in 1986, when the House of Lords formally endorsed *forum non conveniens*, and replaced

---

[1] In this book, the label *forum (non) conveniens* is employed where the discussion is in relation to the English courts' discretionary power to assert or relinquish jurisdiction in both service-out and stay cases. Where the discussion relates only to the courts' discretion to serve proceedings on defendants outside England, the phrase *forum conveniens* is used. In instances where the focus is on the courts' power to give up their (otherwise) soundly founded jurisdiction, following the defendant's stay application, the label *forum non conveniens* is deployed.

[2] *Spiliada Maritime Corporation v Cansulex Ltd* [1987] AC 460 (HL).

[3] Claims in which the basis for the English court's jurisdiction is the defendant's presence in the forum when the claim form is served are commonly referred to as 'as-of-right proceedings'.

[4] *The Atlantic Star* [1974] AC 436 (HL).

[5] This test had been outlined in Scott LJ's oft-quoted judgment in *St Pierre v South American Stones (Gath & Chaves) Ltd* [1936] 1 KB 382 (CA) 398.

[6] *The Atlantic Star* (n 4) 454 (Lord Reid).

[7] *MacShannon v Rockware Glass Ltd* [1978] AC 795 (HL).

the formulation in *MacShannon* with (what is now referred to as) the 'more-appropriate-forum' test as the basis for applying the doctrine.[8]

Under this test, and in a given case, an English court is afforded a discretion to relinquish its (otherwise) properly founded jurisdiction where, as Lord Goff put it, there is 'some other available forum, having competent jurisdiction, which is the appropriate forum for the trial of the action, ie in which the case may be tried more suitably for the interests of all the parties and the ends of justice.[9] The adoption of the more-appropriate-forum test, in turn, signified the English courts' change of tack away from a claimant-friendly approach, under the vexatious-and-oppressive test, and towards one which sought to be more even-handed in its treatment of the litigants' competing interests in seeking to have their dispute litigated in England (or an alternative foreign forum).

Second, the *Spiliada* ruling made it plain that the more-appropriate-forum test applied to both the practice of discretionary staying of actions brought as of right under the *forum non conveniens* doctrine, *and* the related concept of permission to serve proceedings on defendants outside of England, based on its sister doctrine of *forum conveniens*. In this respect, the House of Lords put an end to the confusion which had been generated following Lord Wilberforce's remarks in *Amin Rasheed Shipping Corpn v Kuwait Insurance Co* – namely, that cases concerning stays of as-of-right proceedings were of no assistance in the court's decision to allow service of proceedings on a foreign-based defendant.[10] As a result, the *Spiliada* doctrine has become the modern-day *locus classicus* on the English courts' practice of discretionary exercise of jurisdiction in both stay-of-proceedings and service-out cases.

Although, formally, the *Spiliada* doctrine has been a part of the national rules of jurisdiction in England for a relatively short period of time, it has gained much prominence in the courts' approach to the question of exercising jurisdiction over private-international-law disputes. This development has much to do with London's pre-eminence as a centre for cross-border commercial litigation. A considerable proportion of conflict-of-laws disputes in England over the past three decades or so relates to instances in which, as Lord Templeman described in *Spiliada*, the parties come before the courts in England 'in order to determine where they shall litigate.[11] In the context of these cases, it is very common for defendants in as-of-right proceedings, or claimants, in service-out cases, to seek to rely on the *Spiliada* test. Accordingly, the *forum (non) conveniens* doctrine has become deeply imbedded in the English courts' approach to exercise of jurisdiction in both stay and service-out cases.

---

[8] At the time when the *Spiliada* ruling was handed down, the 'natural forum' test was much more in vogue. Throughout the discussion in this book, terms such as 'the *Spiliada* doctrine' or 'the *Spiliada* test' are used interchangeably to refer to the more-appropriate-forum test, as outlined in the *Spiliada* case.

[9] *Spiliada* (n 2) 476.

[10] *Amin Rasheed Shipping Corpn v Kuwait Insurance Co* [1984] AC 50 (HL) 72.

[11] *Spiliada* (n 2) 464.

The formal acknowledgement of the *forum non conveniens* doctrine in *Spiliada*, with the articulation of the more-appropriate-forum test as the premise for its operation, was not just influential in recasting the English courts' practice of discretionary (non-)exercise of jurisdiction. To varying degrees, it was also instrumental in reshaping the application of equivalent principles across many Commonwealth jurisdictions. For instance, the *Spiliada* doctrine has displaced its counterpart in Scotland, a country which has been widely credited as having 'invented' *forum non conveniens*.[12] What is more, the English doctrine has been deployed (with English cases being frequently consulted and drawn upon) in major and growing centres of international commercial litigation in Singapore and Hong Kong. Even the doctrinal approaches to (non-)exercise of jurisdiction in those Commonwealth jurisdictions that have chosen not to embrace the *Spiliada* doctrine – most notably, Australia and Canada – nevertheless exhibit clear signs of *Spiliada's* influence on them.

At the same time, the path for the *Spiliada* doctrine's development after its adoption in England has been far from smooth. This state of affairs has come about largely as a result of the Europeanisation of English private international law. Even long before *forum non conveniens* was formally recognised in England, there had been considerable doubts about whether the doctrine would be compatible with the jurisdiction rules within the Brussels regime.[13] As noted by the editors of *Anton's Private International Law*, the principal treatise on private international law in Scotland,

> [i]n the negotiations leading to the 1978 Accession Convention, the Working Party, at the request of the UK and Irish Delegations, considered the possible introduction of the doctrine of forum non conveniens into the Brussels Convention, but concluded that the doctrine was inconsistent with the convention's underlying philosophy and rejected the request.[14]

Indeed, following the introduction of the jurisdiction rules set out within the Brussels regime, which came about after the entry into force, in January 1987, of the relevant provisions under the Civil Jurisdiction and Judgments Act 1982 ('CJJA'), the *forum non conveniens* doctrine's scope of operation was rendered much more circumscribed. By virtue of CJJA, s 49, English courts are only able

---

[12] PR Beaumont and PE McEleavy, *Anton's Private International Law* 3rd edn (Edinburgh, W Green, 2011) para 8.405.

[13] The term 'Brussels regime' is used to refer to: Regulation (EU) No 1215/2012 of the European Parliament and of the Council of 12 December 2012 on jurisdiction and the recognition and enforcement of judgments in civil and commercial matters (recast) [2012] OJ L 351/1 (the 'Brussels Ia Regulation'); its earlier incarnations – namely, Regulation (EC) No 44/2001 on jurisdiction and the recognition and enforcement of judgments in civil and commercial matters [2001] OJ L 12/1 (the 'Brussels I Regulation'); the Brussels Convention on Jurisdiction and Enforcement of Judgments in Civil and Commercial Matters 1968 (the 'Brussels Convention'); and the Convention on jurisdiction and the recognition and enforcement of judgments in civil and commercial matters [2007] OJ L 339/3 (the 'Lugano II Convention').

[14] *Anton's Private International Law* (n 12) para 8.400 (citation omitted).

to stay their proceedings under the doctrine if it is 'not inconsistent' with the Brussels regime.

Except for a short period between 1987 and 1991,[15] English courts took the stance that it was entirely consistent with the Brussels regime for them to apply the *forum non conveniens* doctrine and give up their Brussels-based jurisdiction in favour of a more appropriate forum in a non-Member State.[16] However, the decision of the Court of Justice of the European Union in *Owusu v Jackson*,[17] in 2005, made it clear that Brussels-rooted jurisdiction rules were mandatory in nature, and that the *Spiliada* doctrine could not be resorted to as the basis for relinquishing this jurisdiction in favour of a more appropriate foreign forum. As a consequence, the scope for the operation of the *forum non conveniens* doctrine in England was limited to those cases falling within (what are now) Brussels Ia Regulation, Art 6(1)[18] and Lugano II Convention, Art 4(1),[19] or, indeed, altogether outside the scope of the Brussels regime.[20]

More importantly, existential doubts about the *forum (non) conveniens* doctrine – even in its more curtailed, post-*Owusu* form – were raised during the process of revising the Brussels I Regulation. In its report for the review of Brussels I, published in December 2010,[21] the European Commission had proposed for (what was then) Brussels I Regulation, Art 4 – which, subject to certain provisions within the Regulation, allowed courts of Member States to apply their national jurisdiction rules to disputes in cases where the defendant is not domiciled in a Member State – to be erased. The adoption of this proposal would have led to national jurisdiction rules of the Member States to be discarded and replaced by the jurisdictional provisions under the Brussels regime. This proposal was ultimately abandoned, with Brussels I Regulation, Art 4 and its contents, which are now set out under Brussels Ia Regulation, Art 6, surviving and, in turn, enabling Member State courts, where appropriate, to resort to their national rules.

From the brink of being consigned to history, therefore, the *Spiliada* doctrine has lived on to fight another day and remains significant in the context of the

---

[15] See, eg, PM North and JJ Fawcett, *Cheshire & North's Private International Law* 11th edn (London, Butterworths, 1987) 327. This view was upheld in two first-instance decisions: *S&W Berisford plc v New Hampshire Insurance Co Ltd* [1990] 2 QB 631 and *Arkwright Mutual Insurance Co v Bryanston Insurance Co Ltd* [1990] 2 QB 649.

[16] See, in particular, the Court of Appeal's decision in *Re Harrods (Buenos Aires) Ltd (No 2)* [1992] Ch 72 (CA).

[17] Case 281/02 *Owusu v Jackson* [2005] ECR I-1383, [2005] QB 801.

[18] Under Art 6(1): 'If the defendant is not domiciled in a Member State, the jurisdiction of the courts of each Member State shall, subject to Article 18(1), Article 21(2) and Articles 24 and 25 [of the Brussels Ia Regulation], be determined by the law of that Member State.

[19] According to Art 4(1): 'If the defendant is not domiciled in a State bound by this Convention, the jurisdiction of the courts of each State bound by this Convention shall, subject to the provisions of Articles 22 and 23 [of the Lugano II Convention], be determined by the law of that State.'

[20] See, eg, *Cheshire & North's Private International Law* (n 15) 327.

[21] The document's full title is 'Proposal for a Regulation of the European Parliament and of the Council on jurisdiction and the recognition and enforcement of judgments in civil and commercial matters', Brussels, COM (2010) 748 final.

allocation of jurisdiction in England. In fact, the English *forum (non) conveniens* doctrine may well be about to witness an upturn in fortunes. The UK voters' decision in the referendum in June 2016 to leave the European Union, and the triggering of the Treaty on European Union, Art 50 (introduced by the Lisbon Treaty[22]) which marked the formal start to that process, often referred to as 'Brexit', are likely to bring about seismic changes to the private-international-law landscape in England. Inevitably, it will take some time before the dust settles and the precise nature and format of these changes become clear. Nevertheless, it seems likely that the *Spiliada* doctrine will play a greater role in the post-Brexit English private international law.

II. The Objectives of the Book

Commensurate with its prominence, the English *forum (non) conveniens* doctrine has received much attention among scholars in the field of private international law. Over the years, numerous books, law journal articles and case notes have discussed the doctrine and its application in England. For example, the English courts' traditional approach to discretionary non-exercise of jurisdiction under the vexatious-and-oppressive test, particularly in the four decades before *The Atlantic Star*, has been much commented on in the academic literature.[23] Furthermore, there has been an even greater coverage of the developments that followed the decision in *The Atlantic Star*, leading up to the House of Lords' ruling in *Spiliada*.[24] In the same vein, various features of the English courts' post-*Spiliada* practice of discretionary (non-)exercise of jurisdiction have been afforded ample attention.[25] In short, many aspects regarding the history, and subsequent evolution of *forum (non) conveniens* in England are well documented.

Be that as it may, for at least three reasons, there is a strong case for revisiting the doctrine. First, it is argued that certain accounts concerning the English *forum (non) conveniens* doctrine's origins, which have come to be accepted as representing the orthodoxy, are, in fact, open to question. For instance,

---

[22] Treaty of Lisbon amending the Treaty on European Union and the Treaty Establishing the European Community, Lisbon, 13 December 2007, (2007/C 306/01).

[23] See, eg, AS Bell, *Forum Shopping and Venue in Transnational Litigation* (Oxford, Oxford University Press, 2002) paras 3.71–3.77 and RA Brand and SR Jablonski, *Forum Non Conveniens: History, Global Practice, and Future Under the Hague Convention on Choice of Court Agreements* (New York, Oxford University Press, 2007) 11–13.

[24] See, eg, M Pryles, 'Liberalising the Rule on Staying Actions – Towards the Doctrine of Forum Non Conveniens' (1978) 52 *Australian Law Journal* 678, and Brand & Jablonski, ibid 14–20.

[25] See, eg, A Briggs, 'Forum Non Conveniens and Unavailable Courts' (1996) 67 *British Yearbook of International Law* 587, A Briggs, 'The Availability of the Natural Forum and the Definition of the Issue' (1999) 70 *British Yearbook of International Law* 319, L Merrett, 'The Meaning of an "Available" Forum' (2004) *Cambridge Law Journal* 309, L Merrett, 'Uncertainties in the First Limb of the *Spiliada* Test' (2005) 54 *International & Comparative Law Quarterly* 211, and A Briggs, 'Forum Non Satis: *Spiliada* and an Inconvenient Truth' [2011] *Lloyd's Maritime and Commercial Law Quarterly* 329.

some of the characterisations of the operation of the practice of discretionary non-exercise of jurisdiction in England in the late nineteenth and early twentieth centuries may be doubted. In this respect, analysis of the case law from that era, especially in the early twentieth century, points to a more nuanced understanding of the vexatious-and-oppressive test than that which has been suggested in academic commentaries.

Second, there appears to be an almost universal acceptance that Lord Goff's speech in *Spiliada* should be treated as the final word on the development of *forum (non) conveniens* in England. Put differently, the prevailing view is that any additional refinement of the doctrine would be unwarranted. In this context, in *Private International Law in English Courts*, published in 2014, Professor Briggs has considered *Spiliada* as having been (and continuing to be) effective in giving 'the court an overall discretion which is capable of responding to the interests of justice in the individual case'.[26] Elsewhere, and more tellingly, in the latest edition of *Civil Jurisdiction and Judgments*, published in 2015, Professor Briggs has observed that:

> [t]he law as finally put in place by *Spiliada*, striking the balance as it now stands, is the brilliant product of true judicial creativity. As Lord Goff of Chieveley put it, the principle of *forum non conveniens* is 'one of the most civilised of legal principles'. Further comment would be impertinent.[27]

In many ways, these remarks, and those similar to them, which have been made on a number of occasions in the past,[28] capture the spirit with which the decision in *Spiliada* has been received: the law on the practice of discretionary (non-)exercise of jurisdiction in England reached its final destination following the articulation of the more-appropriate-forum test in *Spiliada*. As a result, there has been limited enquiry into whether English *forum (non) conveniens* is in need of reform. But, in fact, an assessment of the relevant cases in this area over the past three decades or so points to a number of shortcomings in the doctrine's application which cannot be remedied without revising certain aspects of the more-appropriate-forum test.

Third, as indicated earlier, the material covering different features of the English *forum (non) conveniens* doctrine is numerous and wide-ranging. Over the years, some books have sought to discuss (and link) the different features of the English doctrine's past, present, and future. Among these, at least two are notable: *Forum Shopping and Venue in Transnational Litigation*,[29] and *Forum*

---

[26] A Briggs, *Private International Law in English Courts* (Oxford, Oxford University Press, 2014) para 4.413.

[27] A Briggs, *Civil Jurisdiction and Judgments* 6th edn (Abingdon, Informa Law from Routledge, 2015) para 4.39.

[28] See, eg, A Briggs and P Rees, *Civil Jurisdiction and Judgments* 4th edn (London, Informa Law, 2005) para 4.20 and A Briggs and P Rees, *Civil Jurisdiction and Judgments* 5th edn (London, Informa Law, 2009) para 4.34.

[29] Bell (n 23).

Non Conveniens: History, Global Practice, and Future Under the Hague Convention on Choice of Court Agreements.[30]

Despite the wealth of learning in these books, their discussion of the English *forum (non) conveniens* doctrine has been mostly incidental to the main issue under consideration. For example, *Forum Shopping and Venue in Transnational Litigation* is predominantly concerned with the significance of venue in the context of cross-border disputes. Likewise, the discussion of the English doctrine in *Forum Non Conveniens: History, Global Practice, and Future Under the Hague Convention on Choice of Court Agreements* is set out in one chapter, and in outline only, in the context of a project that also examines the Hague Choice of Court Convention.[31] As a result, one is hard-pressed to find a single source that has devoted its entire attention to the examination of (and making the connection between) the doctrine's past, present, and possible future development from the perspective of the law in England, which is arguably the jurisdiction in which it is most routinely utilised in international litigation.

This book strives to address the abovementioned shortcomings. Through compiling and analysing material which hitherto has not been accessible in one source, it seeks to advance a more nuanced and coherent understanding of the *forum (non) conveniens* doctrine in England. In this respect, this is the first book-length study devoted entirely to examining the English doctrine's origins, current application, and future. To begin with, and by critically assessing the relevant historical sources, it attempts to refine our understanding of the emergence and evolution of the practice of discretionary (non-)exercise of jurisdiction in England. Then, the book sets out to take stock of the English *forum (non) conveniens* doctrine's contemporary operation. Finally, the enquiry proceeds to build on the analysis of the historical and modern-day developments of the doctrine in England by exploring the case for reforming the law in this area, with the view of rendering it even more consonant with the modern world. The book's ultimate objective is to act as an authoritative and comprehensive reference point for those with an interest in the *forum (non) conveniens* doctrine, in particular, and cross-border private litigation, in general.

III. The Structure and Main Contentions of the Book

This book comprises six chapters. After the introduction in this chapter, Chapter 2 begins the substantive discussion by identifying the place of the *forum (non) conveniens* doctrine within the English national rules of jurisdiction. The analysis seeks to highlight that the doctrine is part of a family of legal principles which English courts employ in promoting and balancing a

---

[30] Brand and Jablonski (n 23).
[31] Convention on Choice of Court Agreements, Hague, 30 June 2005.

number of 'jurisdictional values'. These values – which include 'party autonomy', 'connectedness', and the 'avoidance of parallel or related proceedings' – must be central to any court's decision making on whether to assert jurisdiction over private-international-law disputes.

Chapter 3 examines the *forum (non) conveniens* doctrine's past by outlining the background to the emergence of the modern-day practice of discretionary (non-)exercise of jurisdiction in England. Its main objective is to provide a more detailed (and nuanced) account of the historical developments which preceded the articulation of the more-appropriate-forum test in *Spiliada*. In this respect, the discussion seeks to shed light on certain aspects concerning the earlier origins of the practice of discretionary (non-)exercise of jurisdiction in England which, thus far, have received relatively little attention. At the same time, and through a close inspection of the relevant case law and associated academic commentary, Chapter 3 puts to test some of the widely held views vis-à-vis the English *forum (non) conveniens* doctrine's past. In short, the analysis attempts to map out (and make sense of) the law's evolution in this area from its embryonic form up to the House of Lords' formal recognition of *forum (non) conveniens* in *Spiliada*.

The discussion begins by identifying the first instances in which English courts relied on discretion in asserting (or relinquishing) their jurisdiction. These occasions, which for the most part gained prominence in the nineteenth century included: (i) the so-called *forum conveniens* cases concerning the English courts' discretionary power to serve proceedings on foreign-based defendants; and, (ii) the so-called stay-of-proceedings cases in which courts in England had been asked to stay the proceedings that had been brought before them as of right on the basis that they had been vexatious and oppressive. The analysis of case law and academic commentary in the chapter seeks to demonstrate that the more-appropriate-forum test is mostly English in pedigree, and traceable to the tests applied in service-out and stay cases. The discussion revisits the claim that until the House of Lords' ruling in *The Atlantic Star*, English courts had been plaintiff-centric in their application of the vexatious-and-oppressive test.[32] Based on an assessment of the relevant material, it is contended that although English courts favoured plaintiffs in their application of the vexatious-and-oppressive test in the four decades before the decision in *The Atlantic Star*, at the dawn of the twentieth century, they had actually been markedly more balanced in treating the competing interests of plaintiffs and defendants when applying the test than it has been acknowledged.

Chapter 4, then, sets out to analyse the contemporary application and scope of the English *forum (non) conveniens* doctrine. Its chief aim is to chart the evolution of the doctrine in England in the period after the House of Lords' ruling in *Spiliada*. The analysis in this chapter is conducted from three different perspectives. First, the 'doctrinal' developments in the field of discretionary (non-)exercise of jurisdiction which followed the House of Lords' decision in

---

[32] See, eg, Briggs (n 27) para 1.01.

Spiliada are considered. In this context, the question is whether English *forum (non) conveniens* is a different doctrine today than when *Spiliada* was decided in November 1986. The second perspective from which the modern-day *forum (non) conveniens* doctrine is examined relates to *Spiliada*'s influence in the development of the law in Commonwealth jurisdictions. Third, the discussion in the chapter assesses the degree to which the English *forum (non) conveniens* doctrine's scope has evolved over the past three or so decades.

It will be seen that, today, in staying-of-proceedings cases, the more-appropriate-forum test is applied in the same manner as when it was outlined in *Spiliada*. Likewise, and despite claims to the contrary, principally advanced by Professor Briggs,[33] the current doctrinal application of the test in service-out cases has remained much the same as it was defined in *Spiliada*. In so far as *Spiliada*'s impact outside of England is concerned, the discussion in Chapter 4 illustrates that the formal recognition of the *forum (non) conveniens* doctrine in England has been instrumental in reshaping the approaches to discretionary (non-)exercise of jurisdiction within different Commonwealth jurisdictions. This development is of significance, not least because it has happened in an era when, broadly speaking, Commonwealth courts have become increasingly cautious in following the lead from courts in England when it comes to effecting legal change.[34] At the same time, notwithstanding attempts to expand the scope of the *Spiliada* doctrine to other (broadly related) commercial law concepts, it has remained generally the same as when it was outlined. However, due to the Europeanisation of private international law in England, following the incorporation into English law[35] of jurisdiction rules under the Brussels regime, the *forum (non) conveniens* doctrine's application has become materially curtailed. Consequently, the *Spiliada* doctrine is unavailable to the English courts in those instances where their jurisdiction is rooted in the provisions within the Brussels regime. Of course, given the UK citizens' vote to leave the European Union, this limitation in the doctrine's ambit may ultimately prove to be relatively short lived, with the doctrine's post-Brexit scope returning to the position before the entry into force of the relevant parts of the CJJA.

The focus of the discussion in Chapter 5 turns to the future of the English *forum (non) conveniens* doctrine and, in particular, whether (and, if so, in what way) it should be modified. Through a detailed analysis of a number of post-*Spiliada* English authorities, the chapter aims to demonstrate that the application of the doctrine, in its current form, has given rise to unwelcome side-effects. The main cause for this unsatisfactory state of affairs is the disproportionately broad discretion which the *Spiliada* test has afforded to English courts when deciding whether the foreign court, which has been shown to be the dispute's

---

[33] ibid, para 4.91.

[34] It is, in part, as a result of this caution that in Australia, eg, it has been observed that '[t]oday, it is abundantly clear that there are separate bodies of English and Australian common law': P Finn, 'Common Law Divergences' (2013) 37 *Melbourne University Law Review* 511, 511.

[35] Following the entry into force in 1987 of the relevant provisions under the CJJA.

centre of gravity, can justly dispose of the litigants' claims. For both theoretical and practical reasons, the chapter rejects arguments in favour of maintaining the status quo and explores the possible options for revising the English practice of discretionary (non-)exercise of jurisdiction.

In this respect, it will be argued that, a fruitful doctrinal avenue resides in the context of the protection of a person's right to a fair trial under the European Convention on Human Rights ('ECHR'),[36] Art 6(1), as applied in expulsion proceedings. Accordingly, the chapter's main contention will be that, in both cases concerning service-out applications or staying of proceedings brought as of right, to begin with, English courts should not exercise jurisdiction over a dispute which has been shown to be more closely connected to another available foreign forum. That position should be departed from only where the claimant can establish that sending the matter to its centre of gravity would render the United Kingdom in breach of its ECHR obligations, by virtue of the violation in that forum of the claimant's Art 6(1) rights, as defined in expulsion cases.

Finally, Chapter 6 pulls together the various threads of the discussion. It is very much hoped that this book will serve to enable a richer understanding of one of the most important legal doctrines in the field of English conflict of laws, and prompt further debate in this area.

---

[36] European Convention for the Protection of Human Rights and Fundamental Freedoms, Rome, 4 November 1950, 213 UNTS 221.

2

Locating the Place of *Forum (Non) Conveniens* in the English National Jurisdiction Rules

I. Introduction

The litigation of private-international-law disputes presents many challenges to courts worldwide. These challenges range from addressing questions concerning the substance of the dispute to including issues regarding the trial process. Since these disputes are not purely domestic, arguably the most significant matter which courts must contend with, prior to engaging with the substantive considerations, is to determine the 'jurisdiction questions': do they have jurisdiction to adjudicate on the parties' claims and, if so, are they going to exercise it? In order to respond to these questions, each legal system has developed its own set of 'jurisdiction rules'.

Perhaps the easiest (if somewhat extreme) way in which the jurisdiction rules can resolve the questions is for them to allow courts to treat cross-border disputes as though they were entirely domestic. This approach would allow for jurisdiction to be asserted, regardless of whether the parties and/or the cause of action have any connection with the forum of adjudication. However, in a world consisting of independent sovereign states, this method of responding to the jurisdiction questions would prove implausible (and unappealing), not least because it would increase the likelihood of courts asserting jurisdiction over disputes which should really be entertained in another foreign forum.

Instead, in resolving the jurisdictional question, a far more defensible route to take would be for legal systems to articulate and apply rules which, in the process of allocating jurisdiction, uphold a number of key 'jurisdictional values'. These values include 'party autonomy', 'connectedness', and the 'avoidance of parallel or related proceedings'. Those systems of rules that afford jurisdiction to courts without taking account of these important values run the risk of allowing for the courts to have adjudicatory competence over cases that, put simply, do not belong to them. In order to promote (and balance) the values, English courts have developed and utilised a number of legal doctrines. Prominent among these is the *forum (non) conveniens* doctrine, which is employed by English courts in determining the jurisdiction questions – particularly, whether the courts should exercise jurisdiction.

The chief purpose of this chapter is to locate the place of the *forum (non) conveniens* doctrine within the English national jurisdiction rules, by delineating its sphere of operation from its other doctrinal siblings. The discussion begins, in Part II, by outlining the jurisdictional values and highlighting the type of problems that are likely to arise if they are not upheld in the process of allocating jurisdiction under the English national rules. Part III, then, identifies and introduces the different legal doctrines which English courts have deployed to promote the values. It is in this context that the English *forum (non) conveniens* doctrine's place within the national jurisdiction rules in England is mapped out.

II. Jurisdictional Values and Their Significance in Allocating Jurisdiction

An important starting point for the discussion in this chapter is to identify the main values which systems of jurisdiction rules ought to protect. In an article published in *Current Legal Problems* in 2001, Professor Hill pointed to three main values.[1] The first is party autonomy. In a cross-border dispute, this value is promoted where a court assumes jurisdiction when the parties have submitted to its jurisdiction – or, conversely, fails to exercise jurisdiction, if they have already assented to another court's jurisdiction. Submission, for this purpose, can take the form of the defendant voluntarily consenting to the jurisdiction of the court, or the parties contractually designating a court to hear their claims.

The second value that Professor Hill has identified is connectedness. Connectedness is upheld where a court asserts jurisdiction over a dispute in which the parties and/or the cause of action between them are sufficiently connected with the forum. The underlying idea is that, in the absence of the parties' choice, it is generally legitimate for the forum which has a substantial connection with the parties and/or the litigation to hear the claim. Aside from the general undesirability of allowing for unconnected disputes to be resolved by the forum, failure to promote connectedness would open the courts in the relevant territories to increased risk of 'forum shopping' – a phenomenon whereby a claimant by-passes the dispute's centre of gravity and commences proceedings in a venue from which it anticipates receiving the most favourable judgment.[2]

The final value is the 'avoidance of parallel (or related) proceedings'. This value discourages litigation of the identical (or similar) issues by the same parties before different courts. Plainly, if courts were to routinely assume jurisdiction over cases

---

[1] J Hill, 'Jurisdiction in Civil and Commercial Matters: Is There a Third Way?' (2001) *Current Legal Problems* 439, 458–59.

[2] *Boys v Chaplin* [1971] AC 356 (HL) 401 (Lord Pearson).

involving foreign elements, the likelihood of multiple proceedings involving the same parties and/or issues would be materially increased. As a result, the obvious risk would be the greater prospect of conflicting judgments being given by various courts hearing these identical claims. In such a situation, it would become doubly difficult to know which of those rulings should be given effect to. Then, another potential difficulty may arise: the recognition and enforcement of foreign judgments may be impeded in some courts. For these reasons, it is essential for jurisdictional rules to include measures which seek to avoid the occurrence of parallel (or related) proceedings.

In themselves, certain aspects of English national jurisdiction rules do promote the abovementioned values. For example, party autonomy is upheld by the rule which states that a defendant's submission to the English courts' jurisdiction is sufficient to render the courts competent.[3] Nevertheless, there are many instances in which English courts have to take steps, through articulating and applying different legal doctrines, to protect the values. These occasions tend to (but, do not exclusively) arise in cases in which the English courts' jurisdiction is premised on the defendants' presence in England. It is a long-standing[4] principle of English private international law that a defendant's presence in England, however transient or impermanent, at the time of the commencement of the action, would confer jurisdiction on the English court.[5] Due to its open-textured characteristic, the application of this aspect of the jurisdiction rules can have problematic implications. These implications materialise in three broad types of situation where courts in England technically have jurisdiction, but the claim happens to be: (i) one which has been brought before them in breach of an exclusive jurisdiction clause in favour of another foreign forum; (ii) insubstantially (or not at all) connected with England; or, (iii) already pending in parallel (or related) proceedings elsewhere.

In response to these unsatisfactory consequences, a number of distinct common law doctrines have been developed. These doctrines, which are part of the national jurisdiction rules in England, seek to protect and prioritise the main jurisdictional values in the cases in which the English courts' jurisdiction derives from the defendant's presence in England. Additionally, and linked to these doctrines, there are other principles which enable English courts to uphold jurisdictional values in other (wider) circumstances which arise regardless of the defendants' presence in England. *Forum (non) conveniens* is one of the doctrines through which jurisdictional values are promoted within the English national

---

[3] Eg, *The Messiniaki Tolmi* [1984] 1 Lloyd's Rep 266 (CA), and *Global Multimedia International Ltd v ARA Media Services* [2006] EWHC 3612 (Ch), [2007] 1 All ER (Comm) 1160.

[4] For a detailed account on the development of this basis for assuming jurisdiction in England, see A Dickinson, 'Keeping Up Appearances: The Development of Adjudicatory Jurisdiction in the English Courts' (2016) 86 *British Yearbook of International Law* 6.

[5] Eg, *Colt Industries Inc v Sarlie* [1966] 1 WLR 440 (CA), and *HRH Maharanee Seethadevi Gaekwar of Baroda v Wildenstein* [1972] 2 QB 283 (CA).

jurisdiction rules. Its sphere of operation, along with those of its other doctrinal siblings, are examined in the next part of this chapter. It is worth emphasising that the discussion in this book does not seek to provide an exhaustive account of the doctrines related to *forum (non) conveniens*. However, references will be made to them throughout this book, where it helps the analysis of the *forum (non) conveniens* doctrine's historical evolution, present-day application, and potential future developments.

III. The Doctrinal Measures for Promoting Jurisdictional Values Under the English National Jurisdiction Rules

In this part, sections A to D identify and outline the doctrines which have been developed to address the undesirable situations which may ensue from the application of the presence rule of jurisdiction. Sections E and F, then, discuss those (sister) doctrines which English courts have articulated and deployed in order to uphold jurisdictional values in other (broader) contexts.

A. Promoting Party Autonomy: Stay of Action Brought in Breach of an Exclusive Jurisdiction Clause

One of the circumstances in which the presence-based nature of jurisdiction rules in England could lead to unappealing consequences is where a claimant has commenced proceedings in England in breach of an exclusive jurisdiction clause in favour of another foreign forum.[6] Even in cases where the claim in question and/or the litigants are closely linked with England, it is, without more, problematic for the English courts to simply overlook the parties' choice of forum. After all, such a step would undermine the jurisdictional value of party autonomy.

To address this problem, English courts have developed a doctrinal response. Based on this response, which was distilled in Brandon J's oft-cited judgment in *The Eleftheria*,[7] and more recently reiterated in the House of Lords' ruling in *Donohue v Armco Inc*,[8] the starting point is that the proceedings in England would be stayed, unless the claimant has persuaded the court of the existence of a 'strong cause' to the contrary. The English courts' decision on whether a strong cause has been made for sustaining their jurisdiction in breach of an exclusive jurisdiction

---

[6] For a general discussion, see A Briggs, *Civil Jurisdiction and Judgments* 6th edn (Abingdon, Informa Law from Routledge, 2015) para 4.52, Lord Collins of Mapesbury, *et al*, *Dicey, Morris & Collins on the Conflict of Laws* 15th edn (London, Sweet & Maxwell, 2012) paras 12-149–12-156, and J Hill and A Chong, *International Commercial Disputes: Commercial Conflict of Laws in English Courts* 4th edn (Oxford, Hart Publishing, 2010) paras 9.3.2–9.3.9.

[7] *The Eleftheria* [1970] P 94.

[8] *Donohue v Armco Inc* [2001] UKHL 64, [2002] CLC 440 (HL).

clause, is discretionary in nature.[9] In making that decision, the following factors, set out in *The Eleftheria*, are frequently relied on:

> (4) In exercising its discretion the court should take into account all the circumstances of the particular case. (5) In particular, but without prejudice to (4), the following matters, where they arise, may properly be regarded: (a) In what country the evidence on the issues of fact is situated, or more readily available, and the effect of that on the relative convenience and expense of trial as between the English and foreign courts. (b) Whether the law of the foreign court applies and, if so, whether it differs from English law in any material respects. (c) With what country either party is connected, and how closely. (d) Whether the defendants genuinely desire trial in the foreign country, or are only seeking procedural advantages. (e) Whether the plaintiffs would be prejudiced by having to sue in the foreign court because they would: (i) be deprived of security for their claim; (ii) be unable to enforce any judgment obtained; (iii) be faced with a time-bar not applicable in England; or (iv) for political, racial, religious or other reasons be unlikely to get a fair trial.[10]

This is a non-exhaustive list and English courts are free to take account of other considerations before deciding whether to stay (or, instead, sustain) the as-of-right proceedings that have been brought before them in breach of a jurisdiction clause. Nevertheless, and as highlighted by Professor Briggs, the practical effect of this doctrine is that 'proceedings brought in breach of a jurisdiction agreement for a foreign court will be [stayed] unless the circumstances are exceptional'.[11]

B. Promoting Connectedness: The English Courts' Refusal to Exercise Jurisdiction in 'Non-Justiciable' Cases

The 'presence rule' of jurisdiction in England can also render the courts jurisdictionally competent to entertain claims that, owing to their subject matter, should really be exclusively resolved in another foreign forum. Under English law, there are a number of subject matters which – irrespective of the defendants' submission to the English courts' jurisdiction or wider connections which the claims and/or parties might have with England – have long been deemed as being non-justiciable. For our purposes, two subject matters of this kind are worthy of closer inspection. One concerns disputes in relation to foreign immovable real property,[12] and the other relates to disputes about the validity of foreign intellectual property rights.[13] The main reason why it would be problematic for English courts to assert jurisdiction over these disputes is that they have come to be seen as being innately connected to the foreign forum where the immovable

---

[9] Eg, *The Eleftheria* (n 7) 99 and *El Amria* [1981] 2 Lloyd's Rep 119 (CA) 123.
[10] *The Eleftheria* (n 7) 99–100.
[11] Briggs (n 6) para 4.52.
[12] ibid, paras 4.06–4.08.
[13] ibid, para 4.09.

property is located, or the intellectual property right has been granted. Indeed, this connection is considered to be so strong that even the defendants' submission to proceedings in England – whether by contesting the dispute on its merits, or in the form of an exclusive jurisdiction clause in favour of English courts – will not be enough to make the disputes justiciable in England.

Thus, to promote the value of connectedness, in cases concerning the determination of the ownership of (or possessory rights over) any immovable property situated outside England, English courts – which would otherwise have had jurisdiction because of the defendants' presence in England – have refused to assume jurisdiction.[14] The leading authority in support of this approach is the well-known House of Lords decision in *British South African Company v Companhia de Moçambique*.[15] According to the rule emerging from this decision, which is widely referred to as 'the *Moçambique* rule', English courts treat actions concerning land situated outside England as 'local' issues which must necessarily be dealt with in the courts where the property is located.[16] Therefore, generally, English courts refuse to assert jurisdiction in these disputes.

There are, however, two chief exceptions to the *Moçambique* rule, meaning that English courts could nevertheless proceed with hearing claims concerning immovable property located abroad.[17] Based on the first of these exceptions, outlined in the mid-eighteenth century ruling in *Penn v Lord Baltimore*,[18] English courts can exercise jurisdiction when the claim concerns the enforcement of contractual, fiduciary, or equitable rights pertaining to foreign land. The second exception is statutory and is set out in the Civil Jurisdiction and Judgments Act 1982, s 30. Under this provision, English courts have jurisdiction to entertain proceedings for trespass to (or any other tort affecting) immovable property situated abroad, unless the proceedings are principally concerned with the question of ownership or possession of that property.[19]

A similar logic explains the non-justiciability in England of disputes which have the validity of foreign intellectual property rights as their subject matter.[20] English courts have deemed it to be important to promote the value of connectedness in these cases. Thus, notwithstanding the defendants' submission to the English courts' jurisdiction or the wider considerations which might link the

---

[14] A similar rule is set out under Regulation (EU) No 1215/2012 of the European Parliament and of the Council of 12 December 2012 on jurisdiction and the recognition and enforcement of judgments in civil and commercial matters (recast) [2012] OJ L351/1 (the 'Brussels Ia Regulation'), Art 24(1), which states that 'in proceedings which have as their object rights *in rem* in immovable property or tenancies of immovable property, the courts of the Member State in which the property is situated' shall have exclusive jurisdiction.

[15] *British South African Company v Companhia de Moçambique* [1893] AC 602 (HL).

[16] ibid, 619 (Lord Herschell LC).

[17] For more detail on these exceptions, see Briggs (n 6) paras 4.07–4.08.

[18] *Penn v Lord Baltimore* (1750) 1 Ves Sen 444.

[19] On the scope of this exception, see *Re Polly Peck International plc (in administration) (No 2)* [1998] 3 All ER 812 (CA).

[20] See, Briggs (n 6) para 4.09.

litigants and/or their claim with England, English courts have regarded that the validity of foreign patents, copyrights, and trademarks should be determined by the courts of the forum where the intellectual property rights were issued.

Until the Court of Appeal's decision in *Pearce v Ove Arup Partnership Ltd* in 2000,[21] it was thought that questions concerning the infringement of foreign intellectual property rights, too, were non-justiciable in England.[22] In *Pearce*, however, the Court of Appeal cast doubt on this view. In particular, Roch LJ observed that '[o]n its face the rule in the [*Moçambique*] case does not provide self-evident support for the proposition that a claim for breach of a foreign statutory intellectual property right cannot be entertained by an English court.'[23] More recently, in *Lucasfilms Ltd v Ainsworth*,[24] the UK Supreme Court has favoured the understanding of the position in cases concerning the infringement of foreign intellectual property rights as presented in *Pearce*. As a result, matters relating to the infringement of foreign intellectual property rights are justiciable in England.

C. Promoting Connectedness: Stay of Actions Under the *Forum Non Conveniens* Doctrine

As already indicated, the fact that presence can, by itself, afford jurisdiction to English courts over cross-border disputes increases the risk of litigation being brought in England that does not really belong to that forum. The cases considered here are not those in which the action in England has been brought in breach of an exclusive jurisdiction clause. Neither are they ones which would be non-justiciable in England. Rather, these are cases which, upon closer inspection, are actually more closely connected to another foreign forum than to England and, thus, it would be more appropriate for them to be entertained there.

In response to being faced with disputes that can be more suitably resolved elsewhere, and, in turn, to promote the jurisdictional value of connectedness, English courts rely on the *forum non conveniens* doctrine. The doctrine affords English courts a discretion to stay their proceedings in favour of the forum which is shown to be more appropriate for hearing the case. The current law in this area derives from Lord Goff of Chieveley's speech in the House of Lords' ruling in *Spiliada Maritime Corporation v Cansulex Ltd*.[25] Subject to the provisions within the Brussels regime,[26] and other express or implied statutory

---

[21] *Pearce v Ove Arup Partnership Ltd* [2000] Ch 403 (CA).

[22] Eg, *Tyburn Production Ltd v Conan Doyle* [1991] Ch 75 and *Coin Controls Ltd v Suzo International (UK) Ltd* [1999] Ch 33. See, for general discussion, Briggs (n 6) para 4.09 and Hill and Chong (n 6) paras 9.4.5–9.4.7.

[23] *Pearce* (n 21) 424–25.

[24] *Lucasfilms Ltd v Ainsworth* [2011] UKSC 39, [2012] 1 AC 208 (SC).

[25] *Spiliada Maritime Corporation v Cansulex Ltd* [1987] AC 460 (HL).

[26] The shorthand 'Brussels regime' is employed to cover provisions within the Brussels Ia Regulation, its predecessor instruments, and the Convention on jurisdiction and the recognition and enforcement of judgments in civil and commercial matters [2007] OJ L339/3 (the 'Lugano II Convention').

limitations,[27] the doctrine provides English courts with a 'power to order a stay of proceedings on the basis that England is an inappropriate forum'.[28]

According to the ruling in *Spiliada*, the relevant test based on which English courts determine whether to stay their proceedings under the *forum non conveniens* doctrine – known as the 'more-appropriate-forum test' – is applied in two stages.[29] At the first stage, the onus is on the defendant to convince the English court that there is some other available forum of competent jurisdiction which is more closely connected to the parties' dispute than England.[30] In other words, the defendant has to show not only that the court of the foreign country would assume jurisdiction over the claim, but also that it is the dispute's centre of gravity. In this respect, various factors are examined. None of these considerations is, in itself, definitive in winning the argument for the defendant. Instead, the court's ruling is arrived at through the assessment of all the relevant circumstances surrounding the case. In broad terms, these factors, which are outlined in greater detail in Chapters 4 and 5, include the law governing the dispute, and the degree to which the parties and/or the events giving rise to their claim are linked with the available foreign forum.

If, after its inquiry under the first limb, the English court concludes that the foreign court in question has competence to hear the claim and is more closely connected with the dispute than England, then the second stage of the *Spiliada* test becomes relevant. At this point, the claimant can seek to resist an order for staying of proceedings on the basis that substantial justice would not be obtained in the foreign forum.[31] In this context, the claimant can adduce evidence which points to examples of injustice being caused at virtually any stage in the court process in the dispute's centre of gravity. For the purposes of the second limb of the test in *Spiliada*, the court can take account of:

> risk that justice will not be obtained by a foreign litigant in particular kinds of suits whether for ideological or political reasons, … inexperience or inefficiency of the judiciary, … excessive delay in the conduct of the business of the courts or the unavailability of appropriate remedies.[32]

Any allegations of this nature must be supported by 'cogent evidence'.[33] The stay application would be refused, if the claimant could satisfy the English court that

---

[27] For instance, where the English courts' jurisdiction is based on the Convention for the Unification of Certain Rules Relating to International Carriage by Air, Warsaw, 12 October 1929 (the 'Warsaw Convention').

[28] *Dicey, Morris & Collins* (n 6) para 12R-001.

[29] See, generally, Briggs (n 6) paras 4.17–4.39, A Briggs, *Private International Law in English Courts* (Oxford, Oxford University Press, 2014) paras 4.405–4.415, and *Dicey, Morris & Collins* (n 6) Rule 38(2) paras 12-029–12-046.

[30] *Spiliada* (n 25) 476.

[31] ibid, 478, citing Lord Diplock in *The Abidin Daver* [1984] 1 AC 398 (HL) 411.

[32] *The Abidin Daver*, ibid (Lord Diplock).

[33] *Spiliada* (n 25) 478.

his case would not be justly disposed of if it were sent to the available court in the forum that is more closely connected to the litigation than England.

D. Avoiding Parallel Proceedings: Stay of Proceedings Under the *Lis Alibi Pendens* Doctrine

A slightly different context to that highlighted in Section C, above, in which English courts might regard it undesirable to uphold their (otherwise) properly founded jurisdiction, is one where claims involving similar (or related) parties and/or issues are commenced in England that happen to be subject to court proceedings in a forum elsewhere. As stated in Part II, allowing multiple proceedings to be pursued concurrently in more than one venue could lead to a myriad of problems – both at the litigation stage, but also after the conclusion of the hearings, when, in the event that there are conflicting judgments, there is likely to be confusion over which of them should be recognised or enforced. In order to mitigate these problems, and to protect the value of avoiding parallel proceedings, English courts employ the doctrine of *lis alibi pendens*. Based on this doctrine, courts have a discretion to stay their proceedings if the litigants are also involved in related proceedings against each other in another foreign forum.

The *lis alibi pendens* doctrine's roots in English conflict of laws run deep. As early as the 1880s, courts were entertaining submissions in which defendants in English actions applied for the staying of those proceedings, pointing to a pending hearing in a forum elsewhere.[34] As noted by Baggallay LJ in *The Christianborg* in 1885:

> where a plaintiff sues the same defendant in respect of the same cause of action in two courts, one in this country and another abroad, there is a jurisdiction in the Courts of this country to act in one of three ways, – to put the party so suing to his election, or, without allowing him to elect, to stay all proceedings in this country, or to stay all proceedings in the foreign country – it is not in form a stay of proceedings in the foreign court, but an injunction, restraining the plaintiff from prosecuting the proceedings in the foreign country, which of course cannot be enforced against him if he is a foreigner, and is neither present in this country nor has property here.[35]

For much of the period prior to the articulation of the more-appropriate-forum test in *Spiliada*, it was generally accepted that, broadly, the same considerations governed the English courts' practice of discretionary non-exercise of jurisdiction, regardless of whether concurrent proceedings involving similar (or related) parties and issues were ongoing in a foreign court.[36] As a result, when

---

[34] Eg, *McHenry v Lewis* (1882) 22 Ch D 397 (CA).

[35] *The Christianborg* (1885) 10 PD 141 (CA) 152–53.

[36] See, eg, PM North and JJ Fawcett, *Cheshire & North's Private International Law* 11th edn (London, Butterworths, 1987) 234–37.

entertaining stay applications under the *lis alibi pendens* doctrine, the existence of concurrent proceedings elsewhere was generally regarded as one of the
many factors that linked the dispute to the competing foreign forum.[37] Within
a few months after *Spiliada* was decided, in another House of Lords case in *de
Dampierre v de Dampierre*, Lord Goff confirmed that the *Spiliada* formulation
provided the basis for the courts' decision to relinquish their jurisdiction in
both *forum non conveniens* and *lis alibi pendens* cases.[38] In other words, and not
unlike the pre-*Spiliada* position, the existence of parallel proceedings in another
foreign forum is one of a number of factors which English courts consider before
deciding whether the foreign forum is the dispute's centre of gravity and able to
dispose of the parties' claims justly. Thus, to all intents and purposes, the English
courts' approach to stay applications in cases involving concurrent proceedings
abroad is an aspect of the courts' wider practice under the *forum non conveniens*
doctrine.

E. Promoting Connectedness: The English Courts' Service-out Jurisdiction and the *Forum Conveniens* Doctrine

Thus far, this part of the discussion has outlined doctrines that enable English
courts to uphold the main jurisdictional values in situations where jurisdiction
is based on the defendant's presence in England. As we saw, these doctrines,
in turn, address the potential shortcomings arising from the application of
the presence rule. In addition, English law has developed a number of other
(related) principles which, similar to the doctrines set out in Sections A to D
of this part, seek to promote jurisdictional values in situations other than when
the defendant is present in England. In this respect, they facilitate the hearing
of private-international-law disputes in their home forum. One such principle is
the *forum conveniens* doctrine which is utilised in order to uphold the value of
connectedness. The doctrine enables an English court to serve proceedings on a
foreign-based defendant, provided that the court is persuaded that England is the
proper forum for the dispute.

The English courts' service-out jurisdiction is a long-standing part of its
national jurisdiction rules. It was introduced under the Common Law Procedure
Act 1852. Currently, it is codified in Part 6 of the Civil Procedure Rules ('CPR').[39]
Under CPR, r 6.36, claimants have the right to seek permission to serve proceedings on defendants outside of England in those cases which either fall entirely

---

[37] See, however, JJ Fawcett, 'Lis Alibi Pendens and the Discretion to Stay' (1984) 47 *Modern Law Review* 481.
[38] *de Dampierre v de Dampierre* [1988] AC 92 (HL) 108.
[39] From 1883 until 1999, these rules had been set out under Order 11 of the Rules of the Supreme Court.

outside the material scope of the Brussels regime, or those which are covered by Brussels Ia Regulation, Art 6(1)[40] and Lugano II Convention, Art 4(1).[41]

The English courts' decision whether to issue claim forms outside England has a discretionary basis.[42] The relevant considerations for its application are spelt out in *Seaconsar Far East Ltd v Bank Markazi Jomhouri Islami Iran*,[43] an oft-cited House of Lords authority. According to this ruling, a claimant seeking to serve a claim form on a foreign-based defendant has to establish that: (a) there is a 'serious issue to be tried' in the case; (b) the claim falls within the confines of one of the jurisdictional 'gateways' currently listed within CPR, PD 6B para 3.1; and, (c) England is *forum conveniens* – ie, the proper forum in which the proceedings should be entertained.

When hearing submissions on the *forum conveniens* point, the fundamental issue for the English courts' consideration is whether they are the appropriate venue for resolving the dispute. In many ways, *forum conveniens* is the flip-side of the *forum non conveniens* doctrine. Under both doctrines, English courts are seeking to promote the value of connectedness by identifying the venue which is more closely connected to the dispute and in which justice can be done to the parties involved. As a result, the same range of factors determines the application of both doctrines. The only major difference with *forum non conveniens* cases is that, in *forum conveniens* disputes, claimants have the onus of establishing that England is the proper venue for entertaining the litigation.

F. Promoting Party Autonomy and/or Connectedness: Anti-Suit Injunctions

The other wider context in which the English conflict-of-laws rules seek to promote jurisdictional values – and, in the process, help to allocate the claim to its home forum – concerns situations where, although the dispute is being (or is about to be) litigated before a foreign court, the court in England nevertheless considers that the claim ought not to be continued (or pursued) there. In such a case, the English court grants an anti-suit injunction to prevent the respondent – who is the claimant in the foreign proceedings – from proceeding

---

[40] Under Art. 6(1): 'If the defendant is not domiciled in a Member State, the jurisdiction of the courts of each Member State shall, subject to Article 18(1), Article 21(2) and Articles 24 and 25 [of the Brussels Ia Regulation], be determined by the law of that Member State.'

[41] According to Art. 4(1): 'If the defendant is not domiciled in a State bound by this Convention, the jurisdiction of the courts of each State bound by this Convention shall, subject to the provisions of Articles 22 and 23 [of the Lugano II Convention], be determined by the law of that State.'

[42] *Dicey, Morris & Collins* (n 6) para 11.141.

[43] *Seaconsar Far East Ltd v Bank Markazi Jomhouri Islami Iran* [1994] AC 438 (HL). For a more recent reiteration of these principles, see Lord Collins of Mapesbury's judgment in *Altimo Holdings and Investment Ltd v Kyrgyz Mobil Tel Ltd* [2011] UKPC 7, [2012] 1 WLR 1804 (PC) [71], [81], and [88].

with (or commencing) the foreign hearing.[44] In this instance, anti-suit injunctions are the English courts' response to the problem of having proceedings in – what the English court regards as being – an unsuitable foreign forum.

Anti-suit injunctions are controversial measures because they indirectly interfere with the jurisdiction of foreign courts. Mindful of this controversy, English judges have been at pains to stress that anti-suit injunctions are not intended to limit the jurisdiction of foreign courts; instead, they have characterised them as *in personam* measures which restrain the respondents' actions.[45] Moreover, on a number of occasions, it has been suggested in the case law that anti-suit injunctions are 'exceptional' remedies which are to be applied sparingly.[46] In broad terms, and subject to some limitations,[47] there are two categories of case in which English courts might grant anti-suit injunctions against respondents over whom they have personal jurisdiction. In the first category, the English courts' main pre-occupation is to uphold the value of party autonomy. It involves cases where anti-suit injunctions are issued to restrain the commencement of (or to order the discontinuation of) proceedings that are about to be (or have already been) brought in a foreign court in breach of an exclusive jurisdiction or arbitration clause.[48] In the second class of cases, English courts grant anti-suit injunctions predominantly to promote connectedness. Here, the party seeking an injunction asks the English court to restrain 'unconscionable' proceedings in a foreign court. In this type of situation, the applicant must establish that England is the natural forum – ie, the dispute's centre of gravity – and that the respondent's commencement (or continuation) of proceedings in the foreign forum is vexatious and oppressive.[49]

---

[44] For a general discussion of anti-suit injunctions, see Briggs (n 6) paras 5.32–5.52 and *Dicey, Morris & Collins* (n 6) paras 12-078–12-093.

[45] See, eg, *Fort Dodge Animal Health Limited v Azko Nobel NV* [1998] FSR 222 (CA) 246 (Lord Woolf MR) and *Turner v Grovit* [2001] UKHL 65, [2002] 1 WLR 107 (HL) 117 (Lord Hobhouse).

[46] *ED & F Man (Sugar) Limited v Haryanto (No 2)* [1991] 1 Lloyd's Rep 161, 168 (Steyn J). See, also, Briggs (n 29) paras 5.95–5.96.

[47] The Court of Justice of the European Union has ruled that measures such as anti-suit injunctions should not be granted to restrain litigants from commencing (or continuing) proceedings before a Member State court that fall within the material scope of the Brussels regime, even if that action had been brought in bad faith (as in Case C-159/02 *Turner v Grovit* [2004] ECR I-3565, [2005] 1 AC 101 (CJEU)) or in breach of an arbitration agreement (as in C-185/07 *Allianz SpA (formerly Riunione Adriatica di Sicurtà SpA, Generali Assicurazioni Generali SpA) v West Tankers Incorporation* [2009] ECR I-663, [2009] 1 AC 1138 (CJEU)). For a general discussion regarding the unavailability of anti-suit injunctions in this context, see Briggs (n 6) para 5.34, Briggs (n 29) paras 5.98–5.100 and *Dicey, Morris & Collins* (n 6) paras 12-091–12-093.

[48] See, generally, Briggs (n 6) para 5.37–5.39. In the case of non-exclusive jurisdiction clauses, there are some cases, such as *Sabah Shipyard (Pakistan) Limited v Islamic Republic of Pakistan* [2003] 2 Lloyd's Rep 571 and *Royal Bank of Canada v Corporation Centrak Raiffeisen-Boerenleenbank BA* [2004] 1 Lloyd's Rep 471, which have indicated that the applicant must show vexation and oppression on the part of the other party to be able to obtain an anti-suit injunction.

[49] Eg, *South Carolina Insurance Company v Assurantie Maatschappij 'De Zeven Provincien' NV* [1987] AC 24 (HL) and *Société Nationale Industrielle Aèrospatiale v Lee Kui Jak* [1987] AC 871 (PC). See Briggs (n 29) paras 5.111–5.116.

IV. Conclusion

The main purpose of this chapter has been to identify the place of the *forum (non) conveniens* doctrine within the English national rules of jurisdiction. As the discussion has sought to highlight, the consideration of jurisdictional values – chiefly, party autonomy, connectedness, and the avoidance of parallel or related proceedings – must be at the heart of any court's decision making vis-à-vis its competence to entertain a civil and commercial dispute with international elements. In their own right, not every aspect of the English national rules of jurisdiction are protective of these values. As a consequence, over the centuries, English courts have developed a family of common law doctrines in order to uphold (and promote) these values. In the process of promoting these values, these doctrines enable the private-international-law proceedings to be allocated to the courts to which they really belong. *Forum (non) conveniens* is an important part of this family of principles.

It is the practice of discretionary (non-)exercise of jurisdiction under the *forum (non) conveniens* doctrine which is at the heart of the analysis in this book. Having located *forum (non) conveniens* within the English national jurisdiction rules, the next chapters consider the doctrine's origins, present application, and possible future developments. This discussion begins in earnest in Chapter 3, which focuses on the *forum (non) conveniens* doctrine's past, by outlining the historical background to the emergence of the modern-day practice of discretionary (non-)exercise of jurisdiction in England.

3

Forum (Non) Conveniens – The Past

I. Introduction

After locating the *forum (non) conveniens* doctrine within the English national rules of jurisdiction in Chapter 2, the discussion in this chapter proceeds to outline the background to the emergence of the modern-day practice of discretionary (non-)exercise of jurisdiction in England. The principal aim here is to provide a more detailed (and nuanced) understanding of the historical developments which preceded the articulation of the more-appropriate-forum test in 1986, in the House of Lords' landmark ruling in *Spiliada Maritime Corporation v Cansulex Ltd.*[1] It should be noted that, here as elsewhere in this book, the label *forum (non) conveniens* is employed where the discussion is vis-à-vis the English courts' discretionary power to assert or relinquish jurisdiction in both service-out and stay cases. Where the analysis relates only to the courts' discretion to serve proceedings on defendants outside England, the phrase *forum conveniens* is used. In instances where the focus is on the courts' power to give up their (otherwise) soundly founded jurisdiction over a defendant who was sued while present in England, the label *forum non conveniens* is deployed.

This chapter's contribution is significant for two main reasons. First, it sets out to shed light on those aspects concerning the origins of discretionary (non-)exercise of jurisdiction in England that have received limited attention in the existing sources. In this context, it is true that certain facets – for example, the English courts' traditional approach to granting stays of proceedings under the vexatious-and-oppressive test in the four decades prior to the House of Lords' decision in *The Atlantic Star* in 1973[2] – are well documented.[3] Moreover, there has been an even greater assessment of the changes in the law in the immediate run-up to the decision in *Spiliada*, which had been instigated following the ruling in *The Atlantic Star*.[4] However, and importantly, much less is known about

---

[1] *Spiliada Maritime Corporation v Cansulex Ltd* [1987] AC 460 (HL).

[2] *The Atlantic Star* [1974] AC 436 (HL).

[3] See, eg, AS Bell, *Forum Shopping and Venue in Transnational Litigation* (Oxford, Oxford University Press, 2002) paras 3.71–3.77 and RA Brand and SR Jablonski, *Forum Non Conveniens: History, Global Practice, and Future Under the Hague Convention on Choice of Court Agreements* (New York, Oxford University Press, 2007) 11–13.

[4] See, eg, M Pryles, 'Liberalising the Rule on Staying Actions – Towards the Doctrine of Forum Non Conveniens' (1978) 52 *Australian Law Journal* 678, and Brand and Jablonski, ibid 14–20.

the earlier origins of the practice of discretionary (non-)exercise of jurisdiction in England. More specifically, there has been relatively limited analysis of how the vexatious-and-oppressive test became the relevant principle based on which courts in England granted stays of proceedings. In addition, the way in which the vexatious-and-oppressive test's application evolved in relation to these cases during the period when it was in operation, and the forces behind this evolution, has not been charted in as much detail as it arguably deserves.

The second reason why the coverage in this chapter is of importance is that, by revisiting the relevant case law and academic commentary, it puts to the test some of the widely held views concerning the English *forum (non) conveniens* doctrine's past. For instance, it has been generally accepted that before the English House of Lords' ruling in *The Atlantic Star*, which liberalised the vexatious-and-oppressive test, and put in motion the process of refining the law on discretionary (non-)exercise of jurisdiction, English courts had been plaintiff-centric in their application of the vexatious-and-oppressive test. In this context, in the latest edition of *Civil Jurisdiction and Judgments*, Professor Briggs has observed that, until the decision in *The Atlantic Star*, 'it was assumed, almost without question, that a claimant was entitled to decide whether a defendant would be summoned to court in England, and that a defendant had practically no say in the matter'.[5] This is an apt characterisation of the courts' approach to the practice of discretionary non-exercise of jurisdiction in England from the late 1920s until the mid-1970s. However, an analysis of the case law, especially in the early twentieth century, points to a more nuanced understanding of the operation of the vexatious-and-oppressive test. Indeed, it is argued that, from the beginning of the twentieth century until the late 1920s, English courts were much more even-handed in applying the test than has been acknowledged in the existing legal commentary.

In essence, this chapter attempts to map out (and make sense of) the law's evolution in this area from its embryonic form, up to the House of Lords' articulation of the more-appropriate-forum test in *Spiliada*. The main body of this chapter consists of five parts. The discussion begins, in Part II, by identifying and outlining the earliest examples of discretionary (non-)exercise of jurisdiction in England. As the section proceeds to highlight, the earliest examples of this practice in England can be found in the nineteenth century. Part III, then, looks into the developments in the law in the first three decades of the twentieth century. In particular, the focus is on how English courts came to apply the vexatious-and-oppressive test in the context of staying-of-proceedings cases. It seeks to illustrate that the English courts' approach to the practice of non-exercise of jurisdiction in those years was much the same as its Scottish counterpart under the *forum non conveniens* doctrine. Accordingly, and contrary to suggestions that before the decision in *The Atlantic Star* the law in England had an all but completely

---

[5] A Briggs, *Civil Jurisdiction and Judgments* 6th edn (Abingdon, Informa Law from Routledge, 2015) para 1.01.

plaintiff-centric focus, at least in the first few years of the twentieth century, English courts were, in fact, fairly balanced in their treatment of stay applications. Thereafter, Part IV identifies (and sets out to explain the reasons for) the developments in England which led to the introduction of a much more restrictive (and overly plaintiff-friendly) interpretation of the vexatious-and-oppressive test in the middle third of the twentieth century. To this end, the Court of Appeal's ruling in *St Pierre v South American Stones (Gath & Chaves) Ltd*,[6] and case law immediately before and after it are analysed in detail. Finally, Part V examines the developments which led to the law's piecemeal departure from the vexatious-and-oppressive test and, ultimately, towards the formal recognition of the *forum (non) conveniens* doctrine in England in *Spiliada* in 1986.

For the most part, the relevant analysis is presented chronologically. What is more, and in order to help to contextualise the assessment of the origins and development of *forum (non) conveniens* in England, in various intervals, a comparative methodology has been employed. As a result, references are made to the evolution of the *forum non conveniens* doctrine in Scotland – which is widely credited as being the place where the doctrine was 'invented'.[7] It is worth underscoring, however, that the purpose of this chapter is not to provide an exhaustive account of the doctrine's genesis in Scotland.[8] Rather, the aim of the comparison is to achieve a more textured and coherent understanding of the developments in England, in view of its (dis)similarities with its Scottish counterpart at various stages in the doctrines' evolution in these jurisdictions.

II. The Emergence and Development of the Practice of Discretionary (Non-)Exercise of Jurisdiction in England in the Nineteenth Century

The nineteenth century is a significant period in the development of practices resembling the modern-day *forum (non) conveniens* doctrine. It was in this era that courts in England began to rely on their discretion in deciding whether to assert jurisdiction in the context of private-international-law disputes. As this chapter goes on to illustrate, the roots of the *Spiliada* doctrine are to be found in two separate bodies of precedent in England: (i) the '*forum conveniens* cases' concerning the English courts' discretionary power to serve proceedings on foreign-based defendants; and (ii) the 'stay-of-proceedings cases' where defendants asked courts in England to relinquish jurisdiction over a claim that had been brought before

---

[6] *St Pierre v South American Stones (Gath & Chaves) Ltd* [1936] 1 KB 382 (CA).

[7] Eg, PR Beaumont and PE McEleavy, *Anton's Private International Law* 3rd edn (Edinburgh, W Green/SULI, 2011) para 8.405.

[8] For an in-depth analysis of the doctrine's genesis in Scotland see A Arzandeh, 'The Origins of the Scottish *Forum Non Conveniens* Doctrine' (2017) 13 *Journal of Private International Law* 130.

them during the defendants' presence in England,[9] on the basis that the action had been vexatious and oppressive. In the main, the focus in this chapter is on how these two distinct categories of case law emerged, evolved, and eventually helped to give birth to the *Spiliada* doctrine in England. However, in order to provide added context to this analysis, it is helpful to provide a brief outline of the origins and development of *Spiliada*'s sister doctrine in Scotland.

Scotland is widely considered as the birthplace of *forum non conveniens*. The existence of a discretionary power on the part of the Scottish courts to give up their (otherwise) soundly constituted jurisdiction – akin to the way in which the doctrine is applied today – was clearly acknowledged in *M'Morine v Cowie* in 1845.[10] By the mid-1860s, Scottish courts were faced with the defenders' submissions to stay the proceedings before them, notwithstanding their sound jurisdiction, on the basis that it was 'in the interests of justice and the parties' that the dispute should be entertained in another foreign forum.[11] In these cases, at first, the label '*forum non competens*' was used to characterise the defenders' plea for the staying of Scottish proceedings. Subsequently, and in response to the inadequacies in deploying this label, which denoted lack of competence or jurisdiction on the part of the courts to entertain the claims before them,[12] in the 1873 case of *Macadam v Macadam*,[13] Scottish courts replaced *forum non competens* with the phrase '*forum non conveniens*'. Thereafter, *forum non conveniens* continued to gain prominence in Scotland. In fact, by the end of the nineteenth century, the law in this area had become clear and settled. In many ways, the Scottish courts' preoccupation, when deciding whether to relinquish their jurisdiction, was to find the forum in which the ends of justice would be achieved more appropriately than in Scotland.[14] In the course of this discretionary exercise, the courts' treatment of the parties' competing rights in the case being heard in Scotland, on the one hand, or in the more appropriate foreign forum, on the other, was broadly even-handed. A defender could only secure a stay of proceedings in Scotland, on the basis of *forum non conveniens*, if he could persuade the Scottish court that 'there [was] some other tribunal, having competent jurisdiction, in which the case [could] be tried more suitably for the interests of all the parties and for the ends of justice'.[15] For this purpose, obtaining a stay on the basis of *forum non conveniens* was not dependent on a mere balance of (in)convenience. Rather, the defender had to point to something more in order to convince the court to stay its proceedings.[16]

In deciding whether to stay the action, Scottish courts considered a wide range of factors. By and large, these considerations acted as indicators for identifying

---

[9] In this type of case, the court is said to have jurisdiction 'as of right' to adjudicate the dispute between the parties. These actions are also referred to as 'as-of-right proceedings'.

[10] *M'Morine v Cowie* (1845) 7 D 270 (IH).

[11] Eg, *Longworth v Hope* (1865) 3 M 1049 (IH) and *Clements v Macaulay* (1866) 4 M 583 (IH).

[12] See, especially, *Longworth* (n 11) 1058 (Lord Deas).

[13] *Macadam v Macadam* (1873) 11 M 860.

[14] See A Briggs, 'Forum Non Conveniens – Now We Are Ten?' (1983) 3 *Legal Studies* 74, 78.

[15] *Sim v Robinow* (1892) 19 R 665 (IH) 668 (Lord Kinnear).

[16] ibid.

the relevant dispute's centre of gravity. They included (but were not confined to) the applicable law, the place where the cause of action arose, and the location of the witnesses and the parties. So, in the 1884 case of *Williamson v North-Eastern Railway Company*,[17] which involved a pursuer's claim for compensation following the death of her husband in an accident in England against his employers, Lord Justice Clerk Moncrieff found that the events surrounding the case and the witnesses were connected with England and English law governed some of the issues under consideration in the case.[18] Thus, England was held to be the most suitable venue to hear the case and the defender's application for stay of proceedings in Scotland was successful.

The origins of the practice of discretionary (non-)exercise of jurisdiction in England were markedly different from those in Scotland. As stated at the outset of this part, the modern-day *forum (non) conveniens* doctrine in England is traceable to two separate streams of authorities in the nineteenth century. These were the earliest instances in which English courts relied on their discretion in exercising jurisdiction, in a manner which resembles the *forum (non) conveniens* doctrine as it is applied today.

A. The Discretionary Jurisdiction to Serve Proceedings on Defendants Not Present in England

The first stream of authorities to consider is the so-called *forum conveniens* or service-out cases. These are cases in which English courts have a discretion whether to summon foreign-based defendants to respond to claims which have been brought against them in England. The origins of the English courts' service-out jurisdiction can be traced back to the Common Law Procedure Act 1852. Before its enactment, courts had traditionally only assumed jurisdiction over defendants who had submitted to the English courts' jurisdiction, or those who had been present in England at the time of the commencement of the proceedings. The 1852 Act came about after an inquiry, which had been set up to investigate different aspects of the practices of the common law and Chancery courts, identified numerous instances in which plaintiffs had been unable to commence proceedings against defendants who had left England, after the cause of action had arisen, in order to avoid litigation.[19] At that time, the only way for plaintiffs to seek redress was through 'outlawry proceedings', which enabled them to make applications to English courts for the removal of any protection offered by the law to defendants and their property. However, from the plaintiffs'

---

[17] *Williamson v North-Eastern Railway Company* (1884) 11 R 596 (IH).
[18] ibid, 598 (Lord Young and Lord Rutherfurd Clark concurring, but giving judgments of their own).
[19] For an excellent summary of the background to the introduction of the 1852 Act, see M Pryles, 'The Basis of Adjudicatory Competence in Private International Law' (1972) 21 *International & Comparative Law Quarterly* 61, 67–69.

perspective, the outlawry proceedings were onerous and inefficient. In response, the inquiry proposed that the court should be able to serve a writ on non-resident defendants.[20] These recommendations were enacted under the Common Law Procedure Act 1852, s 18 and s 19.[21]

Not long thereafter, English courts began to serve writs on defendants not present in England. Whether the writ was issued depended on the courts being satisfied that the cause of action had arisen in England. The onus was then on the defendant to challenge the court's decision to serve the writ by showing that the cause of action had not actually occasioned in England.[22] After the enactment of the Judicature Act 1873, and the fusion of the various jurisdictions in England, Order XI of the Rules of the Supreme Court replaced the Common Law Procedure Act 1852, s 18 and s 19.[23] One of the notable changes that occurred after the introduction of Order XI was that plaintiffs had to overcome two obstacles to be able to serve defendants outside of England: to begin with, they had to provide evidence that their cause of action fell within one of the headings included in Order XI. Even if the first hurdle was surmounted, it was still a matter for the English courts' discretion whether permission to serve the foreign-based defendants would be granted. This state of affairs is highlighted in the passage below in Lindley LJ's judgment in *Société Générale De Paris v Dreyfus Brothers* in 1887:

> In the first place, Order XI enumerates certain circumstances under which, and under which alone, the Court can give leave to serve writs out of the jurisdiction. It does not say that when those circumstances occur the Court is bound to give leave. On the contrary, the language is that service out of the jurisdiction 'may be allowed by the Court or a Judge' in certain specified events. This shews that the Court has a discretion and is bound to exercise its discretion.[24]

Thus, the picture which emerges from examining the case law in the late nineteenth century is that, while English courts frequently referred to the discretionary nature of their service-out jurisdiction,[25] the type of factor(s) which determined how that discretion was to be exercised was not clearly outlined. This is to say that, within the authorities in the latter part of the nineteenth century, it

---

[20] Recommendations 7 and 8 of the Copy of the First Report of Her Majesty's Commissioners for Inquiring into the Process, Practice, and System of Pleading in the Superior Courts of Common Law, 16 and 19: cited in Pryles, ibid 68.

[21] Section 18 enacted recommendation 7 and related to writs served on British non-resident defendants. Section 19 placed recommendation 8 on a statutory footing and applied to non-resident defendants who were not British nationals.

[22] *Diamond v Sutton* (1865) LR 1 Ex 130, 132.

[23] Order XI also took over some of the provisions which had existed in equity since 1832 which had given the Court of Chancery a discretionary power to serve writs on defendants outside its jurisdiction. For further information see Pryles (n 19) 67. At the end of the twentieth century, Order 11 was replaced by Part 6 of the Civil Procedure Rules ('CPR'). The source of the English courts' long-arm jurisdiction is presently set out under CPR, r 6.36, with the relevant grounds for serving out of the jurisdiction being listed in CPR PD6B, para 3.1.

[24] *Société Générale De Paris v Dreyfus Brothers* (1887) 37 Ch D 215 (CA) 225.

[25] *Harris v Fleming* (1879) 13 Ch D 208 and *Robey v The Snaefell Mining Company* (1887) 20 QBD 152.

is difficult to identify the grounds on which the courts' discretion was applied in service-out cases. What is more, there is no widespread evidence in the case law in that era to suggest that the phrase *forum conveniens* was in common parlance in England. The House of Lords' decision in *Ewing's Trustees v Ewing*,[26] where references to the phrase *forum conveniens* were made, concerned an appeal from the Court of Session. As the discussion in Part IV of this chapter proceeds to illustrate, it was actually in the twentieth century that English courts began to identify (and rely on) a more readily identifiable set of considerations for exercising their discretion in service-out cases.

B. Stay of Proceedings Brought in England as of Right Under the Vexatious-and-Oppressive Test in *Lis Alibi Pendens* Cases

At around the same time that courts in England sought to include a discretionary element to their assertion of jurisdiction, when asked to entertain claims over foreign-based defendants, they also began to acknowledge that they had a discretion whether to stay proceedings brought before them as of right. In its earliest form, this acknowledgement took place in a specific class of cases in which the defendants had been served with the claim form while present in England: the so-called *lis alibi pendens* cases.

As stated in Chapter 2, *lis alibi pendens* cases are those in which English courts are faced with disputes involving the same (or similar) parties and issues that are also subjected to litigation in another foreign forum. The landmark case, in this context, is the English Court of Appeal's ruling in *McHenry v Lewis* in 1882.[27] This was the first decision in which it was clearly acknowledged that, in *lis alibi pendens* cases, courts in England had a discretion to relinquish their (otherwise) properly established jurisdiction.

In *McHenry*, the plaintiffs had started three separate actions against the defendants, L and his co-trustees. One of the plaintiffs, C, brought the first action in England in 1879, for certain alleged breaches of trust. Another plaintiff, M, commenced the second action in July 1881 in England which concerned broadly similar issues as in the first action. M and others then initiated the third set of proceedings in the United States in August 1881.[28] That claim concerned substantially the same matters as those at the heart of the second action, but involved additional defendants. No judgments had been obtained in any of the hearings. The defendants sought to stay the second action in England, contending that the parties' dispute should be resolved in the ongoing litigation in the United States.[29] The Court of Appeal was chiefly concerned with resolving the following

---

[26] (1885) 10 App Cas 453 (HL).
[27] *McHenry v Lewis* (1882) 22 Ch D 397 (CA).
[28] The case report does not specify where in the United States the action had been brought.
[29] *McHenry* (n 27) 398.

two interrelated questions:[30] (i) did the English court have the power to stay its proceedings on the basis that the defendant was being harassed by the parallel proceedings pending in a foreign forum; and, if so, (ii) what were the ground(s) on which the defendant could obtain a stay of the English proceedings?

The Court of Appeal held that, in principle, courts in England had a discretion to order stays of proceedings in the context of *lis alibi pendens* cases. On the facts of the case, though, the court ruled against staying its proceedings. In exercising its discretion, the court relied on the 'vexatious-and-oppressive' test. However, it was hesitant to provide a clear-cut definition for what amounted to a vexatious-and-oppressive conduct for the purposes of the test. In particular, Bowen LJ observed that:

> it would be most unwise, unless one was actually driven to do so for the purpose of deciding this case, to lay down any definition of what is vexatious or oppressive, or to draw a circle, so to speak, round this Court unnecessarily, and to say that it will not move outside it. I would much rather rest on the general principle that the Court can and will interfere whenever there is vexation and oppression to prevent the administration of justice being perverted for an unjust end. I would rather do that than attempt to define what vexation and oppression mean; they must vary with the circumstances of each case.[31]

Nevertheless, and broadly speaking, the words 'vexation' and 'oppression' were employed as shorthand to refer to proceedings that had been brought 'unconscionably'. To obtain a stay under the vexatious-and-oppressive test, in effect, defendants had to show that the continuation of the proceedings in England vexed or harassed them and/or abused the court process. It was the avoidance of claims of this kind in England which was the predominant consideration in the judges' application of the vexatious-and-oppressive test in *lis alibi pendens* cases.[32]

The vexatious-and-oppressive test has a deep-rooted history in English law. Indeed, it is traceable to the test used in relation to the granting of common injunctions and (later on) anti-suit injunctions. At this juncture, it is helpful to outline briefly the origins and development of the vexatious-and-oppressive test under English law, before explaining how it came to be relied on in the *McHenry* case for granting stays of as-of-right proceedings in England in *lis alibi pendens* cases.

After the break-up of the *aula Regis*, the single court of kingdom, into the Courts of Chancery, King's Bench, Common Pleas, and Exchequer in the latter stages of the Norman period, it was no longer uncommon for a plaintiff to commence proceedings in a court where he would stand to gain an advantage, even though another court was better suited to entertain the claim. Furthermore,

---

[30] ibid, 399. At first instance, Chitty J had rejected the defendants' application: (1882) 21 Ch D 202.
[31] ibid, 407–08.
[32] See Briggs (n 14) 78.

there were occasions where plaintiffs brought proceedings on the same issue and against the same defendant in two or more venues. The vexatious-and-oppressive test is likely to have come into existence as early as in the fifteenth century, when the English Court of Chancery began to issue 'common injunctions', to restrain the commencement (or continuation) of proceedings in other courts of the kingdom which it considered to be vexatious-and-oppressive.[33]

After a considerable period during which the Court of Chancery issued common injunctions to restrain proceedings which it deemed to have been brought unconscionably in other *domestic* courts, it deployed these measures to target vexatious-and-oppressive proceedings in *foreign* courts. The precise point at which this development, which amounted to the birth of (what are now called) anti-suit injunctions, took place is uncertain.[34] Nevertheless, it is possible to detect a number of cases in the nineteenth century in which common injunctions were sought and (at times) granted for the purpose of restraining proceedings in foreign courts which English courts considered to be vexatious and oppressive.

A close inspection of the law in that era suggests that there were broadly two categories of case in which the Court of Chancery in England issued injunctions to restrain foreign proceedings.[35] One category involved cases in which injunctions were sought to prevent the commencement (or continuation) of claims in relation to which final judgments had already been rendered (the 'res judicata cases'). The Court of Chancery almost invariably found foreign proceedings brought in these instances to be vexatious and oppressive, thus granting injunctions to restrain them. For example, in the 1821 case of *Harrison v Gurney*,[36] Lord Eldon LC found unconscionable the defendant's decision to commence proceedings in Ireland, even though an English judgment on the same dispute had already been handed down. Accordingly, an injunction was granted to restrain the continuation of the Irish action on the basis that it was vexatious and oppressive. Similarly, in *Beckford v Kemble*[37] and in *Wedderburn v Wedderburn*,[38] the English Court of Chancery issued injunctions to restrain actions brought in Jamaica and Scotland, respectively. In both sets of proceedings, the actions before the foreign courts were held to be vexatious and oppressive, because English courts had already made rulings in relation to the relevant claims.

While English courts appeared, almost as a matter of course, to issue injunctions in the context of *res judicata* cases, they showed greater restraint in granting

---

[33] See, eg, JH Baker, *An Introduction to English Legal History* 3rd edn (London, Butterworths, 1990) 122.

[34] See the discussion in RH Eden, *A Treatise on the Law of Injunctions* (London, J Butterworth and J Cooke, 1821) 141–42.

[35] See, eg, WW Kerr, *A Treatise on the Law and Practice of Injunctions* 2nd edn (London, William Maxwell & Son, 1878) 514–19.

[36] *Harrison v Gurney* (1821) 2 Jac & W 563. Cited and discussed in Kerr (n 35) 516.

[37] *Beckford v Kemble* (1822) 1 Sim & St 7. Cited and discussed in Kerr (n 35) 516.

[38] *Wedderburn v Wedderburn* (1840) 2 Beav 208. Cited and discussed in Kerr (n 35) 516.

injunctions in those cases in which no earlier judgment had been rendered. In these cases, the court had a discretion to grant an injunction if it concluded, based on a consideration of a wider set of factors, that the ends of justice could not be attained in the foreign proceedings.[39] For instance, in *Bushby v Munday*,[40] decided in 1821, B had owed a gambling debt to Cracroft. In order to secure that debt, he sent a bond to Cracroft's trustee, M. Subsequently, M assigned the bond to Cloves. Thereafter, Cloves and M brought an action against B in Scotland, where B had real property, to recover payment on the bond. In response, B started an action in England in which he argued that the bond in question should be declared null and void. Moreover, B sought an injunction to restrain M and Cloves from pursuing the Scottish action. Sir John Leach V-C granted the injunction, holding that the continuation of the action in Scotland would be vexatious and oppressive.[41] The basis for his decision was that the validity of the bond was a matter for English law and, thus, the court in England was better placed to make a ruling on it.

Another helpful illustration of what could be regarded as a vexatious-and-oppressive conduct can be found in the 1855 case of *Carron Iron Company v Maclaren*.[42] The plaintiff in this case was a Scottish iron company which had brought proceedings against the estate of its deceased agent in Scotland, claiming that a substantial sum of money was owed to it after the agent's death. The executors of the agent's estate made an application to the Master of the Rolls in England for an injunction to restrain the company from further proceedings in Scotland. The injunction was granted. The company appealed to the Privy Council to have the injunction set aside. Citing a number of earlier decisions,[43] Lord Cranworth LC allowed the company's appeal and lifted the injunction. The Lord Chancellor made it plain that there was no doubt about the Court of Chancery's remit to restrain persons within its jurisdiction from initiating vexatious-and-oppressive litigation abroad.[44] In outlining the type of conduct which was vexatious and oppressive, Lord Cranworth LC referred to instances in the case law, such as where an action was about to be commenced in a foreign court while another claim concerning the same issues as those pending in England,[45] or where initiating the action in the foreign court was 'contrary to equity and good conscience'.[46]

---

[39] Kerr (n 35) 517.

[40] *Bushby v Munday* (1821) 5 Madd 297.

[41] ibid, 309.

[42] *Carron Iron Company v Maclaren* (1855) 5 HLC 416 (PC).

[43] Among others, *Lord Portarlington v Soulby* (1834) 3 My & K 104, where an injunction was issued to restrain proceedings in Ireland, and *Jones v Geddes* (1846) 1 Phill 724, where the Scottish action was not deemed to be vexatious and oppressive to warrant the grant of an injunction. The decisions in *Beckford* (n 37), *Bushby* (n 40) and *Wedderburn* (n 38) were also mentioned.

[44] *Carron* (n 42) 436–40.

[45] ibid, 437.

[46] ibid, 439.

These decisions on the application of the vexatious-and-oppressive test were influential in shaping the law on the discretionary staying of proceedings in the context of as-of-right cases in the late nineteenth century. The judges in *McHenry* relied on these decisions in articulating the grounds for the English courts' approach to staying of proceedings in *lis alibi pendens* cases. For instance, in his judgment, Cotton LJ relied on passages from two anti-suit injunction cases in highlighting the conduct that could be characterised as being vexatious and oppressive.[47] One was Lord Cottenham LC's *dictum* in *Wedderburn v Wedderburn*, where the Lord Chancellor had observed that:

> there can be no doubt that the general rule precludes parties from proceeding in any other court for the same purpose for which they are proceeding in this court, whether the other proceedings are taken in this or any other country.[48]

The other passage, cited by Cotton LJ, was taken from Lord Cranworth LC's judgment in the *Carron Iron* case:

> where, therefore, pending a litigation here in which complete relief may be had, a party to the suit institutes proceedings abroad, the Court of Chancery in general considers that act as a vexatious harassing of the opposite party and restrains the foreign proceedings.[49]

Based on these *dicta*, if during the pendency of proceedings in England one of the parties commenced another action concerning the same issues in the courts of another country, the second action was then likely to be seen as vexatious and oppressive. In *McHenry*, the defendants were essentially trying to achieve the reverse of what the applicants had pursued in *Wedderburn* and *Carron Iron* cases – namely, the stay of English proceedings (as opposed to the restraining of litigation in the foreign courts). For this reason, in deciding whether to discontinue the English proceedings, Cotton LJ appeared to apply the vexatious-and-oppressive test by analogy. However, and perhaps mindful of the fact that anti-suit injunction and *lis alibi pendens* cases were not entirely identical, his Lordship added that the discretion to stay proceedings in England was 'to be exercised with very considerable caution'.[50] Cotton LJ reiterated that multiplicity of actions did not, without more, amount to a vexatious-and-oppressive conduct in a *lis alibi pendens* situation.[51] In applying the law to the facts, the Court of Appeal held that the action in England (the second action) and in America (the third action) were both *bona fide*. The plaintiffs could only enforce their claim directly by obtaining judgments in both countries. Thus, the defendants' staying-of-proceedings application was rejected.

[47] *McHenry* (n 27) 405.
[48] *Wedderburn* (n 38) 596.
[49] *Carron* (n 42) 437.
[50] *McHenry* (n 27) 406.
[51] ibid, 407.

III. The Developments at the Beginning of the Twentieth Century: The Flowering of a 'British' Approach to Discretionary Non-Exercise of Jurisdiction

In subsequent *lis alibi pendens* cases towards the end of the nineteenth century, the vexatious-and-oppressive test continued to provide the basis for the English courts' decision on whether to stay their proceedings.[52] The next significant development in the law on discretionary (non-)exercise of jurisdiction came at the dawn of the twentieth century. In a trilogy of cases, decided between 1906 and 1908, English courts gave up their (otherwise) soundly established jurisdiction in favour of foreign courts in disputes that did not involve pending parallel litigation elsewhere. These cases were *Logan v Bank of Scotland (No 2)*,[53] *Egbert v Short*,[54] and *In re Norton's Settlement*.[55] The basis for the courts' exercise of jurisdiction in these cases was the vexatious-and-oppressive test, as developed in *McHenry*. As a consequence, from this point onwards, the same considerations underpinned the courts' ruling on whether to exercise jurisdiction in both *lis alibi pendens* and stay cases.

In themselves, *Logan*, *Egbert*, and *Norton* were path-breaking decisions; outside the context of *lis alibi pendens* cases, they were the first examples of the English courts ordering stays in the context of as-of-right cases. However, as this part seeks to demonstrate, these rulings were also noteworthy for another (albeit less widely-known) reason. The judgments in *Logan*, *Egbert*, and *Norton* highlighted the blossoming, at the start of the twentieth century, of a uniform approach to discretionary staying of proceedings in England and Scotland. Consequently, and as the discussion proceeds to illustrate, during this period, English courts were almost as even-handed as their Scottish counterparts in applying their discretion whether to exercise (or relinquish) jurisdiction in as-of-right cases.

A. *Logan v Bank of Scotland (No 2)*

In *Logan*, reported in 1906, the plaintiff was a Scottish resident who had paid for (and been allotted) a number of preference shares in a Scottish company. Shortly after the purchase of the shares, the plaintiff brought proceedings in England against the defendants for an alleged misrepresentation in the company's prospectus. At first instance, the defendants' application for a stay of English proceedings was refused. The defendants appealed to the Court of Appeal, where they referred, *inter alia*, to the Scottish *forum non conveniens* plea, as well as to the

---

[52] Eg, *The Christianborg* (1885) 10 PD 141 (CA).
[53] *Logan v Bank of Scotland (No 2)* [1906] 1 KB 141 (CA).
[54] *Egbert v Short* [1907] 2 Ch 205.
[55] *In re Norton's Settlement* [1908] 1 Ch 471 (CA).

decision of the New York state court in *Collard v Beach*,[56] as examples of where courts in Scotland and New York had stayed their actions.[57] The defendants were not arguing for the court to adopt the Scottish or New York staying-of-proceedings approaches. Instead, they were relying on the existence of those practices to make more compelling their plea to the English court not to exercise its jurisdiction.

On the facts of the case, the Court of Appeal allowed the defendants' submissions and granted a stay. Sir Gorell Barnes P, who gave the only reasoned judgment in the Court of Appeal,[58] applied the vexatious-and-oppressive test as the basis for staying the proceedings. A process of reasoning by analogy[59] appears to have guided the President towards affording this new function to the vexatious-and-oppressive test. The defendants in *Logan* were essentially pursuing the same objective as the defendants had hoped to achieve in a case like *McHenry* – namely, for the English court to give up its jurisdiction on the basis that the claim had been brought to vex them and/or abuse the court's process. The main difference between the two cases was the absence, in *Logan*, of ongoing parallel or related proceedings elsewhere involving the same parties and cause of action. As a result, Sir Gorell Barnes P drew on the same measure that the Court of Appeal had employed in *lis alibi pendens* cases, such as *McHenry*, in tackling the potential vexation and oppression arising in *Logan*.[60]

In the same vein as Cotton LJ in *McHenry*,[61] the President called for courts facing applications for staying of proceedings to be cautious, stating that they should be careful 'not to check [the plaintiff's] freedom' to initiate proceedings in England as of right.[62] It is unlikely that this call for caution was intended to be interpreted too strictly, as his Lordship proceeded to reiterate that, in staying-of-proceedings cases, the plaintiffs' freedom to commence their claims against defendants present in England had to be balanced against the objective of ensuring that the English courts' 'hospitality' was not 'abused'.[63] According to Sir Gorell Barnes P, in deciding whether to exercise its jurisdiction, the English court had to:

> on the one hand, see clearly that in stopping an action it does not do injustice [to the plaintiff], and, on the other hand, I think the Court ought to interfere whenever there is such vexation and oppression that the defendant who objects to the exercise of the jurisdiction would be subjected to such injustice that he ought not to be sued in the

---

[56] *Collard v Beach* (1904) 93 AD 339. In that case, the court stayed its proceedings on the basis that the matter before it could have been better dealt with in the litigants' home forum (Connecticut) and that entertaining it in New York would have unduly congested its dockets.

[57] *Logan* (n 53) 143.

[58] Collins MR and Romer LJ concurring.

[59] On the significance of analogical reasoning as an engine for common law development, see LL Weinreb, *Legal Reason: The Use of Analogy in Legal Argument* (New York, Cambridge University Press, 2005).

[60] *Logan* (n 53) 150.

[61] *McHenry* (n 27) 406.

[62] *Logan* (n 53) 150.

[63] ibid.

Court in which the action is brought, to which injustice he would not be subjected if the action were brought in another accessible and competent Court.[64]

Applying the law to the facts, the President found that the inconvenience of trying a case in England inflicted sufficiently serious injustice on the defendants to render the English action vexatious and oppressive. As such, the defendants' appeal was allowed, and the proceedings were stayed.

The decision in *Logan* is significant because it was the first instance of its kind in which an English court granted a stay of proceedings brought as of right, based on the vexatious-and-oppressive test. But, it is also noteworthy because of the way in which the wider ambit of the English practice of discretionary staying of proceedings was defined. In the course of his judgment, Sir Gorell Barnes P remarked on how the English practice compared with its Scottish equivalent under the plea of *forum non conveniens*. In this regard, and having discussed a number of Scottish cases such as *Longworth* and *Williamson*,[65] the President emphasised that the approaches to granting stays of as-of-right proceedings in the two jurisdictions shared many similarities. Tellingly, his Lordship considered that:

> it may, however, be that there is not really any very substantial difference between the practice in Scotland [under *forum non conveniens*] and that of our Courts as expressed by various judges – viz, that the Court will interfere to prevent vexatious proceedings which would have the effect of preventing the due administration of justice.[66]

Indeed, Sir Gorell Barnes P went on to observe that he was doubtful that there was 'any substantial difference between the two' practices in England and Scotland.[67] It is argued that, not only does this part of the President's judgment show that he regarded the English and Scottish approaches to be broadly similar in substance, but it also signified that it was not inconceivable to have envisaged a complete alignment of this aspect of the laws in England and Scotland before long.

B.   The Decisions in *Egbert v Short* and *In re Norton's Settlement*

The other two cases which followed *Logan* in quick succession were *Egbert* and *Norton*. These decisions reiterated the approach in *Logan* on the practice of discretionary staying of English proceedings in as-of-right cases. Moreover, they exemplified similarities in the English and Scottish approaches to discretionary (non-)exercise of jurisdiction at the beginning of the twentieth century.

In *Egbert*, a first-instance case decided in 1907, the plaintiff was an Indian domiciliary. She brought an action against the defendant, a solicitor working in

---

[64] ibid.
[65] ibid, 148–49.
[66] ibid, 149.
[67] ibid, 151.

India, while he was on holiday in England. In those proceedings, the plaintiff sought to recover damages for an alleged breach of duty on the part of the defendant. In *Norton*, a Court of Appeal decision from 1908, a claim was commenced before the English court concerning a deed of settlement which had been executed in India. The plaintiff and the defendant were a married couple who were both British subjects, though, at the time of the action, the husband was resident in India and the wife had just begun living in England. While the defendant was on a short visit to England, the plaintiff commenced an action against him to recover all moneys subject to the trusts of the settlement which the defendant had received or had transferred to others.

In both cases, the defendants were successful in obtaining stays of proceedings in England. In the course of their reasoning, the judges in *Egbert* and *Norton* placed reliance on the judgment of Sir Gorell Barnes P in *Logan*. To begin with, their Lordships restated that the courts' discretion to give up jurisdiction in as-of-right proceedings had to be exercised cautiously.[68] Subsequently, they conduced broadly the same analysis as that which helped to bring about the decision in *Logan*. For example, in *Egbert*, Warrington J drew on,[69] among others, the following passage from Sir Gorell Barnes P's judgment:

> It seems to me clear that the inconvenience of trying a case in a particular tribunal may be such as practically to work a serious injustice upon a defendant and be vexatious. This would probably not be so if the difference of trying in one country rather than in another were merely measured by some extra expense; but where the difficulty for the defendant of trying in the country in which the action is brought is such that it is impracticable to properly try the case by reason of the difficulty of procuring the attendance of busy men as witnesses, and keeping them during a long trial, and of having to deal with masses of books, documents, and papers which are not in the country where the action is brought, and of dealing with law foreign to the tribunal, it appears to me that a case of vexation in some circumstances may be made out if the plaintiff chooses to sue in that country rather than in that where everybody is and where all the witnesses and material for the trial are.[70]

Applying the principles in *Logan* to the facts of the case in *Egbert*, Warrington J concluded that the plaintiff's commencement of the proceedings in England had amounted to vexatious-and-oppressive conduct. Thus, he granted an order based on which the court relinquished its jurisdiction.[71]

Similarly, in *Norton*, Vaughan Williams LJ stated that 'something more should exist than a mere balance of convenience in favour of proceedings in some other country'.[72] According to his Lordship, the party seeking a stay had to establish that 'either the expense or the difficulties of trial in this country are so great that

---

[68] See *Egbert* (n 54) 212 and *Norton* (n 55) 479.
[69] *Egbert* (n 54) 213.
[70] *Logan* (n 53) 151.
[71] *Egbert* (n 54) 214.
[72] *Norton* (n 55) 479.

injustice will be done – ... that it will be very difficult, or practically impossible, for [him] to get justice in this country'.[73] On the facts, the court granted a stay of proceedings on the basis that the English action had been brought vexatiously.

It is noticeable that there were similarities between these pronouncements and those made in the context of the application of *forum non conveniens* in Scotland. Throughout its nineteenth-century development in Scotland, courts had emphasised that they should not readily allow the defenders' stay applications.[74] Furthermore, they had frequently stated that the fact that the balance of convenience pointed in favour of trial in the foreign forum was not, by itself, sufficient in determining whether stay would be granted. In this respect, in *Sim v Robinow*, an influential judgment handed down in 1892, Lord Kinnear had opined that:

> I am not aware that the court has ever refused to exercise its jurisdiction upon the ground *of a mere balance of convenience and inconvenience*, and the reason is that such a ground of judgment would make it necessary for the court to proceed upon facts and circumstances the full force of which it cannot appreciate without an inquiry into the whole merits of the case.[75]

Academic commentary in the early twentieth century, too, reflected this apparent similarity between the English and Scottish staying-of-proceedings approaches. Perhaps the most notable example, in this context, was Gibb's *The International Law of Jurisdiction in England and Scotland*. This book was published in 1926, soon after the House of Lords' formal application of the *forum non conveniens* plea, in an appeal from the Court of Session, in *Société de Gaz de Paris v Société Anonyme de Navigation 'Les Armateurs Français'*.[76] Gibb's account of the approaches in England and Scotland to staying of actions leaves readers with the impression that, fundamentally, both jurisdictions applied the same principle. Gibb commented on the plea of *forum non conveniens* in 'England and Scotland' in the same chapter, noting that 'there [was] so little ... difference between the attitudes of English and Scots law' in relation to the practice of discretionary staying of proceedings.[77] Furthermore, he observed that courts (whether English or Scottish), would not stay their proceedings

> unless there be, in the circumstances of the case, such hardship on the party setting up the plea as would amount to vexatiousness or oppression if the court persisted in exercising jurisdiction. The inconvenience, then, must amount to actual hardship, and this must be regarded as a condition *sine qua non* of success in putting forward the defence

---

[73] ibid. See, also, Kennedy LJ's statement in *Norton* that '[t]he question of staying the action cannot ... be decided on considerations, more or less speculative, as to the balance of convenience; but one must inquire whether or not injustice will result if the proceedings are not stayed, and whether or not there has been an oppressive use of the process of the court which is sought to be put in force': ibid, 486.

[74] See, especially, *Clements* (n 11) 593 (Lord Justice-Clerk Inglis).

[75] *Sim* (n 15) 668 (emphasis added).

[76] *Société de Gaz de Paris v Société Anonyme de Navigation 'Les Armateurs Français'* 1926 SC (HL) 13.

[77] AD Gibb, *The International Law of Jurisdiction in England and Scotland* (Edinburgh, William Hodge & Co, 1926) 212.

of *forum non conveniens*. For the general rule is that a court possessing judiciary must exercise it unless the reasons to the contrary are clear and cogent.[78]

In many ways, this passage represents a hybrid statement which draws on doctrinal elements in both the English and Scottish case law. Gibb referred to 'vexatiousness' and 'oppression' – the terminology used by the courts in England in stay-of-proceedings cases – alongside 'inconvenience' – a term used in equivalent cases in Scotland.[79]

In these circumstances, and perhaps more importantly, it is contended here that the picture that emerges from the analysis of cases such as *Logan*, *Egbert*, and *Norton*, regarding the law on discretionary staying of proceedings in England, is actually more nuanced than the one discernible in the legal literature. For instance, as stated in this chapter's introductory section, Professor Briggs has remarked that, up until the English House of Lords' ruling in *The Atlantic Star*, in 1973, English courts had applied their discretion whether to stay their proceedings in a plaintiff-centric manner.[80] However, as this part has attempted to show, at the beginning of the twentieth century, English courts were generally balanced in their application of the vexatious-and-oppressive test. Indeed, in all three cases discussed above, the defendants were successful in their stay applications. The fact that, in that era, judges and commentators considered the English practice to be broadly akin to its Scottish equivalent under *forum non conveniens* is yet another reason for revisiting our understanding of this aspect of the historical developments predating the articulation of the modern-day staying-of-proceedings practice in England.

IV. The Developments in the Middle Third of the Twentieth Century: The Emergence in England of a Plaintiff-Centric Approach to Staying of Proceedings

In these circumstances, it may have been anticipated that the momentum generated by the decisions in *Logan*, *Egbert*, and *Norton* would ultimately drive the test for exercising jurisdiction in stay and *lis alibi pendens* cases in England closer to the Scottish *forum non conveniens* doctrine. Indeed, in view of the documented parallels between the two approaches, it might even have been thought that English courts would promptly proceed to import (and adopt) the Scottish doctrine for the purpose of granting stays of proceedings brought as of right.

These developments were not forthcoming, however. In fact, from the late 1920s until the mid-1970s, in stay and *lis alibi pendens* cases heard in England,

---

[78] ibid, 212–13.

[79] Indeed, observers in other jurisdictions, too, appeared to regard the English and Scottish staying-of-proceedings practices as being similar: see, especially, P Blair, 'The Doctrine of Forum Non Conveniens in Anglo-American Law' (1929) 29 *Columbia Law Review* 1.

[80] Briggs (n 5) para 1.01.

courts were no longer as balanced in treating the parties' competing interests regarding where the case should be entertained as they had been at the start of the twentieth century. In this respect, they became exceedingly plaintiff-centric in their application of the vexatious-and-oppressive test.[81] This change of emphasis was so stark that it was almost impossible, during this period, for a defendant in English proceedings to obtain a stay of proceedings that had been commenced against him during his presence in England. In other words, what had seemed to be a largely balanced approach to discretionary staying of proceedings in England, in the early years of the twentieth century, became highly one-sided in favour of those who wished to bring their claims for litigation in England.

The main objective here is to explain this unexpected about-turn. One point has to be made from the outset: as the discussion highlights, the fact that English courts almost completely failed to allow stay-of-proceedings applications was not immediately apparent. Thus, it does not seem to have been widely picked up on at the time by judges, counsel, or academics. It is only through a retrospective analysis of the sources between the late 1920s and early 1970s that the overly restrictive nature of the English discretionary non-exercise of jurisdiction becomes apparent.

A. The Immediate Build-up to the English Courts' Change of Approach

The brakes were slammed on the momentum generated by the decisions in *Logan*, *Egbert*, and *Norton* towards the adoption in England of a discretionary staying-of-proceedings practice, resembling the Scottish *forum non conveniens* doctrine, in two first-instance decisions. These were *The Janera*,[82] reported in 1927, and *The London*, decided in 1930.[83] Both were *lis alibi pendens* cases.

The dispute in *The Janera* arose in the context of a collision between two foreign vessels in Egyptian waters. While an action was pending in Egypt,[84] owners of the vessel M, who were the defendants in the Egyptian hearing, initiated proceedings in England against the owners of the vessel J. In turn, the owners of J made a

---

[81] In the meantime, incidentally, Scottish courts continued to follow the approach as endorsed in *Les Armateurs Français*, without any noticeable changes to it: see, among others, *Lawford v Lawford's Trustees* 1927 SC 360 (IH), *Robinson v Robinson's Trustees* 1929 SC 360 (IH), *Robinson v Robinson's Trustees* 1930 SC (HL) 20, *Owners of SS 'Sheaf Lance' v Owners of SS 'Barcelo'* 1930 SLT 445 (IH), *Woodbury v Sutherland's Trustees* 1938 SLT 371 (OH), *Woodbury v Sutherland's Trustees* 1938 SC 689 (IH).

[82] *The Janera* (1927) 29 Ll L Rep 273.

[83] *The London* (1930) 38 Ll L Rep 126.

[84] The owners of the vessel J, who had an office in England, had commenced proceedings against the owners of the other vessel M, in Egypt. The Egyptian court appointed an expert to present a report on the collision. The report was favourable towards the owners of J. Consequently, the Egyptian court made an order for the owners of M to be arrested. The owners of M sought to set aside that order but were unsuccessful.

conditional appearance and applied to have the English action set aside for being vexatious and oppressive. Broadly speaking, the owners of J had three bases for their application:[85] first, the Egyptian action between the parties was still pending; second, all the material facts, witnesses and evidence were to be found in Egypt, where the collision had taken place; and, finally, the owners of M only commenced the English action after they had discovered that they had slim chances of success in Egypt. Accordingly, they argued that the English action had been brought with the intention of vexing and harassing them. Hill J was unpersuaded by the defendants' submissions. He stated that the fact that the plaintiffs in the English hearing were defendants in the Egyptian trial was not enough to warrant the court relinquishing its jurisdiction.[86] Accordingly, he dismissed the defendants' stay application.

The Janera was relied on in *The London*.[87] In this case, a Dundee steamship, L, and a Norwegian vessel, G, collided in Dundee Roads. An action for damages had been commenced in Scotland by the owners of L and a similar action in England was then brought by the owners of G. The owners of L sought a stay of the English action, arguing that the collision had taken place in Scottish waters and that a process had been commenced against the owners of G in Scotland. Moreover, they argued that the English action was *prima facie* vexatious and oppressive because it was brought while a similar action involving the same parties was pending in another court in the United Kingdom.[88] Langton J dismissed the defendants' application and sustained the proceedings in England. He considered that the court's decision whether to give up its jurisdiction was discretionary in nature and that, on the facts, the plaintiffs should not be deprived of their right to commence proceedings in England. Thus, he rejected the defendants' stay application.[89]

At one level, it might be observed that the English courts' approach in *The Janera* and *The London* to the defendants' pleas for staying the actions was in keeping with the approach which had been employed in England in the early twentieth century. After all, the judges in both cases employed the vexatious-and-oppressive test in deciding whether to exercise jurisdiction. Be that as it may, the prevailing conclusion that can be drawn from the short judgments in both cases is that the judges were more preoccupied with not doing injustice to the plaintiffs, in depriving them from the right to commence the as-of-right proceedings in England, as opposed to the injustice to the defendants in sustaining the English proceedings. Put differently, the balancing exercise that had been a conspicuous

---

[85] *The Janera* (n 82) 274.

[86] ibid, 275.

[87] *The London* (n 83).

[88] ibid, 126–27. This submission appeared to have had support in the academic commentary at the time, most notably the third edition of *Dicey's Conflict of Laws*. Citing the decision in *McHenry*, the editors observed that, in the context of a *lis alibi pendens* case, if the foreign court in which the proceedings are pending 'is a Court of the United Kingdom or of any country forming part of the British dominions, the plaintiff's proceedings are *prima facie* vexatious': AV Dicey and AB Keith *Conflict of Laws* 3rd edn (London, Stevens & Sons, 1922), Sub-Rule 79.

[89] *The London* (n 83) 128.

feature of the courts' decision making in *Logan*, *Egbert*, and *Norton*, was absent in *The Janera* and *The London*.

B. The Court of Appeal's Ruling in *St Pierre*

The momentum created by the decisions in *Logan*, *Egbert*, and *Norton* towards the possible adoption in England of a discretionary staying-of-proceedings practice resembling the Scottish *forum non conveniens* doctrine came to a halt following the Court of Appeal's decision in *St Pierre*. This *lis alibi pendens* ruling, decided in 1935, is widely regarded as the English law's first *locus classicus* on discretionary non-exercise of jurisdiction, whether in stay or *lis alibi pendens* cases.

St Pierre concerned an action in England between B, the representatives of a Chilean landlord, and CS and SAS, two English companies. CS and SAS were the lessee and the guarantor under the lease, respectively. Under the lease, which had been drawn up in Spanish and was subject to Chilean law, rent was to be paid at the option of the lessors either in Chile, or remitted to Europe according to their instructions. CS claimed that Chilean legislation prevented them from remitting the rent from Chile without official authorisation by the Chilean government, which had refused to ratify the payment. As a result, they commenced proceedings in Chile, seeking a declaration that the rent owed under the lease was payable in Chilean pesos in Chile. While the Chilean action was pending, the defendants in those proceedings commenced a hearing in England claiming that the rent should be payable in sterling. In response, the defendants in the English action applied for the proceedings to be stayed. Among others, they argued that all the evidence in the case was connected to Chile: not only did the contract relate to land in Chile, but it was also drawn up in Spanish between Chilean subjects and a company which had all its activities in Chile.[90] They, therefore, contended that the English action had been brought to vex and oppress them.

The defendants' argument in favour of a stay of English proceedings was rejected by Potter J at first instance and, subsequently, by a unanimous Court of Appeal.[91] In his judgment in the Court of Appeal, and in outlining the principles underpinning the English courts' decision on whether to allow the defendants' applications for non-exercise of jurisdiction in stay or *lis alibi pendens* cases, Scott LJ formulated the following test:

> (i) A mere balance of convenience is not a sufficient ground for depriving a plaintiff of the advantages of prosecuting his action in an English Court if it is otherwise properly brought. The right of access to the King's Court must not be lightly refused. (ii) In order to justify a stay two conditions must be satisfied, one positive and the other negative: (a) the defendant must satisfy the Court that the continuance of the action would work an injustice because it would be oppressive or vexatious to him or would be an abuse of

[90] *St Pierre* (n 6) 386.
[91] Greer, Slesser and Scott LJJ.

the process of the Court in some other way; and (b) the stay must not cause an injustice to the plaintiff. On both, the burden of proof is on the defendant. These propositions are, I think, consistent with and supported by the following cases: *McHenry v Lewis*; *Peruvian Guano Co v Bockwoldt*; *Hyman v Helm*; *Thornton v Thornton*; and *Logan v Bank of Scotland (No 2)*.[92]

It is this passage that came to be regarded as the standard test based on which English courts considered whether to give up their (otherwise) properly founded jurisdiction in stay or *lis alibi pendens* cases.

At first blush, Scott LJ's formulation did not say anything which was radically new. He explicitly cited (and relied on) the main authorities in the late nineteenth and early twentieth century. The first limb of the test affirms the position in *Logan* and *Norton* that a balance of convenience is not, *ipso facto*, sufficient to warrant a stay of English proceedings. By the same token, Scott LJ's observation that '[t]he right of access to the King's Court must not be lightly refused' essentially embodies Cotton LJ's note of caution that the court should be careful not to deprive a plaintiff from his entitlement to initiate proceedings in England as of right. Similarly, the second limb of the *St Pierre* test was very much consistent with Sir Gorell Barnes P's statement in *Logan* that the court has to conduct a balancing exercise in deciding whether it should stay its proceedings. Moreover, the coverage of the decision in *St Pierre* in the leading private-international-law treatise published in its immediate aftermath did not elicit a change in the operation of the discretionary staying-of-proceedings practice in England. For instance, in the first edition of Morris's *Cases on Private International Law*, published in 1939, no mention was made of *St Pierre* in the section concerned with *lis alibi pendens*.[93] In the same vein, in the second edition of *Private International Law* published in 1938, Cheshire only referred to *St Pierre* in a footnote.[94] To all outward appearances, therefore, *St Pierre* represented a development of the earlier practice by simply consolidating it into a defined rule. Accordingly, the comment made earlier – namely, that the momentum generated by the decisions in *Logan*, *Egbert*, and *Norton* towards the potential adoption in England of a discretionary staying-of-proceedings practice akin to the once characterised under the Scottish *forum non conveniens* doctrine came to a standstill – might be regarded as an exaggeration.

C. Stay of Proceedings in England after *St Pierre*

However, a retrospective study of the way in which the post-*St Pierre* cases applied the test illustrates that, in fact, the English courts' approach to discretionary staying of proceedings became much more restrictive, making it almost impossible for defendants to obtain a stay of English proceedings. From the decision in

---

[92] *St Pierre* (n 6) 398 (citations omitted).
[93] JHC Morris, *Cases on Private International Law* 1st edn (Oxford, Clarendon Press, 1939) 387–94.
[94] GC Cheshire, *Private International Law* 2nd edn (Oxford, Clarendon Press, 1938) 119–25.

St Pierre, in 1935, until the mid-1970s, there appears to be only one reported case in which a stay was granted in England.[95] In almost all post-*St Pierre* stay or *lis alibi pendens* cases, the courts' main priority was the protection of the plaintiffs' right to commence proceedings in England. Such was the level of prominence afforded to the plaintiffs' entitlement to have their claims heard in England that, in effect, it was made impossible for defendants to convince the courts to relinquish their jurisdiction. In other words, no amount of connection with the foreign forum seemed to be sufficient to render the English action vexatious and oppressive and, thus, one that had to be stayed. In practice, the requirements under the first limb of the test almost completely overshadowed those under its second part – which required courts to balance the competing interests of both plaintiffs and defendants in sustaining (or staying) the proceedings.

Consider, in this context, *The Quo Vadis*,[96] a *lis alibi pendens* case. This first-instance case concerned disputes arising from a collision involving a Belgian ship, R, and a Dutch ship, QV, in Dutch territorial waters. The owners of QV had initiated an action in the Netherlands. Subsequently, the owners of R brought proceedings against the owners of QV in England. The defendants in the English proceedings applied for a stay of those proceedings, pointing to the ongoing litigation in the Netherlands. For the most part, the defendants premised their stay application on the fact that a claim concerning the same issues under examination in the English trial were being heard by the Dutch courts. Moreover, they contended that the collision had occurred in Dutch territorial waters and concerned Dutch and Belgian vessels.[97] Notwithstanding these submissions, and the lack of any meaningful connection between the parties and the dispute with England, the stay application was turned down. Relying on the decisions in *The Janera* and *The London*, Pilcher J stated that the plaintiffs had 'a *prima facie* right' to decide where to initiate their claim.[98] According to the judge, '[u]nless it can be clearly shown that to permit' the plaintiffs to bring the action in England 'would be vexatious and oppressive, I can see no possible reason for staying their action'.[99] The gravitational pull of the Dutch court was not enough to render the English action vexatious and oppressive and, in turn, persuade the court to deny the plaintiff its right to initiate proceedings in England.

The fact that the *St Pierre* ruling is regarded as a turning point in the English courts' approach to staying of proceedings – by making it much more restrictive than the way it was applied at the start of the twentieth century – was largely due to how Scott LJ's formulation in that case was perceived (and deployed) in later authorities and/or academic discussions. This state of affairs is chiefly a by-product of judicial doctrinal development at common law being as much the result of how

---

[95] *The Marinero* [1955] P 68 (a *lis alibi pendens* case).
[96] *The Quo Vadis* [1951] 1 Lloyd's Rep 425. See, also, *The Monte Urbasa* [1953] 1 Lloyd's Rep 587.
[97] ibid, 426.
[98] ibid, 428.
[99] ibid.

a landmark decision has been understood in succeeding cases and commentary, as what was actually stated in that decision. This position is a unique characteristic of the common law because common law courts are, in the words of Rudden, in dialogue 'with the past'.[100] Although a common law court is bound by an existing authority, it often has a relatively free hand in interpreting a particular decision or test. In the common law, it is perfectly possible that what a certain case or legal principle stands for could well depend on the picture which emerges from the subsequent body of cases and commentaries.

It was in these circumstances that, by the mid-twentieth century, English courts had become plaintiff-centric in their approach to discretionary non-exercise of jurisdiction in England. Cases such as *Logan*, *Egbert*, and *Norton* had become relegated to mere footnotes, illustrating an exceptional group of cases in which courts in England had granted stays of their proceedings.[101]

D. Murmurs of a Need to Depart from the *St Pierre* Approach

It was not until the mid-1960s that commentators began to come to terms with the fact that, after the decision in *St Pierre*, discretionary staying of proceedings in England had become all but non-existent. Thereafter, there was a period of active debate within academic circles which aimed to re-appraise the law as it was being applied under the *St Pierre* test.[102] The main argument which emerged from those discussions was that, in deciding whether to stay the as-of-right proceedings brought before them, English courts should rely on their discretionary approach, based on which they assume jurisdiction in service-out cases.

As set out in Part II of this chapter, from the mid-nineteenth century onwards, English courts had developed a practice that would allow them to assert jurisdiction over defendants who were not present in England on a discretionary basis. To convince the court to serve a writ on a defendant outside England, first, the plaintiff had to establish that the subject matter of the dispute fell within the relevant provisions of Order XI of the Rules of the Supreme Court. Thereafter, the court could decide whether to allow for the defendant to be served. For a considerable period after the introduction of the service-out jurisdiction, there were no clear pronouncements in the cases about the type of factors which influenced the exercise of this discretion.[103] It was really from the mid-1920s onwards that the type

---

[100] B Rudden, 'Courts and Codes in England, France and Soviet Russia' (1973–1974) 48 *Tulane Law Review* 1010, 1016–17. In explaining the judicial method at the common law, Rudden also points to the court's dialogue with the counsel before it, the discussions among the judges hearing a specific case and also the dialogue 'with the future'.

[101] See especially GC Cheshire, *Private International Law* 5th edn (Oxford, Clarendon Press, 1957) 124.

[102] See, particularly, BD Inglis, 'Jurisdiction, the Doctrine of *Forum Conveniens*, and Choice of Law in Conflict of Laws' (1965) 81 *Law Quarterly Review* 380, JD McClean, 'Jurisdiction and Judicial Discretion' (1969) 18 *International & Comparative Law Quarterly* 931, and Pryles (n 19).

[103] See, eg, *The Hagen* [1908] P 189 (CA).

of instances which influenced the courts' discretionary power to summon foreign-based defendants to appear in hearings in England became clearer.

A close inspection of some of the main authorities in that era highlights that, in making their decision whether to assert jurisdiction, English courts were essentially consulting factors which were broadly similar to those applicable under the proper-law doctrine in cases where the parties had not chosen the contract's governing law.[104] In those cases, the contract's proper law was said to be the legal system 'with which the transaction ha[d] its closest and most real connection'.[105] As stated by the editors of the eighth edition of *Cheshire's Private International Law*, published in 1970, the range of considerations which courts took into account in identifying the closest and most real connection included:

> the domicil and the residence of the parties; the national character of a corporation and the place where its principal place of business is situated; the place where the contract is made and the place where it is to be performed; the style in which the contract is drafted, as, for instance, whether the language is appropriate to one system of law, but inappropriate to another; the fact that a certain stipulation is valid under one law but void under another; the nationality of the ship in maritime contracts; the economic connexion of the contract with some other transaction; the fact that one of the parties is a sovereign State; the nature of the subject-matter or its *situs*; the head office of an insurance company, whose activities range over many countries; and, in short, any other fact which serves to localize the contract.[106]

As the final sentence of the passage reiterates, the courts' main preoccupation, when identifying the disputes' proper law in the absence of the parties' choice, was to pinpoint the contract's centre of gravity. Mostly by coincidence, the factors consulted in ascertaining a contract's proper law were, in many respects, akin to the ones which were consulted by Scottish courts when deciding whether to stay their proceedings under *forum non conveniens*. In essence, when faced with a stay application, courts in Scotland had to rule on where the dispute's centre of gravity was located. Stays would have been granted if the defender persuaded the Scottish court that, on balance, the case 'belonged' to the foreign forum.

As a result, though not widely acknowledged at the time, the English courts' exercise of their discretion in service-out cases in the middle third of the twentieth century in many ways resembled the Scottish courts' application of their discretion under the *forum non conveniens* doctrine. Indeed, it was around this time that in a number of service-out cases, courts began to use the phrase '*forum conveniens* considerations' to refer to the factors for assessing whether they should exercise their discretion in favour of admitting service-out applications.[107]

---

[104] For more detail regarding the application of this common law choice-of-law rule, see the decision in *Bonython v Commonwealth of Australia* [1951] AC 201 (PC).

[105] ibid.

[106] GC Cheshire and PM North, *Cheshire's Private International Law* 8th edn (London, Butterworths, 1970) 203–04 (citations omitted).

[107] See, *Rosler v Hilbery* [1925] Ch 250 (CA), *In re Schintz* [1926] Ch 710 (CA), *Ocean Steamship Company Ltd v Queensland State Wheat Board* [1941] 1 KB 402 (CA), and *Vitkovice Horni A Hutni Tezirstvo v Korner* [1951] AC 869 (HL).

The use of the label, though, appears not to be due to any influence of the Scottish *forum non conveniens* doctrine. The neo-Latin phrase was employed simply as shorthand.

In this context, one illustrative service-out case worthy of consideration is *Rosler v Hilbery*.[108] This case, which was decided in 1925, concerned an action by members of a Belgian company against a Belgium resident for the recovery of a sum of money which they claimed to have belonged to them. On the facts, the Court of Appeal rejected the plaintiffs' appeal and declined to give permission for the writ to be served on the defendant. The main reason for the court's finding was that, in substance, the action had no connection with England.[109] In reaching this conclusion, Pollock MR took into account that Belgian law was the law applicable to the dispute and that the issues giving rise to the case had happened in Belgium.[110] Likewise, in *Kroch v Rossell & Cie*,[111] a 1937 defamation case, the Court of Appeal, consisting incidentally of two of the judges who decided *St Pierre*,[112] dismissed the plaintiff's application to summon Belgium- and France-based defendants. The judges were of the view that the case 'would be better tried' outside England, as the language of the case was French and French law governed the dispute.[113]

One of the first commentators to propose that courts in England should apply the same discretionary principles that govern the exercise of their discretion in service-out cases to staying of as-of-right actions was Inglis. In an innovative article, published in the *Law Quarterly Review* in 1965,[114] he advocated that the *forum conveniens* principle, as applied in the context of service-out cases, should also have a role to play in the English courts' decision making in stay cases.[115] Somewhat radically, perhaps, Inglis considered that the defendants' presence in England was 'the type of factor which has to be weighed, along with the other circumstances of the case, in determining the true "centre of gravity" of the plaintiff's action' and that, of its own, it 'possess[ed] no inherent magic'.[116] He argued that the English practice of staying of proceedings, as applied in cases such as *Logan*, *Egbert*, and *Norton*, was reconcilable with the *forum conveniens* analysis in service-out cases.[117] According to Inglis:

> [t]he significant feature of [stay] cases, … , is that although the final decision in each of them was arrived at in terms of the abuse of the court's process, in all of them the

---

[108] *Rosler* (n 107).

[109] ibid, 261.

[110] ibid, 259–60.

[111] *Kroch v Rossell & Cie* [1937] 1 All ER 725 (CA). The case report does not specify the plaintiff's nationality.

[112] Slesser and Scott LJJ.

[113] *Kroch* (n 111) 731.

[114] Inglis (n 102). Inglis also made broadly similar proposals in an article published a year earlier: BD Inglis, 'Forum Conveniens – Basis of Jurisdiction in the Commonwealth' (1964) 13 *American Journal of Comparative Law* 583.

[115] Inglis (n 102) 386.

[116] ibid.

[117] ibid, 387–90.

'abuse' arose purely because of the inappropriateness of [England as the forum for entertaining the dispute], and in all of them the abuse could just as easily have been expressed in terms of the principle of *forum conveniens*.[118]

He, therefore, favoured a 'universal' *forum (non) conveniens* doctrine which would be applicable both in the context of stay of as-of-right proceedings and service-out cases, with the only difference being the shifting of the burden of proof. If the English action is brought during the defendant's presence in England, then the onus is on the defendant to seek a stay of those proceedings. Conversely, where permission is sought to initiate a claim against a defendant outside England, it is the plaintiff who shoulders the burden of establishing that England is *forum conveniens*.[119]

However, in view of the state of the law at the time, Inglis's proposals for legal reform in stay and *lis alibi pendens* cases, was liable to be deemed ambitious and unrealistic. This point was, in fact, noted by Professor McClean in his article, published in the *International & Comparative Law Quarterly* in 1969.[120] While supporting the thrust of Inglis's thesis, Professor McClean noted that Inglis had taken 'too rosy a view of the developments' at the time.[121] Nevertheless, he was on the same page as Inglis, contending that 'the element of judicial discretion', which was important in relation to service-out cases, was 'remarkably understated' where jurisdiction was assumed as of right.[122] In other words, Professor McClean, too, considered that the best way for a court to decide whether to stay its as-of-right proceedings was by relying on its approach to the assumption of jurisdiction in service-out cases.

A broadly similar viewpoint was advanced by Professor Pryles in another law journal publication in 1972.[123] He also questioned the logic in the English courts' refusal to apply the *forum conveniens* principles in deciding whether as-of-right proceedings in England should be stayed (or sustained).[124] He observed that, ever since the enactment of the Common Law Procedure Act in 1852, the presence of the defendant in England was no longer the cornerstone of the English courts' adjudicatory competence, because they could summon defendants who were not present in England.[125] Based on these considerations, Professor Pryles went on to argue that the same factors which governed the English courts' decision whether to assert jurisdiction in service-out cases should also assist them in determining whether they should exercise (or relinquish) their jurisdiction in as-of-right cases.[126]

---

[118] ibid, 387.
[119] ibid, 390–91.
[120] McClean (n 102).
[121] ibid, 948.
[122] ibid, 934.
[123] Pryles (n 19).
[124] ibid, 72.
[125] ibid.
[126] ibid.

As can be seen, arguments by these legal scholars were effectively the first real attempts at revising the post-*St Pierre* practice of discretionary staying of proceedings in England. Their suggested route was particularly attractive because, if it were to be adopted, it would have, to a significant extent, aligned the rules for exercise of jurisdiction with those for determining the proper law of a contract in the absence of the parties' designation. Had it occurred, this development would have meant that, more often than not, the dispute would have been resolved on the basis of the laws of the forum which was most closely connected to the dispute. In turn, and significantly, such an advancement in the law would have brought the staying-of-proceedings practice in England much closer its Scottish counterpart. Nevertheless, the proposals in these articles did not have an instant impact. Courts continued to treat stay applications as restrictively as they had in the post-*St Pierre* era.[127] Moreover, these arguments did not immediately create a wider appetite for reforming the law within academic circles. For instance, *Cheshire's Private International Law*, in its eighth edition in 1970, merely pointed, in two footnotes, to the discursive elements within Professor McClean's article.[128]

It might, therefore, be tempting to disregard the importance of these articles when surveying the historical development of staying of proceedings in England. That, though, would be an unduly hasty step. As the discussion in Part V of this chapter goes on to highlight, eventually, the law on discretionary staying of proceedings in England began to undergo piecemeal evolution. These changes, which were put in motion in the mid-1970s, progressed at such pace that, by the mid-1980s, the House of Lords held that the same considerations governed the English courts' (non-)exercise of jurisdiction in both as-of-right and service-out cases. Because of their effectively foreshadowing of what ultimately came to be the modern-day staying-of-proceedings practice in England, the attempts of Inglis and Professors McClean and Pryles to reshape this area of law must be acknowledged.

V. Developments in England in the 1970s and 1980s: The Gradual Departure from *St Pierre*

A. The Problematic Implications Arising from the Narrow Application of the *St Pierre* Test

Soon after the first arguments in favour of reforming the English staying-of-proceedings approach under the *St Pierre* test were made, it became abundantly apparent that the application of the test had problematic implications. The first (and, arguably, most pressing) shortcoming was the greater frequency in the

---

[127] See, eg, *Ionian Bank v Couvreur* [1969] 1 WLR 781 (CA).
[128] *Cheshire's Private International Law* (n 106) 115–16.

instances of 'forum shopping' in England. As briefly touched on in Chapter 2, forum shopping arises where a litigant by-passes the dispute's 'home' and, instead, initiates proceedings in a venue from which it expects to receive the most favourable judgment, notwithstanding the fact that the forum has little (or no) connection with the claim.[129]

By the mid-twentieth century, it had become commonplace for plaintiffs to forum shop in England. At least in part, this situation had been brought about due to the English courts' slowness, in that era, in relinquishing their jurisdiction under the *St Pierre* test. Indeed, as noted by Dr Bell, back then, the courts' approach in England to staying of proceedings, in effect,

> constituted something of an inducement towards forum shopping, or at least provided no effective bar, even in blatant cases. For, as long as a plaintiff was able to serve the defendant while present in [England], however fleeting or fortuitous that presence might be, there was little chance of a stay being secured.[130]

Forum-shopping cases can take different forms. Arguably, the most blatant examples of these cases are those in which the claim form is served on a person who happens to be passing through the English jurisdiction. Almost invariably, the only factor linking the dispute to England in those cases is the defendant's (transient) presence in the forum. Perhaps the starkest example of this category of case is *HRH Maharanee Seethadevi Gaekwar of Baroda v Wildenstein* in 1972.[131]

The case concerned, *inter alia*, an action for rescission of contract brought before the English court by an Indian princess, who resided in France, against a French citizen who was an art expert. The writ was served on the defendant, some nine months after it was issued, when he was in England to attend the Ascot races. He, in turn, sought a stay of the English proceedings on the basis that they had been vexatious and oppressive. The defendant's submission was successful at first instance, with Bridge J granting a stay. He concluded, relying on the *dictum* of Sir Gorell Barnes P in *Logan*,[132] that in cases where the defendant is served with a writ while on a short visit, '*a presumption arises* that the proceedings are oppressive' unless the plaintiff could present evidence of 'absence of oppression to the defendant or … injustice to the plaintiff'.[133]

On the plaintiff's appeal, the Court of Appeal unanimously overturned Bridge J's judgment, holding that, the circumstances of the case did not render

---

[129] *Boys v Chaplin* [1971] AC 356 (HL) 401 (Lord Pearson).

[130] Bell (n 3) para 3.78, citing Wilson and Toohey JJ in *Oceanic Sun Line Special Shipping Co Inc v Fay* (1988) 165 CLR 197, 212.

[131] *HRH Maharanee Seethadevi Gaekwar of Baroda v Wildenstein* [1972] 2 QB 283 (CA).

[132] According to the President: 'if, for instance, as was put in argument, a dispute of complicated character had arisen between two foreigners in a foreign country, and one of them were made defendant in an action in this country by serving him with a writ while he happened to be here for a few days' visit, I apprehend that, although there would be jurisdiction in the court to entertain the suit, it would have little hesitation in treating the action as vexatious and staying it': *Logan* (n 53) 152.

[133] *Maharanee of Baroda* (n 131) 286 (emphasis added).

the plaintiff's commencement of the proceedings in England vexatious and oppressive.[134] The Court of Appeal exhibited no concern for the fact that the case before it was only tenuously linked with England – through the defendant's brief presence in the forum. Tellingly, in this respect, Edmund Davies LJ opined that, in bringing her claim in England, the plaintiff 'was doing no more than our law permits, even though it may have ruined [the defendant's] day at the races. Some might regard her action as bad form; none can legitimately condemn it as an abuse of legal process'.[135]

A few months later, in yet another statement in a different case, which was very much representative of the English courts' relaxed attitude in the middle third of the twentieth century to entertaining disputes that, to all intents and purposes, did not belong to England, Lord Denning MR (in)famously observed that:

> No one who comes to these courts asking for justice should come in vain. ... This right to come here is not confined to Englishmen. It extends to any friendly foreigner. He can seek the aid of our courts if he desires to do so. You may call this 'forum-shopping' if you please, but if the forum is England, it is a good place to shop in, both for the quality of the goods and the speed of service.[136]

These pronouncements show that the vexatious-and-oppressive test, as it had been applied post-*St Pierre*, provided too weak a barrier to limit instances of forum shopping in England. In those circumstances, unless there were to be a more balanced application of the principles for granting stays of proceedings, the problem of forum shopping could in fact have become even more exacerbated.[137]

Second, and aside from fostering the problem of forum shopping, the narrow application of the *St Pierre* test had rendered this aspect of English law out of step with the emerging socio-economic realities in the mid-twentieth century. It was from that era onwards that the volume of global commercial transactions expanded dramatically. As highlighted by Professor Pryles, by the mid-1970s, this development had gained greater urgency.[138] The United Kingdom's accession to (what was then called) the European Economic Community in that period was a further significant contributing factor towards a surge in cross-border commercial relations. The way the *St Pierre* test had come to be applied and interpreted in cases in the middle third of the twentieth century depicted an approach which had little respect for foreign legal systems and was arguably out of step with the changing legal landscape in the mid-1970s.[139] Thus, there were growing socio-economic pressures on English courts to become less inward-looking in applying their discretionary staying-of-proceedings practice.

---

[134] ibid, 292 (Lord Denning MR). Edmund Davies and Stevenson LJJ concurred, though they gave slightly different reasons for their decision.

[135] ibid, 294.

[136] *The Atlantic Star* [1973] QB 364 (CA) 381G and 382C.

[137] Bell (n 3) paras 3.78–3.79.

[138] M Pryles, 'Judicial Darkness on the Oceanic Sun' (1988) 62 *Australian Law Journal* 774, 775.

[139] This lack of respect is well-illustrated in Lord Denning MR's *dictum* in *The Atlantic Star* (n 136) 381G and 382C.

B. The House of Lords' Ruling in *The Atlantic Star*: The Law's Return to the Pre-*St Pierre* Position

The prevalence of these problems with the law in England on staying of proceedings had made it undesirable to continue with the narrow application of the vexatious-and-oppressive test. In response, in a 13-year period, the House of Lords engaged in a step-by-step revision of the law in this area. As the analysis in this section shows, a gradual refinement of the law, and the stewardship and input of individuals, provided the impetus for the English courts' departure from the vexatious-and-oppressive test in *St Pierre* and, ultimately, the adoption of the *forum non conveniens* doctrine.

The first step towards revising the law was taken in *The Atlantic Star*. The dispute arose from a collision involving Dutch vessels, AS and BS, and a Belgian vessel, H, in Belgian waters.[140] The owners of H started proceedings against the owners of AS in the Antwerp Commercial Court. While those proceedings were still pending, the owners of BS brought an action against the owners of AS before the English High Court.[141] In response, the defendants asked for a stay of the English action. The defendants argued that the English action had been vexatious and oppressive because:

> the Commercial Court in Antwerp, rather than the Admiralty Court [in England], was the convenient *forum* for the determination of the plaintiff's claim; that the balance of convenience [in favour of the trial taking place in Belgium] was so strong as to be overwhelming; and that because of this overwhelming balance of convenience, it was vexatious or oppressive for the plaintiff to sue the defendants [in England].[142]

Additionally, the defendants contended that 'so far as attaching importance to convenience of forum is concerned, there should in principle be no difference between the approach of the Court [in service-out cases], on the one hand, and when asked to stay an [as-of-right] action'.[143] This line of reasoning broadly chimed with the proposals of Inglis and Professors McClean and Pryles for reforming the law on discretionary staying of proceedings, which were discussed earlier.

Brandon J, however, rejected these arguments. On the facts of the case, his Lordship found that although the Belgian court was better placed for resolving the dispute, for 'practical reasons', the defendant had failed to convince the English court that the action before it was vexatious and oppressive.[144] As for the defendants' other contention, Brandon J stated that service-out cases 'afforded little or no guidance to the exercise of the Court's discretion to stay' as-of-right proceedings

---

[140] The collision had taken place between AS and BS. Consequently, BS collided with H, amounting to the sinking of both BS and H.
[141] *The Atlantic Star* [1972] 1 Lloyd's Rep 534 (Queen's Bench Division, Admiralty Court).
[142] ibid, 538 (Brandon J summarising the defendants' submissions).
[143] ibid, 540.
[144] ibid, 539–40.

in England.[145] Brandon J's decision to decline to stay the proceedings in England was subsequently upheld by the Court of Appeal.[146]

Ultimately, the owners of AS appealed to the House of Lords.[147] Robert Goff QC, as he then was, was the lead counsel arguing the appeal on their behalf. He criticised the English courts' preoccupation with upholding the plaintiffs' right to initiate proceedings in England, contending that it favoured plaintiffs, encouraged forum shopping, and went against international comity.[148] Robert Goff QC pursued a bold argument which had not hitherto been directly advocated before English courts: he exhorted the court to recognise in England (what he called) the 'Scottish and American approach' to the staying of proceedings – under which the court could give up its jurisdiction in favour of a more appropriate forum elsewhere under the *forum non conveniens* doctrine.[149]

Nevertheless, the House of Lords unanimously rejected Robert Goff QC's invitation to adopt the *forum non conveniens* doctrine into English law. Lord Reid, a Scottish Law Lord, considered the doctrine to be 'peculiar [to] the Scottish method of establishing jurisdiction by arrestment *ad fundandem jurisdictionem*'.[150] Lord Wilberforce was equally unpersuaded by the arguments in favour of embracing the *forum non conveniens* doctrine. As his Lordship noted, 'for some 100 years the law of England [on discretionary staying of proceedings] ha[d] taken a divergent path with its own rules, defined and adjusted in numerous cases, some of high authority'.[151]

However, their Lordships' refusal to transplant the *forum non conveniens* doctrine into English law did not signify the House of Lords' contentment with (or, indeed, endorsement of) how the *St Pierre* test had come to be applied by English courts in stay-of-proceedings or *lis alibi pendens* cases. In a three-to-two majority decision, which was later described by Lord Diplock as a 'landmark in the development of English law',[152] the House of Lords acknowledged the undesirability of the approach in *St Pierre* and triggered a process of departure from it.[153] In particular, Lord Reid was critical of Lord Denning MR's apparent endorsement of forum shopping, evidenced in his abovementioned remarks in the Court of Appeal in

---

[145] ibid, 540.

[146] *The Atlantic Star* (n 136).

[147] Lord Reid, Lord Morris of Borth-Y-Gest, Lord Wilberforce, Lord Simon of Glaisdale and Lord Kilbrandon.

[148] *The Atlantic Star* (n 2) 441.

[149] ibid, 442. Robert Goff QC made specific reference to the House of Lords' decision in the *Les Armateurs Français* case (n 76) and the federal American decisions in *Canada Malting Company Limited v Paterson Steamship Limited* (1932) 285 US 413 and *Gulf Oil Corp v Gilbert* (1947) 330 US 501.

[150] ibid, 454.

[151] ibid, 464. Lord Morris (ibid, 456) and Lord Kilbrandon, another Scottish Law Lord, (ibid, 476) raised a similar reason in rejecting Robert Goff QC's argument. Lord Simon did not mention his specific reason(s) for not adopting the *forum non conveniens* doctrine, though he generally agreed with Lord Morris's speech.

[152] *The Abidin Daver* [1984] AC 398 (HL) 407.

[153] Lord Reid, Lord Wilberforce and Lord Kilbrandon spoke for the majority; Lord Morris and Lord Simon dissented.

The Atlantic Star. In his Lordship's opinion, the Master of the Rolls' *dictum* recalled 'the good old days, the passing of which many may regret, when inhabitants of this island felt an innate superiority over those unfortunate enough to belong to other races'.[154] Accordingly, Lord Reid stated that 'time [was] ripe for a re-examination of the rather insular' approach to granting stays following *St Pierre*.[155]

In this respect, Lord Reid opted for a more 'liberal' construction of the *St Pierre* test as the most prudent course of action in reforming the law – and addressing the problem of forum shopping.[156] Lord Wilberforce, too, favoured liberalising the *St Pierre* test. In his Lordship's view 'vexatious' had been 'a word of illustration rather than limitation', and that 'too close and rigid an application of it may defeat the spirit which lies behind it'.[157] Lord Wilberforce proceeded to combine his reluctance to replace the *St Pierre* test with his preference for a more liberal interpretation of the test, arriving at the following construction:

> First, a plaintiff should not lightly be denied the right to sue in an English court, if jurisdiction is properly founded. The right is not absolute. The courts are open, even to actions between foreigners, relating to foreign matters. But they retain a residual power to stay their proceedings ... Secondly, in considering whether a stay should be granted the court must take into account (i) any advantage to the plaintiff; (ii) any disadvantage to the defendant: this is the critical equation, and in some cases it will be a difficult one to establish.[158]

The first limb of Lord Wilberforce's test was noticeably more balanced than the first stage of the *St Pierre* test: it explicitly underscored that the plaintiffs' right to commence proceedings in England was not absolute and was subject to the courts' 'residual power' to stay their proceedings. What is more, and as highlighted by the second part of the liberalised test, Lord Wilberforce placed greater emphasis on a need for English courts to weigh equitably the competing interests of the litigants in deciding whether to stay (or sustain) proceedings commenced in England as of right. Consequently, the liberalisation of the vexatious-and-oppressive test led to it being applied in a much more similar fashion as it had been in cases such as *Logan, Egbert,* and *Norton* at the start of the twentieth century. Applying these principles to the facts of the case, the defendants' appeal was allowed, and the English proceedings were stayed.

In many ways, it was not surprising that in *The Atlantic Star* the House of Lords decided to depart from Scott LJ's formulation in *St Pierre*, and introduce a test which made it easier for defendants to obtain stays of as-of-right proceedings in England. Given all the ever-increasing (and hard-to-ignore) shortcomings with the English courts' application of the vexatious-and-oppressive test after *St Pierre*, any other step would have been unrealistic and, arguably, imprudent. Nevertheless,

---

[154] *The Atlantic Star* (n 2) 453.
[155] ibid.
[156] ibid, 454.
[157] ibid, 466 and 468.
[158] ibid, 468.

the formulation which the majority Law Lords arrived at in their final analysis was somewhat curious. Putting all of *St Pierre's* ills to one side, one thing was virtually certain about the approach under it: once the English court had assumed jurisdiction over a dispute, it was highly resistant to relinquishing it. The liberalised formulation, however, rendered the test for the staying of as-of-right proceedings in England imprecise and vague, as it hinted at greater scope for granting stays without providing much in terms of detail on the kind of considerations which influence the courts' decision making.

It might, therefore, be questioned why the majority Law Lords – who included Lord Reid and Lord Wilberforce, two of the finest legal minds of that era – opted for their favoured tack. It is argued that the majority Law Lords' decision to simply liberalise the *St Pierre* test was largely influenced by their Lordships' desire to effect an *incremental* (as opposed to a *wholesale*) reform to the law on discretionary non-exercise of jurisdiction. After all, it had been settled law for around 40 years that English courts would hardly ever decline to exercise jurisdiction in stay or *lis alibi pendens* cases under the vexatious-and-oppressive test.[159] Any re-articulation of the test other than one which maintained the relevant principles in *St Pierre*, but in a watered-down form, could have been seen as being too radical at that time, and likely to have created uncertainty for litigants.

Despite some confusion surrounding the House of Lords' decision in *The Atlantic Star*, the case is regarded as a turning point in the English courts' approach to discretionary non-exercise of jurisdiction. The sources within the literature were quick in identifying this changing landscape. For example, the ninth edition of *Cheshire's Private International Law*, published in 1974, contained a section entitled 'forum non conveniens'.[160] No such section had featured in the previous editions of this influential book. Moreover, commenting on the decision in *The Atlantic Star* in the *British Yearbook of International Law*, Carter considered that the impact of the majority's ruling went beyond mere liberal interpretation of the words 'vexatious' and 'oppressive' with the result that, when deciding whether to stay its proceedings, the court became engaged in balancing the differing interests of the parties involved.[161] Put simply, the pronouncements of the majority in *The Atlantic Star* had defined the path for the future developments of this aspect of the English law. As the discussion in the remainder of this chapter proceeds to demonstrate, the same incrementalism, which was at the heart of the majority's approach to doctrinal reform, continued to act as the principal engine for the law's evolution.

---

[159] This consideration may have played a part in the dissenting Law Lords' preference for an Act of Parliament to provide the basis for displacing the English approach to the staying of proceedings as outlined in the *St Pierre* test: Lord Morris (ibid, 462) and Lord Simon (ibid, 473).

[160] PM North, *Cheshire's Private International Law* 9th edn (London, Butterworths, 1974) 123–26.

[161] PB Carter, 'Staying of Actions and the Doctrine of Forum Non Conveniens' (1972–1973) 46 *British Yearbook of International Law* 428, 430. See, similarly, A Maclean, 'Foreign Collisions and *Forum Conveniens*' (1973) 22 *International & Comparative Law Quarterly* 748, 478.

C. *MacShannon v Rockware Glass Ltd*: The Next Step Away from the *St Pierre* Test

As already indicated, the majority Law Lords' liberalisation of the vexatious-and-oppressive test in *The Atlantic Star* amounted to a welcome step away from the unsatisfactory implications which had resulted from the plaintiff-friendly way in which the vexatious-and-oppressive test had been applied after *St Pierre*. The liberalised formulation, though, had its own problems. Chief among these was the lack of sufficient guidelines within the test for litigants to be able to form a clear sense of whether, in a given case, stay of proceedings in England would be granted. In other words, the test in *The Atlantic Star* provided too imprecise a basis for the courts' decision making in stay cases and, thus, had the propensity to lead to unpredictable outcomes. As a result, and in order to counter this shortcoming, further refinement of the law had to be made.

By far the most important reform came around four years after the decision in *The Atlantic Star*, in *MacShannon v Rockware Glass Ltd*.[162] *MacShannon* concerned an action by plaintiffs, four Scotsmen living and working in Scotland, against the defendant English companies. The dispute arose from injuries sustained by the plaintiffs in industrial accidents in Scotland. The defendant companies applied to stay the action in England, pointing to Scotland as the venue in which the plaintiffs' claims should be heard.

At first instance, Robert Goff J rejected the defendants' application for a stay of the English action. He summarised the principles in *The Atlantic Star* and stated:

> [t]hirdly, *possibly a negative point*, it is clear from *The Atlantic Star*, both from arguments and judgments, that English courts have rejected the principle of forum non conveniens as a criterion for deciding whether or not stay of execution should be granted.[163]

This statement might be regarded as an indirect criticism of the House of Lords' rejection of his invitation, as counsel in *The Atlantic Star*, to embrace the *forum non conveniens* principle. Robert Goff J's apparent criticism, however, was not shared by the Court of Appeal upon the defendants' appeal. Stephenson LJ considered that the House of Lords had made its position clear by unanimously deciding not to embrace the doctrine in *The Atlantic Star*.[164] As for the substance of the appeal, however, the Court of Appeal upheld Robert Goff J's judgment in a majority decision.[165] In arguably the most revealing sign of how far the law on discretionary staying of proceedings in England had evolved, from the position

---

[162] *MacShannon v Rockware Glass Ltd* [1978] AC 795 (HL).
[163] Cited in Stephenson LJ's judgment at the Court of Appeal level: [1977] 1 WLR 376 (CA) 383–84 (emphasis added).
[164] ibid, 384–85.
[165] Stephenson and Waller LJJ spoke for the majority; Lord Denning MR dissented.

in the intervening years between the rulings in *St Pierre* and *The Atlantic Star*, Lord Denning MR, dissenting, observed:

> [p]reviously we were disposed to think too much of our own legal system. It was so superior to all others that, if a plaintiff managed to serve a defendant while he was in this country, we nearly always let him continue with it. Time and time again we said that when a plaintiff has validly invoked the jurisdiction of these courts – by serving the defendant here without having to ask the leave of anyone – he is prima facie entitled to pursue it to the end. No matter that his action arose in a far off land, it was not to be stayed unless it was vexatious or oppressive or otherwise an abuse of the process of the court. ... Those good old days are gone. Our entry into the Common Market has brought many changes. One of them is the recognition that the legal systems of other countries have their merits, too: and we must learn to live with them.[166]

These observations represented a major U-turn on the part of the Master of the Rolls from the stance he had adopted in *Maharanee of Baroda* and *The Atlantic Star*.[167] Nevertheless, he was in the minority in concluding that the English action should be stayed in favour of courts in Scotland. However, on the defendants' subsequent appeal to the House of Lords, their Lordships were unanimous in reaching the decision that the proceedings in England should be stayed.

Lord Keith of Kinkel and Lord Diplock delivered the two main speeches.[168] While Lord Keith preferred to apply the test in *The Atlantic Star*, Lord Diplock was not content with keeping the law as it was. At the same time, analysis of Lord Diplock's speech indicates that he was no revolutionary and sought to continue the law's advancement in a more piecemeal fashion. The following passage in his speech is illustrative of this point:

> It would not be consonant with the traditional way in which judicial precedent has played its part in the development of the common law of England, to attempt to incorporate holus-bolus from some other system of law, even so close as that of Scotland, doctrines or legal concepts that have hitherto been unrecognised in English common law. The progress of the common law is gradual. It is undertaken step by step as what has been stated in a previous precedent to be the law is re-examined and modified so as to bring it into closer accord with the changed conditions in which it falls to be applied today. But this is not to say that the result of proceeding by the latter course of reasoning will necessarily be very different from that which would have been achieved by adopting into English law a concept from some other legal system. Destinations that are very close to one another may be reached by different routes. So there would be nothing surprising in the fact that in rejecting as the appropriate route the importation into English common law of the Scots doctrine of forum non conveniens in favour of the more traditional method of developing this branch of the common law from where the

---

[166] *MacShannon* (n 163) 380.
[167] See also Pryles (n 4) 681.
[168] Lord Salmon, Lord Fraser of Tullybelton and Lord Russell of Killowen made shorter concurring speeches.

precedent in *St Pierre* … had left it in 1936, the majority of the House had nevertheless [allowed for the Scottish doctrine to be admitted by the back door].[169]

Accordingly, Lord Diplock very much picked up from where the majority in *The Atlantic Star* had left off. His Lordship regarded that the balancing of the parties' conflicting interests (as to where the litigation should be brought) was at the heart of the liberalised vexatious-and-oppressive test. The prominence of this balancing exercise, he noted, had placed the English and Scottish staying-of-proceedings approaches much closer to one another, albeit the English courts had chosen to develop the law in a more step-by-step manner.[170] In view of the changes to the law since the decision in *The Atlantic Star*, Lord Diplock considered that the continued reference to the words 'vexatious' and 'oppressive' in any new formulation for non-exercise of jurisdiction was likely to cause confusion.[171] His Lordship, therefore, proceeded to reformulate the test for staying of as-of-right proceedings in England as follows:

> (2) In order to justify a stay two conditions must be satisfied, one positive and the other negative: (*a*) the defendant must satisfy the court that there is another forum to whose jurisdiction he is amenable in which justice can be done between the parties at substantially less inconvenience or expense, and (*b*) the stay must not deprive the plaintiff of a legitimate personal or juridical advantage which would be available to him if he invoked the jurisdiction of the English court.[172]

Put differently, in the first place, the defendant had to identify another foreign forum which is the 'natural and appropriate forum' for the dispute's litigation and would also take jurisdiction over it. However, the court would refrain from granting a stay if that would prevent the plaintiff from obtaining a legitimate personal or juridical advantage.

One noticeable change from the *St Pierre* formulation was that the *MacShannon* test did not explicitly indicate that English courts should be slow in granting a stay of proceedings. Although Lord Diplock did not include the term 'vexatious and oppressive' in the new test, the second limb continued to echo the second part of limb two of the *St Pierre* test. In relation to the burden of proof, Lord Diplock made it clear that the defendant had to satisfy the first limb of the test, and the plaintiff had to prove the second part. Nevertheless, there were passages in the other Law Lords' speeches which suggested that the burden was entirely on the defendant to convince the court that the English action should be stayed. For example, Lord Salmon considered that 'the question for the English court is whether the defendant … can establish that to refuse a stay would produce injustice'.[173] Similarly, Lord Russell stated that '[i]t must, I apprehend, be for the

---

[169] *MacShannon* (n 162) 811, citing a passage from Lord Simon's dissenting speech in *The Atlantic Star* (n 2) 473.
[170] ibid.
[171] ibid.
[172] ibid, 812.
[173] ibid, 819.

defendant to show cause why in any given case a stay ought in the exercise of judicial discretion to be ordered'.[174]

This apparent lack of clarity in relation to the burden-of-proof question was the main subject of Carter's critique of the case.[175] He concluded his analysis by expressing doubt about the existence of support in the case for Lord Diplock's statement that the burden of proof was to shift from the defendant to the plaintiff once the first stage of the test has been satisfied.[176] More generally, Carter was underwhelmed by the decision, deeming it to be 'unmomentous'.[177]

However, Carter's view of *MacShannon* was not widely shared among others with an interest in the field. For instance, Professor Pryles greeted the ruling with much more enthusiasm, and considered it a landmark which did not 'merely re-affirm the majority opinion in *The Atlantic Star* but arguably [went] further'.[178] Furthermore, Professor Pryles welcomed the effect of the *MacShannon* test on the English courts' approach to discretionary non-exercise of jurisdiction, arguing that:

> [t]he common law jurisdiction rules are not entirely satisfactory and can lead to the assumption of jurisdiction in the most tenuous circumstances where there is really no significant connection between the litigation and the forum. In these circumstances a liberal rule as to the staying of actions is required. It cuts down local parochialism as regards judicial adjudication, and is consistent with a spirit of international legal cohesion and integration. Moreover, empowering courts to decline to hear cases having little connection with the forum reduces the workload of the courts and avoids difficult choice of law problems which such cases often entail. The [*MacShannon*] rule is very similar to the Scottish and American doctrine of forum non conveniens, in substance if not in form.[179]

The commentary in the tenth edition of *Cheshire and North's Private International Law*, published in 1979, also suggests that the decision was anything but unmomentous.[180] In this edition, the decisions in *Logan*, *Egbert*, and *Norton*, which had been all but ignored in earlier editions, were extensively discussed in the main body of the text.[181]

In sum, by the late 1970s, and after four decades of near irrelevance, the practice of discretionary staying of proceedings in England had been resurrected, with Lord Diplock's test in *MacShannon* replacing the *St Pierre* formula. The result was that, in deciding whether to (dis)continue the as-of-right proceedings in England,

---

[174] ibid, 823.
[175] PB Carter, 'Jurisdiction: The Propriety of an English Forum' (1978) 49 *British Yearbook of International Law* 291.
[176] ibid, 293.
[177] ibid, 291.
[178] Pryles (n 4) 681.
[179] ibid, 684–85.
[180] PM North, *Cheshire and North's Private International Law* 10th edn (London, Butterworths, 1979) 119–22.
[181] ibid, 119–20.

the English courts' approach had become much closer to their Scottish counter-parts' practice under the *forum non conveniens* doctrine.

D. Staying of Proceedings in England Immediately after the Introduction of the *MacShannon* Test

Soon after its introduction, the *MacShannon* test began to be applied in other areas of private international law. For example, in *Castanho v Brown & Root* in 1981,[182] a unanimous House of Lords ruled that the *MacShannon* test was to be relied on in determining whether anti-suit injunctions should be issued.[183] Lord Scarman, who gave the only reasoned speech in *Castanho*, transposed the test in *MacShannon* into the context of the case before him. Accordingly, under the new test, in order to justify the grant of an injunction the applicant must establish:

> (a) that the English court is a forum to whose jurisdiction they are amenable in which justice can be done at substantially less inconvenience and expense, and (b) the injunction must not deprive the plaintiff of a legitimate personal or juridical advantage which would be available to him if he invoked the [foreign] jurisdiction.[184]

As touched on in Chapter 2, anti-suit injunctions are discretionary measures which English courts might issue in order to restrain a litigant from commencing (or continuing) proceeding in a foreign forum. Although, *forum (non) conveniens* and anti-suit injunctions are similar – in that they are both utilised in order to uphold jurisdictional values – they are conceptually different doctrines. As a result, the House of Lords' decision to recalibrate the test for granting anti-suit injunctions in line with the *MacShannon* test marked a significant development.[185]

Despite the *MacShannon* test's growing prominence, doctrinally, it was not the finished product. There were still a number of important aspects concerning its application and interpretation which required further clarification. For example, the conflicting passages in the Law Lords' speeches in *MacShannon* had made it difficult to form a clear view about the precise meaning (and future interpretation) of each of the elements of the test. These imperfections and uncertainties with the test had to be addressed.

For the most part, the task of refining the law in this area fell on individuals in the judiciary and academia. It is notable that, compared to the immediate

---

[182] *Castanho v Brown & Root* [1981] AC 557 (HL).
[183] Lord Scarman, Lord Wilberforce, Lord Diplock, Lord Keith of Kinkel and Lord Bridge of Harwich concurring.
[184] *Castanho* (n 182) 575.
[185] For a criticism of this decision, see A Briggs, 'No Interference with Foreign Court' (1982) 31 *International & Comparative Law Quarterly* 189.

aftermath of *The Atlantic Star*, where academics were somewhat responsive to the developments at the court level, after *MacShannon* they played a more proactive role in recasting the approach to staying of proceedings in England. As the discussion in the remainder of this chapter demonstrates, collectively, these individuals played a major part in the reform of this aspect of the English conflict-of-laws rules in the 1980s.

In the early 1980s, and as a High Court judge, Robert Goff J was particularly influential in elaborating the law in relation to the first limb of the *MacShannon* test. For instance, in *Trendtex Trading Corp v Credit Suisse*,[186] he stated that where a foreign law is the law applicable to a dispute, the courts of that forum, rather than England, might be a more natural or appropriate venue for the resolution of the dispute.[187] In *European Asian Bank v Punjab and Sind Bank*,[188] he observed that the first limb of the *MacShannon* test was not satisfied where the party seeking a stay could not point to a *single* alternative forum which was the dispute's centre of gravity.[189] Indeed, when the litigation in *European Asian Bank v Punjab and Sind Bank* reached the Court of Appeal, Stephenson LJ recognised Robert Goff J's industry in instigating the change of tack in England in relation to the practice of discretionary staying of proceedings – both as counsel in *The Atlantic Star* and as a first-instance judge – observing that 'no Judge on the bench has had to study and state the principles on which proceedings in this country are stayed more often and more carefully than [Robert Goff J]'.[190]

While the bases for the application of the *MacShannon* test were being gradually clarified in stay cases in England, contributions by legal scholars were also being made regarding how the law in this area might be refined further. In this respect, a salient contribution was made by Professor Briggs in an article published in *Legal Studies* in 1983.[191] This article took stock of the fast-moving developments in the law in the aftermath of the House of Lords' ruling in *The Atlantic Star*. In it, Professor Briggs observed that following the departure from the *St Pierre* test, staying of proceedings in England was premised on the defendant's identifying of the natural forum for the dispute, but also 'an evaluation and maybe a balancing of the advantages to the plaintiff of being allowed to sue in [England], and disadvantages to the defendant of being sued there instead of in the natural forum'.[192] He questioned the merit of focusing on 'personal advantage' as a basis for the new stay-of-proceedings practice in England.[193]

---

[186] *Trendtex Trading Corp v Credit Suisse* [1980] QB 629 (CA).

[187] See, also, *The Hida Maru* [1981] 2 Lloyd's Rep 510 (CA), where the Court of Appeal sustained the action in England as English law governed the contract between the parties.

[188] *European Asian Bank v Punjab and Sind Bank* [1981] 2 Lloyd's Rep 651.

[189] In this case, the alternative forums in whose favour the defendants sought to obtain a stay were India and Singapore.

[190] *European Asian Bank v Punjab and Sind Bank* [1982] 2 Lloyd's Rep 356 (CA) 363.

[191] Briggs (n 14).

[192] ibid, 82.

[193] ibid, 83–84.

According to Professor Briggs, '[although] the weighing of advantages and disadvantages is attractively easy in theory, its theoretical justifications seems obscure alongside the identification of a natural forum, and its operation in practice is less easy than at first sight'.[194]

In attempting to improve the *MacShannon* test – by affording it clearer and more predictable grounds of application – Professor Briggs proposed that, for the purpose of the first limb of the test, the natural forum was to be regarded as 'the courts of the jurisdiction with which [the dispute] has the most real and substantial connection [and] will hear that action'.[195] He noted that the test for identifying the natural forum was broadly similar to the one applied in determining the proper law of a contract in the absence of parties' express designation.[196] As for the second limb of the *MacShannon* test, he identified the following instances as warranting for courts in England to sustain their proceedings, notwithstanding the fact that the foreign court has been shown to be the natural forum: (i) when proceedings in the natural forum would amount to the denial of justice to the plaintiff – to the point that judgment rendered in that forum would be refused recognition or enforcement in England; (ii) the action is time-barred in the natural forum; and (iii) an Act of Parliament in England forbids the action from being litigated in the natural forum.[197]

When considered at a general level, Professor Briggs's suggestions for the refinement of the English staying-of-proceedings practice had certain resemblances with the reform option advanced by Inglis and Professors McClean and Pryles in the late 1960s and early 1970s. They had contended, it is recalled, that in deciding whether to stay as-of-right proceedings, English courts should apply the test for assuming jurisdiction in service-out cases. As discussed earlier, the factors under which leave for summoning a foreign-based defendant would be granted were not much different from those which helped the court to identify a contract's proper law in the absence of the parties' stipulation. In spirit, therefore, Professor Briggs's contribution revived broadly the same themes as those which had been advanced in a different form in earlier decades.

E. The Ruling in *The Abidin Daver*: A Further Step Closer to the Outright Adoption of *Forum Non Conveniens* in England

The first real opportunity for Professor Briggs's proposals for reforming the *MacShannon* test to have an impact on the law's development arose when the litigation in *The Abidin Daver*,[198] a *lis alibi pendens* case, reached the House of Lords.

---

[194] ibid, 84.
[195] ibid, 85.
[196] ibid.
[197] ibid, 89–93.
[198] *The Abidin Daver* (n 152).

However, in this case, their Lordships exhibited little enthusiasm in advancing the law by embracing reform options such as the one articulated by Professor Briggs. Instead, they simply endorsed the way courts in England had interpreted and applied the *MacShannon* test.

The Abidin Daver concerned a dispute following a collision between a Turkish vessel, AD, and a Cuban vessel, LM, in Turkish waters. While an action by the owners of AD against the owners of LM was pending in Turkey, the owners of LM initiated a claim in England. In return, the owners of AD sought to stay the English proceedings. At first instance, Sheen J held that the English proceedings should be stayed. The LM's owners' appeal to the Court of Appeal, however, was unanimously allowed and the stay order was reversed.[199] The Court of Appeal ruled that Sheen J had given too much weight to the existence of pending proceedings in Turkey. Subsequently, the owners of AD appealed to the House of Lords. The House unanimously allowed their appeal and stayed the English proceedings.

In the House of Lords, the main question for consideration concerned the significance that had to be attached to the existence of parallel proceedings in Turkey for the purposes of the stay application. Lord Diplock, who delivered one of the two main speeches in the case,[200] stated that the existence of *lis alibi pendens* was simply one of the factors which the court had to take into account in deciding whether to give up its jurisdiction.[201] Furthermore, and in relation to the second limb of the *MacShannon* test, he clarified that it was for the plaintiff to show, using 'cogent evidence', that staying the proceedings in England in favour of the natural forum would cause him an injustice.[202] Lord Diplock proceeded to remark that in view of the developments in the law in the years following the decision in *The Atlantic Star*, the law in England on discretionary staying of proceedings in stay and *lis alibi pendens* cases was 'indistinguishable' from the Scottish *forum non conveniens* doctrine.[203]

In some ways, the decision in *The Abidin Daver* amounted to a welcome development. In particular, it put an end to nearly six years of confusion generated following the *MacShannon* ruling by making it plain that the party resisting the stay had to bear the onus of establishing the requirements under the second limb of the test.[204] Nevertheless, academic commentators persisted with their call for

---

[199] *The Abidin Daver* [1983] 1 WLR 884 (CA) (Sir John Donaldson MR, Dunn and Purchas LJJ).

[200] Lord Brandon of Oakbrook delivered the other main speech. Lord Edmund-Davies, Lord Keith of Kinkel and Lord Templeman gave short opinions.

[201] *The Abidin Daver* (n 152) 410.

[202] ibid, 411.

[203] ibid (Lord Edmund-Davies, Lord Keith and Lord Templeman concurring).

[204] Although in *MacShannon* Lord Diplock had suggested that the burden was on the plaintiff to establish the second limb of the test, certain passages in Lord Salmon's and Lord Russell's speeches in the same case had appeared to point to the burden of proof being on the defendant. Indeed, in a subsequent case – namely, *European Asian Bank* – Robert Goff J had stated at first instance that the burden of proving that the plaintiff would not face a personal or juridical disadvantage if sent to the alternative foreign forum was on the defendant: (n 188) 656. This approach had been followed in a number of subsequent authorities such as *Castanho* (n 182), *European Asian Bank*

more reform. In one significant contribution, published in the *International &
Comparative Law Quarterly* in 1986, Professor Schuz analysed the *MacShannon*
test, particularly from the viewpoint of its effectiveness in controlling forum
shopping.[205] A large part of her article concerned an outline of the law in England
on the discretionary staying of proceedings.[206] She noted that, although, thanks
to the *MacShannon* test, the law was doctrinally in a more satisfactory place than
under the *St Pierre* formula, it still suffered from a number of shortcomings.[207]
Among others, she pointed to the 'great difficulty and uncertainty [arising] over
the identification of legitimate advantages', for the purpose of the second limb of
the formulation, and the fact that the balancing of all the circumstances involved
in the case 'cannot be performed on any more practicable basis than judicial
instinct', as being some of the main defects in the law in this area.[208]

Building on Professor Briggs's proposed approach to discretionary non-
exercise of jurisdiction in his *Legal Studies* article, though by reworking certain
aspects of it, Professor Schuz argued that English courts should adopt the following test for granting stays of proceedings brought in England as of right:

> the courts of another country have a closer and more real connection with the action
> and that the foreign court has jurisdiction to hear the dispute *unless the plaintiff proves
> that in all the circumstances of the case it would be unjust for the action to be tried in that
> foreign court.* Provided always that (i) no action shall be stayed if the judgment of the
> foreign court would not be entitled to be recognised in England; and (ii) no action shall
> be stayed where to do so would be contrary to express statutory provision.[209]

Given that this test embraced many aspects of Professor Briggs's proposed formulation, it is contended that Professor Schuz's suggested formulation bears many
similarities with the test applied by English courts when determining the proper
law of a contract in the absence of the parties' stipulation – which, as pointed out
earlier, broadly resembled considerations at the heart of the English courts' exercise of jurisdiction in service-out cases. In that respect, in much the same vein
as Professor Briggs's *Legal Studies* article, Professor Schuz's contention on how
the English courts' approach to staying of proceedings in as-of-right cases should
evolve touched on themes which had already been explored in the academic
contributions of Inglis and Professors McClean and Pryles in the period between
the mid-1960s and early 1970s.

(n 190), *The Messiniaki Tolmi* [1983] 1 Lloyd's Rep 666 – all cited in R Schuz, 'Controlling Forum-
Shopping: The Impact of *MacShannon v. Rockware Glass Ltd.*' (1986) 35 *International & Comparative
Law Quarterly* 374, 399.

[205] Schuz, ibid. See, also, A Briggs, 'The Staying of Actions on the Ground of "Forum Non Conveniens"
in England Today' [1984] *Lloyd's Maritime and Commercial Law Quarterly* 227.

[206] Schuz (n 204) 378–99.

[207] ibid, 408.

[208] ibid.

[209] ibid, 411 (emphasis in the original, citation omitted).

F. *Spiliada Maritime Corporation v Cansulex Ltd*: The Adoption of *Forum Non Conveniens* in England

A few months after the publication of Professor Schuz's article, the litigation in *Spiliada Maritime Corporation v Cansulex Ltd* went before the House of Lords. *Spiliada* was a service-out case in which the main question was whether the English court should give permission for proceedings to be served on a company incorporated in British Columbia. Although, the issue of staying of as-of-right proceedings was not directly in contention, a considerable proportion of their Lordships' speeches was devoted to discussing the law in England on that matter. In what has become one of the most important judicial pronouncements in English conflict of laws in the twentieth century, the House of Lords finally recognised the doctrine of *forum non conveniens* as the basis for granting stays of proceedings brought in England as of right. What is more, the ruling made it plain that the same test governed the English courts' (non-)exercise of jurisdiction in *both* stay and service-out cases.

Coincidentally (or otherwise), Lord Goff of Chieveley – whom as Robert Goff QC in *The Atlantic Star* had argued in favour of the adoption of the *forum non conveniens* doctrine – delivered the main speech in the case.[210] Citing (with implicit approval) Lord Diplock's statement in *The Abidin Daver* – namely, that the English and Scottish laws on discretionary non-exercise of jurisdiction were indistinguishable – Lord Goff deemed it appropriate to examine a number of Scottish cases which spelt out the framework for staying of actions in Scotland.[211] In this respect, his Lordship quoted the following passage in Lord Kinnear's judgment in *Sim v Robinow* as representing the law in both England and Scotland:

> the plea can never be sustained unless the court is satisfied that there is some other tribunal, having competent jurisdiction, in which the case may be tried more suitably for the interests of all the parties and for the ends of justice.[212]

Additionally, Lord Goff drew on a number of other leading Scottish *forum non conveniens* decisions,[213] before moving on to refine the *MacShannon* formula.[214] The combined result of this analysis was the following 'basic principle', which has become known as the 'more-appropriate-forum test':

> ... a stay [would] only be granted on the ground of forum non conveniens where the court [was] satisfied that there [was] some other available forum, having competent jurisdiction, which [was] the appropriate forum for the trial of the action, i.e. in which

---

[210] Lord Keith, Lord Griffiths and Lord Mackay of Clashfern concurred; Lord Templeman reached the same decision, giving different reasons.

[211] *Spiliada* (n 1) 474.

[212] *Sim* (n 15) 668.

[213] Eg, *Longworth* (n 11) and *Les Armateurs Français* (n 76).

[214] *Spiliada* (n 1) 474.

the case may be tried more suitably for the interests of all the parties and the ends of justice.[215]

Evidently, Scottish cases and commentary were influential in shaping Lord Goff's conception of staying of proceedings in English law under the *forum non conveniens* doctrine.[216] As far as the wording of Lord Goff's basic principle was concerned, it was virtually identical to (if not, indeed, a paraphrase of) the test articulated in Lord Kinnear's *dictum* in *Sim*. Furthermore, the amendment of the second limb of the *MacShannon* test went some way towards freeing the staying-of-proceedings practice in England from the overhanging influence of the *St Pierre* test and gave the impression that the English court fully embraced the Scottish *forum non conveniens* doctrine. In these circumstances, it might be concluded, as some seem to have,[217] that Lord Goff's basic principle signified a wholesale transplantation into English law of the Scottish *forum non conveniens* doctrine. It is argued, however, that this would not be an entirely convincing conclusion to reach.

An assessment of Lord Goff's basic principle in *Spiliada* points to the continued significance of the earlier English developments in the way in which the *Spiliada* doctrine was shaped. One of the most notable differences between the *Spiliada* and the Scottish doctrines was the number of steps in which they were being applied. Throughout its existence as a legal doctrine, Scottish *forum non conveniens* had been applied in one stage:[218] the justice to the pursuers in sustaining the Scottish proceedings was considered in conjunction with all other factors – such as the proper law of the contract or the location of the evidence and witnesses – in deciding whether a foreign forum was more connected to the case in hand. In this context, the following passage from Lord Jauncey's judgment in *Credit Chimique v James Scott Engineering Group Ltd* provides a helpful illustration of the operation of the Scottish *forum non conveniens* doctrine:

(1) ... the burden of satisfying the tribunal that the case submitted to it for decision should not be allowed to proceed lie[d] upon the defender who table[d] the plea; (2) ... this burden [could] only be discharged where weighty reasons [have been advanced] why an admitted jurisdiction should not be exercised, mere balance of inconvenience being insufficient; (3) ... there [was] another court of competent jurisdiction in which the matter in question [could] be litigated; and (4) ... considerations

---

[215] ibid, 476.

[216] AE Anton, *Private International Law* 1st edn (Edinburgh, W Green & Son Ltd, 1967) 150.

[217] JG Collier, 'Staying of Actions and Forum Non Conveniens. English Law Goes Scotch' (1987) 46 *Cambridge Law Journal* 33, and E Blackburn, 'Lis Alibi Pendens and Forum Non Conveniens in Collision Actions After the Civil Jurisdiction and Judgments Act 1982' [1988] *Lloyd's Maritime and Commercial Law Quarterly* 91.

[218] See, eg, *Lawford* (n 81), *Robinson* (n 81), *Robinson v Robinson's Trustees* (n 81), *Sheaf Lance* (n 81), *Woodbury* (n 81), *Woodbury v Sutherland's Trustees* (n 81), *Struth v Laing* 1943 SLT 11 (ShCt), *MacLean v MacLean* 1947 SC 79 (IH), *Jubert v Church Commissioners for England* 1952 SC 160 (OH), *Babington v Babington* 1955 SC 115 (IH), *Argyllshire Weavers Ltd v A Macaulay (Tweeds) Ltd* 1962 SC 388 (IH), *Balshaw v Kelly (otherwise Balshaw)* 1966 SLT 297 (OH), *Balshaw v Balshaw* 1967 SC 63 (IH). However, as will be discussed in chapter four, the Scottish *forum non conveniens* doctrine has been applied differently after the decision in *Spiliada*.

of these reasons [led] to the conclusion that the interests of the parties [could] more appropriately be served and the ends of justice [could] more appropriately be secured in that other court.[219]

Additionally, a close inspection of the relevant sections in the first edition of Anton's *Private International Law*,[220] the leading treatise on private international law in Scotland, lends support to the contention that the Scottish *forum non conveniens* doctrine had been applied as a one-stage test.

It is suggested that, notwithstanding the lack of explicit mention in Lord Goff's speech, he considered that the basic principle in *Spiliada* was to be applied in two stages. Influenced by the analysis in Professors Briggs's and Schuz's articles,[221] he effectively separated the process for the application of the *Spiliada* test into two stages. In the first stage, marked as points (a) and (b) in his summary of the law in *Spiliada*, Lord Goff outlined that the burden of establishing that another forum was more closely connected to the dispute rested on the defendant.[222] In point (f), however, he stated that it was only where the defendant was able to point to the more closely connected forum that the plaintiff could challenge the stay by pointing to 'circumstances which go beyond those taken into account when considering connecting factors with other jurisdictions'.[223]

Given that Professors Briggs's and Schuz's proposals for reforming the law on discretionary staying of proceedings were broadly speaking a reformulation of the *MacShannon* test, echoes of the second part of the second limb of the *St Pierre* test still continued to resonate under the *Spiliada* doctrine. It is for this reason that the borrowing of the Scottish doctrine is hedged around the existing norms and principles in England. Accordingly, and despite their many similarities, the *Spiliada* doctrine manifests an English understanding of the Scottish *forum non conveniens* principle and not the unreserved adoption of it.

As touched on earlier, the *Spiliada* ruling was also significant because of Lord Goff's remarks about the extent to which the same principles governed the (non-)exercise of jurisdiction in hearings initiated as of right, on the one hand, and those concerning the issuing of proceedings on foreign-based defendants, on the other.[224] In particular, his Lordship stated that it was 'inevitable that the question in both groups of cases must be ... to identify the forum in which the case can be suitably tried for the interests of the parties and for ends of justice'.[225] In other words, whether English courts would exercise their jurisdiction in as-of-right and service-out cases depended on the same set of considerations. This pronouncement, in turn, put an end to the confusion which had been generated

---

[219] *Credit Chimique v James Scott Engineering Group Ltd* 1979 SC 406 (OH) 410.
[220] Anton (n 216) 148–54.
[221] Although the Scottish sources were clearly influential in forming Lord Goff's decision, he also singled out Professors Briggs's and Schuz's articles in the course of his speech: *Spiliada* (n 1) 488.
[222] *Spiliada* (n 1) 476.
[223] ibid, 478.
[224] ibid, 478–82.
[225] ibid, 480.

following Lord Wilberforce's remarks in *Amin Rasheed Shipping Corpn v Kuwait Insurance Co* that cases concerning stays of as-of-right proceedings were of no assistance in the court's decision to allow service of proceedings on a foreign-based defendant.[226] Accordingly, and as emphasised by Lord Goff, in the application of the courts' discretionary power under the more-appropriate-forum test in the context of service-out cases:

> [t]he effect is, not merely that the burden of proof rests on the plaintiff to persuade the court that England is the appropriate forum for the trial of the action, but that he has to show that this is clearly so. In other words, the burden is, quite simply, the obverse of that applicable where a stay is sought of proceedings started in this country as of right.[227]

This burden is typically deemed to have been discharged where the English court concludes that, on balance, England is the dispute's centre of gravity.[228] Even when England is not the more closely connected forum, the English court may nevertheless rule that it is *forum conveniens*, if it is persuaded that the foreign forum, to which the action really belongs, cannot justly entertain the parties' claims.[229]

Applying the relevant principles to the facts of the case, their Lordships allowed the plaintiffs' appeal and granted permission for the proceedings to be served out of England. The *Spiliada* ruling marked the final step in a long line of earlier judicial pronouncements, which had sought to gradually refine the English law on staying of proceedings by making it more even-handed in its treatment of the litigants' competing interests in having their disputes litigated in England (or an alternative foreign forum). It is for this reason that it is widely considered to be one of the most important rulings in the field of private international law in England.

VI. Conclusion

This chapter has sought to outline the background to the emergence of the modern-day practice of discretionary (non-)exercise of jurisdiction in England. Its principal aim has been to provide a more detailed (and nuanced) understanding of the historical developments which preceded the articulation of the more-appropriate-forum test in *Spiliada*. To achieve this purpose, the analysis has sought to shed light on certain aspects concerning the earlier origins of the practice of discretionary (non-)exercise of jurisdiction in England which, hitherto, have received relatively little attention. At the same time, and through an

---

[226] *Amin Rasheed Shipping Corpn v Kuwait Insurance Co* [1984] AC 50 (HL) 72.
[227] *Spiliada* (n 1) 481.
[228] L Collins, *et al*, *Dicey, Morris & Collins on the Conflict of Laws* 15th edn (London, Sweet & Maxwell, 2012) para 11-143. Another expression which is used is that England has to be 'shown to be the proper place in which to bring the claim': Briggs (n 5) para 4.88.
[229] ibid, para 11-144.

examination of large volume of case law and associated academic commentary, it has attempted to put to challenge some of the views concerning the English *forum (non) conveniens* doctrine's past that have come to represent the orthodoxy.

Part II highlighted that it was in two separate lines of judicial decisions in England in the nineteenth century when courts began to rely on a discretion whether to exercise jurisdiction in private-international-law disputes: (i) cases concerning the service of proceedings on foreign-based defendants; and (ii) cases where courts in England had been asked to stay the proceedings that had been brought before them during the defendants' presence in the forum. The courts' ability to relinquish their (otherwise) soundly founded jurisdiction in as-of-right cases, on a discretionary basis, was first acknowledged towards the latter part of the nineteenth century. In its earliest form, this acknowledgement happened in *McHenry* in 1882, a *lis alibi pendens* case. In this context, and through a process of analogical reasoning, the court relied on the vexatious-and-oppressive test – which itself had been used by courts in England for centuries in issuing of common injunctions and (later) anti-suit injunctions.

Subsequently, Part III illustrated that the next major development in the law on staying of proceedings in England came at the dawn of the twentieth century when courts ruled in favour of giving up jurisdiction, regardless of whether parallel proceedings were pending elsewhere. In this regard, in three cases decided between 1906 and 1908 – namely, *Logan*, *Egbert*, and *Norton* – the vexatious-and-oppressive test was relied on as providing the basis for the courts' (non-)exercise of jurisdiction in as-of-right actions. The examination of these cases and associated academic commentary in Part III, in turn, illustrated that, in the first two decades of the twentieth century, the law on discretionary staying of proceedings in England was, in fact, much the same as its Scottish counterpart under the *forum non conveniens* doctrine. Indeed, in view of the similarities between the two approaches, it might even have been thought that English courts would promptly proceed to import and adopt the Scottish doctrine for the purpose of staying of proceedings. Therefore, contrary to the view that, before the mid-1970s, English staying-of-proceedings practice was almost entirely plaintiff-centric in focus, at the start of the twentieth century, English courts were broadly even-handed in their treatment of stay applications.

However, as discussed in Part IV, from the late 1920s until the mid-1970s, the courts' treatment of stay applications in England became much more slanted against the defendants, with courts becoming exceedingly plaintiff-friendly in how they exercised their discretion under the vexatious-and-oppressive test. In this context, the Court of Appeal's ruling in the *St Pierre* case – with its consolidation of the English courts' earlier pronouncements on discretionary staying of proceedings into a defined rule – is widely considered as the turning point in the law's development. Although, on the face of things, the test in *St Pierre* appeared to be premised on earlier authorities, including *Logan*, *Egbert*, and *Norton*, in almost all post-*St Pierre* stay or *lis alibi pendens* cases, the protection of the plaintiffs' right to commence proceedings in England became the courts' main priority. This state of affairs, it was argued, was partly due to the way in which the *St Pierre* rule was perceived (and applied) in later authorities and/or academic contributions. As explored in Part V, the restrictive application of the vexatious-and-oppressive test after the *St Pierre* ruling had encouraged forum shopping in England and rendered English staying-of-proceedings law incongruous with the wider socio-economic realities of the mid- to late twentieth century. The increasing prevalence of these problems prompted the triggering of a gradual departure from a strict application of the vexatious-and-oppressive test in the House of Lords' ruling in *The Atlantic Star* in 1973. In a 13-year period, following the decision in *The Atlantic Star*, the law underwent a step-by-step revision which, finally, led to the formal recognition of *forum (non) conveniens* in England in the *Spiliada* case in 1986 as the doctrine which would be applicable both in the context of stay of as-of-right proceedings and service-out cases. The next chapter seeks to build on the historical background presented here by assessing the contemporary status and application of the English *forum (non) conveniens* doctrine.

4

Forum (Non) Conveniens – The Present

I. Introduction

The previous chapter re-evaluated the historical developments which preceded the introduction of the more-appropriate-forum test in *Spiliada Maritime Corporation v Cansulex Ltd*,[1] as the basis for the practice of discretionary (non-)exercise of jurisdiction in England. In this chapter, the discussion moves on to examine the present-day application and scope of the English *forum (non) conveniens* doctrine. The fundamental aim here is to take stock of the evolution of the doctrine in the three or so decades following the decision in *Spiliada* and, thereby, facilitate a more complete understanding of the law's development during this period.

Inevitably, aspects of what is closely inspected in this chapter will be familiar to those with an interest in this subject area. The *Spiliada* doctrine has rapidly gained in importance, even though it has formally been a part of the national rules of jurisdiction in England for a relatively short period of time. In service-out cases, the doctrine is at the heart of the courts' decision making on whether jurisdiction could be asserted over foreign-based defendants. Additionally, and in the related (though conceptually different) context of cases in which defendants are sued in England while present within the forum,[2] the test in *Spiliada* forms the basis for the courts' (non-)exercise of their (otherwise) soundly established jurisdiction. Because of its prominence, therefore, the doctrine has received extensive treatment in the existing literature.

Nevertheless, in order to realise this book's objective of providing an authoritative and a comprehensive reference point for those with an interest in the origins, current application, and potential future developments of *forum (non) conveniens* in England, it is necessary to study closely the doctrine's contemporary application and scope. In much the same manner as the analysis in Chapter 3, the discussion here seeks to assess the main accounts on the application of *forum (non) conveniens* in England in the period after the House of Lords' ruling in *Spiliada*.

For the purposes of this chapter, the *Spiliada* doctrine's modern-day operation and ambit is explored from three different perspectives. First, the post-*Spiliada* 'doctrinal' developments in the field of discretionary (non-)exercise of jurisdiction in England are examined in Part II. The main issue for consideration in this

---

[1] *Spiliada Maritime Corporation v Cansulex Ltd* [1987] AC 460 (HL).
[2] The so-called 'as of right' proceedings.

part is whether, today, *forum (non) conveniens* in England is a different doctrine than when it was articulated in *Spiliada* in November 1986. It is argued that, in staying-of-proceedings cases, the more-appropriate-forum test is applied today in the same manner as when it was outlined in *Spiliada*. Likewise, and despite claims to the contrary, advanced chiefly by Professor Briggs,[3] the current application of the test in service-out cases is not, in doctrinal terms, significantly different from that set out in the *Spiliada* case. The second perspective from which the *forum (non) conveniens* doctrine in its contemporary form is assessed, in Part III, relates to *Spiliada*'s impact on the development of equivalent principles concerning the practice of discretionary (non-)exercise of jurisdiction across the Commonwealth. As this part of the chapter attempts to demonstrate, the *Spiliada* doctrine has been the main source of inspiration in (re)shaping the modern practice in these jurisdictions. The third (and final) perspective from which the current English *forum (non) conveniens* doctrine is explored, in Part IV, concerns the way in which its scope of application has evolved over the past 30 years. This aspect of the discussion seeks to illustrate that, despite efforts to expand the scope of the *Spiliada* doctrine to other (broadly related) commercial conflict-of-laws concepts – namely, the granting of anti-suit injunctions or the staying of proceedings brought in breach foreign jurisdiction agreements – it has generally remained unchanged. However, due to the Europeanisation of English private international law, which began after the introduction in England[4] of jurisdiction rules under the Brussels regime,[5] the *forum (non) conveniens* doctrine's overall scope of application has become materially limited.[6] This state of affairs was confirmed in 2005 in *Owusu v Jackson*,[7] after the Court of Justice

---

[3] A Briggs, *Civil Jurisdiction and Judgments* 6th edn (Abingdon, Informa Law from Routledge, 2015) para 4.91.

[4] Following the entry into force in 1987 of the relevant provisions under the Civil Jurisdiction and Judgments Act 1982.

[5] The Brussels regime covers provisions within the Regulation (EU) No 1215/2012 of the European Parliament and of the Council of 12 December 2012 on jurisdiction and the recognition and enforcement of judgments in civil and commercial matters (recast) [2012] OJ L351/1 (the 'Brussels Ia Regulation'), its predecessors, and the Convention on jurisdiction and the recognition and enforcement of judgments in civil and commercial matters [2007] OJ L339/3 (the 'Lugano II Convention').

[6] Aside from the limitations placed on the applicability of the *forum non conveniens* doctrine by the introduction into English law of the Brussels-based jurisdiction rules, there are other statutory constraints on the doctrine's operation. For example, in the context of proceedings brought in England based on the Convention for the Unification of certain rules relating to international carriage by air, implemented into English law by the Carriage by Air Acts (Application of Provisions) Order 1967, the *Spiliada* doctrine has been held to be inapplicable: *Milor SRL v British Airways plc* [1996] QB 702 (CA). Similarly, English courts are unable to rely on the doctrine to relinquish their jurisdiction where it is rooted in the provisions within the Convention on the Contract for the International Carriage of Goods by Road (CMR), Geneva, 19 May 1956 (the 'CMR Convention'): *Royal Sun Alliance Insurance plc v MK Digital Fze (Cyprus) Ltd* [2005] EWHC 1408 (Comm), [2005] 2 CLC 146. Aikens J's judgment was reversed on appeal, but his pronouncements regarding the inapplicability of the *Spiliada* test in the context of the CMR Convention was not overruled: [2006] EWCA Civ 629, [2006] 2 Lloyd's Rep 110 (CA). For the purposes of this book, the main focus is on the Brussels-inspired limitations on the *forum (non) conveniens* doctrine's application.

[7] Case C-281/02 *Owusu v Jackson* [2005] ECR I-1383, [2005] QB 801.

of the European Union (the 'Court of Justice') ruled that the doctrine is incompatible with the jurisdiction scheme under the Brussels regime. Part IV rehearses the debate at the time concerning the (in)applicability of a discretionary principle such as *Spiliada* in cases where the basis for the English courts' adjudicatory competence was rooted in the Brussels regime. It also enquires into the extent to which courts in England have adhered to the *Owusu* ruling in the years that have followed it. It is argued that this multi-faceted assessment of the evolution of the English *forum (non) conveniens* after *Spiliada* helps to provide a more complete understanding of the doctrine's present-day scope and operation.

II. Post-*Spiliada* Doctrinal Developments

The first perspective from which to explore the *forum (non) conveniens* doctrine today relates to the question whether the basic principle set out in Lord Goff of Chieveley's speech in *Spiliada* marked the final step in its *doctrinal* advancement. Put differently, the issue for consideration is whether, doctrinally, there have been any changes to the more-appropriate-forum test in the years following its articulation in *Spiliada*.

In this context, it is suggested that, a helpful step might be to examine the English courts' application of the test in cases concerning staying of as-of-right proceedings separately from how they have applied it when asked to grant permission for claim forms to be served on defendants outside of England. This method of analysis enables us to see the extent to which the doctrine has evolved in either (or both) of these distinct (but related) concepts.

A. Stay of As-of-Right Proceedings

Before critically reviewing the more-appropriate-forum test's doctrinal journey over the past 30 years in the context of staying-of-proceedings cases, the relevant grounds for its application must be revisited. As discussed in Chapter 3, the courts' decision whether to relinquish their (otherwise) properly established jurisdiction on a discretionary basis is premised on the following 'basic principle', set out in Lord Goff's speech in *Spiliada*:

> … a stay will only be granted on the ground of forum non conveniens where the court is satisfied that there is some other available forum, having competent jurisdiction, which is the appropriate forum for the trial of the action, i.e. in which the case may be tried more suitably for the interests of all the parties and the ends of justice.[8]

This basic principle is to be applied in two stages. In the first stage, the onus is on the defendant to convince the English court that there is some other available

---

[8] *Spiliada* (n 1) 476.

forum of competent jurisdiction which is also more closely connected to the parties' dispute than England.[9] In other words, the defendant has to show that, not only the court in the foreign country would assume jurisdiction over him and/ or the claim against him, but that it is also the dispute's centre of gravity. Various factors are examined by the courts in determining whether the available forum elsewhere is indeed the more closely connected forum to the dispute. None of these factors is, by itself, decisive in determining whether the English proceedings should be stayed. Typically, the factors under consideration include the degree to which the parties, the events giving rise to their claim, and also the law governing the dispute are connected with a particular country. Additionally, where relevant, the court takes into account the fact that the litigants before it are also involved in related proceedings in another foreign forum.[10]

If the defendant fails to establish that an available and more closely connected foreign forum exists, then the proceedings in England would be sustained. However, if the English court arrives at the opposite conclusion, then the stay application can only be resisted if the claimant is able to point to 'circumstances which go beyond those taken into account when considering connecting factors with other jurisdictions'.[11] At this juncture, the claimant can adduce evidence which highlights examples of injustice being caused at virtually any stage in the civil litigation process in the more closely connected forum. As succinctly stated by Lord Diplock in *The Abidin Daver*, these instances include (but are not confined to):

> risk that justice will not be obtained by a foreign litigant in particular kinds of suits whether for ideological or political reasons, … inexperience or inefficiency of the judiciary, … excessive delay in the conduct of the business of the courts or the unavailability of appropriate remedies.[12]

Any allegations of this kind must be based on 'cogent evidence'.[13] Provided that the claimant can satisfy the English court that his claim would not be justly dealt with in the more closely connected forum, then the stay application would be refused. In such circumstances, the English court would sustain the proceedings before it.[14]

---

[9] ibid. For the sake of simplicity, the forum which is identified by the first stage of the *Spiliada* test is referred to as 'the more closely connected forum'.

[10] For a more detailed account of the considerations under the *Spiliada* doctrine's first limb, and how the courts apply them when hearing stay applications, see Briggs (n 3) paras 4.19–4.29, and P Torremans, *et al, Cheshire, North & Fawcett's Private International Law* 15th edn (Oxford, Oxford University Press, 2017) 365–69 and 395–400.

[11] ibid, 478.

[12] *The Abidin Daver* [1984] 1 AC 398 (HL) 411.

[13] *Spiliada* (n 1) 478, citing Lord Diplock's statement in *The Abidin Daver* (n 12).

[14] For a more detailed account of the considerations under the *Spiliada* doctrine's second limb, and how the courts apply them when hearing stay applications, see Briggs (n 3) paras 4.30–4.35, and *Cheshire, North & Fawcett* (n 10) 400–09.

An assessment of the case law and related commentary on the operation of the more-appropriate-forum test in stay cases shows that, by and large, it has been applied in the same manner as when it was outlined in *Spiliada*. Nevertheless, at least one aspect of the doctrinal developments in this context, over the past three decades, deserves closer attention. This facet concerns (what seemed to be) an unintended (and, ultimately, short-lived) move on the part of the English courts towards doctrinal reinterpretation of the *Spiliada* test, by broadening the scope of 'availability' of the alternative foreign forum under the doctrine's first limb.

Establishing availability was made an explicit condition of granting a stay of the English proceedings after the introduction of the test in *MacShannon v Rockware Glass Ltd*.[15] As highlighted in Chapter 3, under the *MacShannon* test, the party seeking a stay, *inter alia*, had to establish that he was 'amenable' to the jurisdiction of the alternative foreign forum.[16] For the purposes of the *MacShannon* test, a defendant was regarded as being amenable if the foreign court would assume jurisdiction over him. Availability of the alternative foreign forum has continued to be a necessary ingredient for obtaining a stay of the English proceedings following the articulation of the more-appropriate-forum test. In *Spiliada*, Lord Goff defined an available forum as one which has 'competent jurisdiction' over the defendant.[17] Although Lord Goff did not specifically spell out what he meant by a court with competent jurisdiction, there was no reason to think that his Lordship sought to attribute to it a different meaning to the one ascribed by the House of Lords under the *MacShannon* test.

In the majority of the reported cases in the late 1980s and early 1990s, the issue of availability of the foreign forum under the *Spiliada* test was rarely (if ever) in contention.[18] Nevertheless, in the handful of cases in that era in which availability was discussed, it was clear that it was one of the requirements that had to be established by the defendant under the first limb of the *Spiliada* test, and

---

[15] *MacShannon v Rockware Glass Ltd* [1978] AC 795 (HL).
[16] ibid, 812.
[17] *Spiliada* (n 1) 476.
[18] See, eg, *EI du Pont de Nemours & Company v Agnew* [1987] 2 Lloyd's Rep 285, *Mitsubishi Corporation v Aristidis I Alafouzos* [1988] 1 Lloyd's Rep 191, *The Emre II* [1989] 2 Lloyd's Rep 182, *Meadows Indemnity Company Ltd v Insurance Corporation of Ireland plc* [1989] 1 Lloyd's Rep 181 – overruled on different grounds: [1989] 2 Lloyd's Rep 298 (CA), *The Irish Rowan* [1991] 2 QB 206 (CA), *The Vishva Ajay* [1989] 2 Lloyd's Rep 558, *Kloeckner & Co AG v Gatoil Overseas Inc* [1990] 1 Lloyd's Rep 177 – overruled on different grounds: *Times*, 9 April 1990 (CA), *Cleveland Museum of Art v Capricorn Art International SA and Another* [1990] 2 Lloyd's Rep 166, *S & W Berisford plc and Another v New Hampshire Insurance Co* [1990] 2 QB 631, *Arkwright Mutual Insurance Co v Bryanstan Insurance Co Ltd and Others* [1990] 2 QB 649, *The Po* [1990] 1 Lloyd's Rep 418, *The Vishva Abha* [1990] 2 Lloyd's Rep 312, *Re Harrods (Buenos Aires) Ltd* [1990] BCC 481 – overruled on different grounds: [1992] Ch 72 (CA), *Banco Atlantico SA v The British Bank of the Middle East* [1990] 2 Lloyd's Rep 504, *The Golden Mariner* [1990] 2 Lloyd's Rep 215 (CA), *The Oinoussin Pride* [1991] 1 Lloyd's Rep 126, *The Po* [1991] 2 Lloyd's Rep 206 (CA), *The Maciej Rataj* [1991] 2 Lloyd's Rep 458. This state of affairs was also reflected in the academic commentary at the time: PM North and JJ Fawcett, *Cheshire & North's Private International Law* 11th edn (London, Butterworths, 1987) 223–225 and L Collins, *et al*, *Dicey & Morris on the Conflict of Laws* 12th edn (London, Sweet & Maxwell, 1993) 403.

only related to the alternative foreign court having jurisdiction to entertain the claim. Therefore, the fact that the plaintiff faced practical difficulties or injustice in bringing his claim in the foreign forum had no bearing on its availability. For instance, in *New Hampshire Insurance Co v Strabag Bau AG,*[19] it was held that the fact that the German court had competent jurisdiction over the defendants was sufficient to render it available. Similarly, in *Connelly v RTZ Corporation,*[20] the Court of Appeal stated that the practical difficulties in bringing the action in Namibia (which was more closely connected to the dispute than England), due to lack of legal-aid provisions there, was a matter that had to be considered under the second limb of the *Spiliada* test. In so far as the first limb was concerned, their Lordships observed, the circumstances of the case had not rendered Namibia unavailable.

This understanding of the meaning of availability was, however, thrown into doubt by the Court of Appeal's decision in *Mohammed v Bank of Kuwait and the Middle East KSC* in 1996.[21] *Mohammed* was the first post-*Spiliada* case in which determining the meaning of availability was the main issue for the court's consideration. The case concerned an action by the respondent, M, an Iraqi citizen, against the appellants, BKME, a Kuwaiti bank (and his former employer), for an amount which M alleged BKME owed him under the contract of employment. In response, BKME sought, *inter alia*, a stay of the English proceedings on the basis of *forum non conveniens*, pointing to courts in Kuwait as being the appropriate venue for litigating the dispute. At first instance, BKME succeeded at obtaining a stay of the English proceedings. In the course of their submissions before the Court of Appeal, BKME argued that availability formed part of the analysis under the first limb of the *Spiliada* test and referred only to the foreign court's ability to assert jurisdiction over the dispute.[22] Evans LJ, however, rejected this argument, stating that, for the purposes of the *Spiliada* doctrine, availability had a wider meaning. According to his Lordship, for the alternative foreign forum to be available, it had to be shown that substantial justice would be attainable there.[23] On the facts, Evans LJ concluded that Kuwait was not an available forum and, therefore, M's stay application was rejected.

To all intents and purposes, the Court of Appeal's decision in *Mohammed* redrew the boundaries of the *Spiliada* test and made it a different doctrine. It afforded a far wider meaning to availability than that which had been envisaged when the more-appropriate-forum test was initially articulated. As indicated earlier, under the *Spiliada* doctrine, whether the party resisting the stay of the English proceedings could obtain justice in the alternative foreign forum had

---

[19] *New Hampshire Insurance Co v Strabag Bau AG* [1992] 1 Lloyd's Rep 361 (CA).
[20] *Connelly v RTZ Corporation* [1996] QB 361 (CA).
[21] *Mohammed v Bank of Kuwait and the Middle East KSC* [1996] 1 WLR 1483 (CA).
[22] ibid, 1489.
[23] ibid, 1490.

no bearing on that forum's availability. Rather, (un)availability hinged solely on whether the foreign court would entertain the case against the defendant.

This divergence in *Mohammed* from the original parameters of availability under the *Spiliada* doctrine attracted widespread criticism within the academic commentary.[24] In this respect, perhaps the main problem with the decision, as identified by Professor Briggs, was that the Court of Appeal blurred the boundaries between the first and second limb of the *Spiliada* doctrine.[25] He noted that, by broadening the scope of availability of the foreign forum to include the sound administration of justice there, the Court of Appeal effectively placed an additional burden on the party that seeks to obtain a stay of proceedings in England. All things being equal, this development was liable to make it increasingly more difficult for defendants to succeed in their stay applications.[26] According to Professor Briggs, a better approach would have been to return to the position before the *Mohammed* case and address questions concerning injustice to the plaintiff in staying the action in England under the second (as opposed to the first) limb of the *Spiliada* test.[27]

However, as adverted to earlier, this unintended departure from tradition was short-lived. In *Connelly v RTZ Corporation* in 1997,[28] the House of Lords restored the narrow interpretation of availability under the English *forum non conveniens* doctrine. In this case, the plaintiff commenced proceedings in England against the defendant corporation, his former employers. His claim was that he had contracted cancer due to the defendants' negligence, while he had been working at their mines in Namibia. There was little doubt that Namibia was the dispute's centre of gravity: it was there where the alleged tort had occurred – and all the mines, witnesses, and documents were located. In the proceedings before the House of Lords, both parties had conceded that Namibia was the forum more closely connected with their dispute than England. The plaintiff had stated that he had limited means and would not be able to bring his claim without some form of legal aid – which he contended was unavailable in Namibia. In these circumstances, the main issue for the House of Lords' determination was whether the Namibian court could justly dispose of the plaintiff's claim.

The House of Lords found that the plaintiff's contention regarding the lack of financial means in Namibia, to enable him to conduct the litigation in that forum, did not put in question the *availability* of the Namibian court as the dispute's centre of gravity under the first limb of the *Spiliada* test. Instead, it was a factor that affected the Namibian court's ability to deal justly with the claim under *Spiliada*'s

---

[24] Eg, A Briggs, 'Forum Non Conveniens and Unavailable Courts' (1996) 67 *British Yearbook of International Law* 587 and E Peel, 'Forum Non Conveniens and the Impecunious Plaintiff – Legal Aid and Conditional Fees' (1997) 113 *Law Quarterly Review* 43.

[25] Briggs, ibid, 588.

[26] ibid.

[27] ibid, 589.

[28] *Connelly v RTZ Corporation* [1998] AC 854 (HL).

second limb. In a four-to-one majority decision, it was held that the absence of legal-aid provisions in Namibia had meant that its courts were not appropriate to hear the plaintiff's claim. Thus, the English proceedings were sustained.[29] The dissenting voice, Lord Hoffmann, did not disagree with the manner in which the *Spiliada* doctrine was applied by the majority. Rather, he favoured a lower threshold for justice than them. According to his Lordship, the overwhelming connection between Namibia and the dispute meant that justice would still have been done in Namibia, even though the quality of its delivery may not have been as high as it would have been if the proceedings had been conducted in England.[30]

Although there was no explicit discussion of the merits (or shortcomings) of the decision in *Mohammed*, the ruling in *Connelly* marked a step towards restating the original *Spiliada* principle. As noted by Professor Briggs,[31] the decision in *Connelly* reiterated that issues such as lack of legal-aid provisions in the more closely connected forum was 'part of the plaintiff's armoury for contending that it would be unjust to dispatch him to the natural forum' and had to be 'taken account of under the second *Spiliada* limb'.[32] Therefore, the *Connelly* ruling rendered 'untenable' the Court of Appeal's analysis in *Mohammed* on the meaning of availability.[33]

For the most part, the House of Lords' decision in *Connelly* ended any prospect for the reinterpretation of the first limb of the *Spiliada* test, through the expansion of the meaning of the availability of the more closely connected forum.[34] As a consequence, in so far as the application of the *Spiliada* test in the context of staying-of-proceedings cases is concerned, the doctrine has continued to be applied in the same manner as when it was outlined in *Spiliada*.

B. Service-out Cases

As illustrated in Chapter 3, the *Spiliada* ruling made it plain that the more-appropriate-forum test applied to both the practice of discretionary staying of

---

[29] ibid, 874 (Lord Goff). Lord Lloyd of Berwick, Lord Hope of Craighead and Lord Clyde concurred.
[30] ibid, 875–76.
[31] A Briggs, '*Forum Non Conveniens* and the Cost of Litigation' (1997) 68 *British Yearbook of International Law* 357.
[32] ibid, 358.
[33] ibid.
[34] For arguably the most notable authority that nonetheless conceived of availability in the same manner as the decision in *Mohammed*, see *889457 Alberta Inc v Katanga Mining Ltd* [2008] EWHC 2679, [2009] 1 BCLC 189. In this case, the claimants accused the defendants of dishonest attempts to dispossess him of his interest in a Congolese mining company. The Democratic Republic of Congo ('DRC') was the dispute's centre of gravity. However, the English court found that, due to the major political upheaval in the DRC at the time of the hearing, the country lacked a 'developed infrastructure' for the rule of law to thrive: 204–09. As a result, the defendants' application for a stay of the English proceedings was rejected because the court found it impossible 'to regard the DRC as an available forum for the resolution of [the] dispute': 209–10. In this respect, and contrary to *Connelly*'s interpretation of availability, the judgment in *Katanga* has echoes of *Mohammed*.

proceedings, *and* the related concept of permission to serve claims on defendants outside England.[35] Thus, the same set of considerations, which were discussed earlier, are consulted by courts in England in deciding whether to exercise their jurisdiction in as-of-right and service-out cases. In applying the more-appropriate-forum test in a service-out case, however, the claimant shoulders the burden of convincing the court that England is the more appropriate forum for the litigation.[36] This burden is typically discharged where the English court concludes that, on balance, England is the dispute's centre of gravity,[37] or the 'proper forum in which to bring the claim'.[38] Even when England is not the proper forum, the English court may nevertheless rule that it is *forum conveniens*, if it is persuaded that the foreign forum cannot justly dispose of the parties' claims.[39]

With one major exception, a close inspection of the leading commentators' accounts regarding the application of the more-appropriate-forum test in service-out cases indicates that this aspect of the law is doctrinally applied in much the same way as when it was set out in *Spiliada*.[40] The one account that stands alone is that which Professor Briggs has advanced. Following two fairly recent decisions in England by the Court of Appeal (*Cherney v Deripaska*)[41] and the Privy Council (*Altimo Holdings and Investment Ltd v Kyrgyz Mobil Tel Ltd*),[42] he has proffered the view that the doctrine's operation in service-out cases has in fact evolved from its position in 1986. Before considering Professor Briggs's reasoning for this stance in more detail, it is necessary to examine the disputes in *Cherney* and *Altimo Holdings*.

For present purposes, it suffices to state that these cases broadly concerned allegations on the part of the claimants that they had been defrauded on a substantial scale. The litigants in *Cherney* were Russian nationals with significant connections with their homeland. They had entered an agreement in London, concerning the ownership of a large aluminium company in Russia. The claimant sought damages for losses which he contended had been caused by the defendant. *Altimo Holdings* was a case that had initially been brought before the courts in the Isle of Man. It had arisen following a protracted dispute regarding the ownership of a mobile telephone company in Kyrgyzstan. It was clear in both *Cherney* and *Altimo Holdings* that England was not the venue more closely connected

---

[35] *Spiliada* (n 1) 478–482.

[36] ibid, 480.

[37] L Collins, *et al*, *Dicey, Morris & Collins on the Conflict of Laws* 15th edn (London, Sweet & Maxwell, 2012) para 11-143.

[38] Briggs (n 3) para 4.88.

[39] *Dicey, Morris & Collins* (n 37) para 11-144.

[40] Eg, compare, on the one hand, the accounts in PM North and JJ Fawcett, *Cheshire and North's Private International Law* 12th edn (London, Butterworths, 1992) 204–08 and *Dicey & Morris* (n 18) 316–18, and the ones in *Cheshire, North & Fawcett* (n 10) 365–78, and *Dicey, Morris & Collins* (n 37) paras 11-140–11-144.

[41] *Cherney v Deripaska* [2009] EWCA Civ 849, [2009] 2 CLC 408 (CA).

[42] *Altimo Holdings and Investment Ltd v Kyrgyz Mobil Tel Ltd* [2011] UKPC 7, [2012] 1 WLR 1804 (PC) (also known as *AK Investment CJSC v Kyrgyz Mobil Tel Ltd*).

with the claims; the forums to which the actions really belonged were Russia and Kyrgyzstan, respectively. Nevertheless, in each of these cases, the claimants argued that their claims against the defendants would not be justly disposed of in Russia and Kyrgyzstan.[43] In the end, and notwithstanding that England was not the proper forum in either case, it was held to be *forum conveniens* in both instances, with the claimants obtaining permission to serve the foreign-based defendants.

In two case notes, published in the *British Yearbook of International Law*[44] and the *Lloyd's Maritime and Commercial Law Quarterly*,[45] Professor Briggs discussed the decisions in *Cherney* and *Altimo Holdings*. In particular, he was critical of the courts' finding that England was *forum conveniens*, when it was patently clear that the dispute was more closely connected to Russia and Kyrgyzstan. In relation to the judgment in *Cherney*, Professor Briggs observed that it was 'the first occasion on which the [English] court had found that it was justified in authorizing service out even though the foreign court was the natural forum',[46] concluding that the court had taken 'a false step'.[47] Professor Briggs was equally disparaging in his assessment of the judgment in *Altimo Holdings*. In a passage that captures the heart of Professor Briggs's critique of the Privy Council's decision, he opined that:

> [t]he proposition that service out should be permitted even though England was not the natural forum is not what *Spiliada* had seemed to say; the proposition that service out should be allowed when there was a natural forum which was plainly elsewhere was even less obviously what *Spiliada* had authorised; and the proposition that service out should be permitted because the [English] court perceives there to be a 'risk' that the courts of the natural forum will not do justice according to the law is, one has to say, pretty astonishing.[48]

Professor Briggs considered that, what made the decision in *Altimo Holdings* (and, for that matter, *Cherney*) 'surprising' was that the courts had allowed for doubts about the ability of the Kyrgyz and Russian courts to justly entertain the claimants' disputes to '*drive* the entire application for permission to serve out'.[49] In his view, a better course of action would have been for the English court to apply the *Spiliada* test in such a way whereby 'if England is not the natural forum, …, [then] service out of the jurisdiction will not be authorised, even if the foreign court is not much good'.[50]

---

[43] *Cherney v Deripaska* [2008] EWHC 1530 (Comm), [2009] 1 All ER (Comm) 333, [198] and *Altimo Holdings*, ibid 1810 and 1816.
[44] A Briggs, 'Russian Oligarchs and the Conflict of Laws' (2008) 79 *British Yearbook of International Law* 543.
[45] A Briggs, 'Forum Non Satis: *Spiliada* and an Inconvenient Truth' [2011] *Lloyd's Maritime and Commercial Law Quarterly* 329.
[46] Briggs (n 44) 546.
[47] ibid, 547.
[48] Briggs (n 45) 331.
[49] ibid, 330 (emphasis in the original, citation omitted).
[50] ibid, 333 (citation omitted).

In the same vein, and more recently, in the latest edition of *Civil Jurisdiction and Judgments* published in 2015, Professor Briggs has described the precedent set in *Cherney* and *Altimo Holdings*, concerning the application of the *Spiliada* test in service-out cases, as being 'controversial' and 'unsettling'.[51] To begin with, Professor Briggs identified cases 'where the administration of civil justice has utterly broken down or has utterly degenerated' in the dispute's centre of gravity.[52] In this context, one of the decisions which he drew upon was *Oppenheimer v Louis Rosenthal & Co AG*.[53] *Oppenheimer* was a service-out case in which a German national of the Jewish faith sought to commence proceedings before the English court against his German employer. Although Germany was clearly the dispute's 'home', the court issued an order, summoning the defendant to appear in the English proceedings. The chief basis for the court's decision was that if the matter had been remitted to Nazi-ruled Germany, there was every prospect that the plaintiff would not receive a fair hearing and could well be captured and harmed.[54]

In Professor Briggs's view, in cases like *Oppenheimer* – where there has been a failure of the rule of law in the forum to which the dispute really belongs – it is legitimate for the English court to find itself *forum conveniens*, even though it is not otherwise the proper forum.[55] However, he regarded *Cherney* and *Altimo Holdings* as being distinguishable from this group of cases. As he noted, the contention in *Cherney* and *Altimo Holdings* was not that the rule of law had collapsed in Russia and Kyrgyzstan. Instead, it was that there was 'a risk that [the claimants] would not receive justice' in those jurisdictions, 'perhaps because there [was] a State interest in the matter which would pervert the course of justice'.[56] In other words, these were cases in which the injustice complained of was not so extreme and self-evident to warrant the English courts' service-out permission, in a situation when it was not the proper forum for hearing the claim.

It is argued that, while the courts' rulings in *Cherney* and *Altimo Holdings* might be the first examples of their kind, where claimants could serve foreign-based defendants, they should not be seen as signifying an evolution in the application of the *Spiliada* doctrine. After all, the courts' approach to its (non-)exercise of jurisdiction in these authorities was, in broad terms, consistent with how the more-appropriate-forum test has always been applied in relation to service-out applications. In these cases, just as in those concerning stay applications, if the claimant can persuade the English court that regardless of the lack of connection between the claim and England, the proceedings cannot be justly handled in the

---

[51] Briggs (n 3) para 4.91.
[52] ibid (citations omitted).
[53] *Oppenheimer v Louis Rosenthal & Co AG* [1937] 1 All ER 23 (CA). Another example was *Katanga* (n 34) in which, due to major political unrest in the DRC, there had been complete breakdown of the rule of law in that forum – which happened to have the greatest connection with the dispute.
[54] ibid, 25 (Greer LJ).
[55] Briggs (n 3) para 4.91.
[56] ibid (citations omitted).

more closely connected forum elsewhere, then the balance is tipped in favour of the finding that England is *forum conveniens*. An assessment of the case law in this area highlights that the ground(s) based on which the English court would find itself *forum conveniens* – when it is not the proper forum for the litigation of the dispute, yet is persuaded that the claimant cannot receive justice in the foreign forum – need not be as extreme as the ones in cases like *Oppenheimer*.

Consider, in this respect, the Court of Appeal's judgment in *Roneleigh Ltd v MII Exports Inc*.[57] In this service-out case, an English plaintiff brought breach-of-contract proceedings in England against a New Jersey-based company. Owing to the tenuous connection between England and the dispute, the plaintiffs were unable to establish that England was the proper forum. However, the plaintiffs contended that there was a significant costs advantage to them if the case was litigated in England – as their litigation costs would have been much greater if they sued in New Jersey. This consideration alone was sufficient to persuade the court to grant permission to serve the proceedings outside England. Similarly, in *Islamic Arab Insurance Co v Saudi Egyptian American Reinsurance Co*,[58] the Emirati plaintiffs were able to obtain an order to serve proceedings on a Panamanian defendant, notwithstanding limited connection between the dispute and England. The submission that courts in Saudi Arabia, as the forum that was claimed to be more closely connected to the dispute, lacked the expertise or specialism to handle insurance disputes, was the factor that nudged the English court towards the finding that it was *forum conveniens*.

In these circumstances, it is difficult to regard the decisions in *Cherney* and *Altimo Holdings* as breaking new ground in the application of the *Spiliada* doctrine. Instead, they should be treated as classic examples of denial of justice in the foreign forum and, thus, consistent with the existing case law in this area. For these reasons, and contrary to Professor Briggs's observations, it is argued that the more-appropriate-forum test is currently applied in service-out cases in broadly the same manner as when it was articulated in *Spiliada*.

III. The *Spiliada* Doctrine's Global Influence

Thus far, the discussion has evaluated *Spiliada's* doctrinal developments over the past three decades, concluding that it is generally unchanged in both stay and service-out cases. The next step is to explore the modern-day English *forum (non) conveniens* doctrine's influence (or otherwise) on the evolution of the equivalent principles concerning discretionary (non-)exercise of jurisdiction across the Commonwealth.

---

[57] *Roneleigh Ltd v MII Exports Inc* [1989] 1 WLR 619 (CA).
[58] *Islamic Arab Insurance Co v Saudi Egyptian American Reinsurance Co* [1987] 1 Lloyd's Rep 315.

As the analysis proceeds to illustrate, the *Spiliada* doctrine has been influential in (re)shaping the current practice in these jurisdictions. Before examining the English doctrine's global impact in more detail, it is helpful to briefly consider the approach in Commonwealth countries to discretionary (non-)exercise of jurisdiction prior to the articulation of the more-appropriate-forum test in *Spiliada*.

A. The Approach in Commonwealth Jurisdictions before *Spiliada*

For decades prior to the formal endorsement of the *forum (non) conveniens* doctrine in England, and the introduction of the more-appropriate-forum test, the English courts' approach to discretionary (non-)exercise of jurisdiction set the benchmark for similar practices in Commonwealth jurisdictions. As a consequence, for much of the twentieth century, the legal principles in this area were fundamentally alike.

In Australia, for example, in *Maritime Insurance Ltd v Geelong Harbour Trust Commissioners*,[59] decided in 1908, the Australian High Court relied on the vexatious-and-oppressive test, as set out in decisions such as *Logan v Bank of Scotland (No 2)*[60] and *Egbert v Short*,[61] in ruling on whether to stay its proceedings on a discretionary basis. In this case, GHTC, a Victorian corporation, brought an action against MI, an English company, for the recovery of a sum of money pursuant to an insurance agreement between the parties. In response, MI applied for a stay of the proceedings in the Victorian Supreme Court. MI's main contention was that the Australian action was vexatious and oppressive, and that Natal in South Africa was the 'proper and more convenient' forum for the litigation of the matter.[62] Various passages from *Logan* and *Egbert* featured prominently in Griffith CJ's judgment, who gave the only reasoned decision.[63] He dismissed the defendants' appeal, concluding that the injustice done to the plaintiffs, by preventing them from continuing with their action in Victoria, would be greater than the injustice that would be inflicted on the defendants, if their stay application was turned down.[64]

The situation in Canada was much the same as that in Australia. Consider, in this regard, the judgment in *First Natchez Bank v Coleman*,[65] reported in 1901.

---

[59] *Maritime Insurance Ltd v Geelong Harbour Trust Commissioners* (1908) 6 CLR 194.
[60] *Logan v Bank of Scotland (No 2)* [1906] 1 KB 141 (CA).
[61] *Egbert v Short* [1907] 2 Ch 205.
[62] *Maritime Insurance* (n 59) 196.
[63] Barton, O'Connor and Higgins JJ concurring.
[64] See, similarly, *Rutt v Metropolitan Underwriters* (1929) SASR 426, *Cope Allman (Australia) Ltd v Celermajer* [1968] 11 FLR 488 and *Telford Panel and Engineering Works v Elder Smith Goldsborough* (1969) VR 193 (all interstate cases).
[65] *First Natchez Bank v Coleman* [1901] 2 OLR 159.

This was a *lis alibi pendens* case in which proceedings had been brought in Ontario while a broadly similar dispute was being heard in Louisiana. In the Divisional Court in Ontario, Meredith CJ rejected the stay application. In reaching this conclusion,[66] he stated that the law in England, as outlined in cases such as *McHenry v Lewis*,[67] ought to govern the Ontarian court's exercise of its discretion.[68]

By the mid-twentieth century, courts in Commonwealth jurisdictions continued to be receptive to the developments in the English staying-of-proceedings practice. In Canada, for instance, courts at different levels began to apply the vexatious-and-oppressive test, as outlined in Scott LJ's judgment in *St Pierre v South American Stones (Gath & Chaves) Ltd*,[69] in deciding whether to stay their proceedings.[70] By the same token, the House of Lords' decision, in *The Atlantic Star*,[71] to liberalise its application of the vexatious-and-oppressive test, and the subsequent introduction of a revised formulation in the *MacShannon* case, prompted courts in Australia[72] and Canada[73] to revisit their approaches to discretionary staying of proceedings.

B. The Approach in Commonwealth Jurisdictions after *Spiliada*: An Overview

In these circumstances, it must have been thought that Commonwealth courts would adopt with alacrity the new English *forum (non) conveniens* doctrine following the decision in *Spiliada*. Indeed, this is what happened in New Zealand, in *McConnell Dowell Constructors Ltd v Lloyd's Syndicate 396*.[74] And, likewise, in Singapore, in *Brinkerhoff Maritime Drilling Corp v PT Airfast Services Indonesia*

---

[66] ibid, 161–62 (Lount J concurring).

[67] *McHenry v Lewis* (1882) 22 Ch D 397 (CA).

[68] See, also, the decision in *Marine Trust Co v Weining* [1935] 3 DLR 282, where *First Natchez Bank* was cited in support of the notion that in exercising their discretion whether to stay or sustain their proceedings, Canadian courts ought to rely on the English cases.

[69] *St Pierre v South American Stones (Gath & Chaves) Ltd* [1936] 1 KB 382 (CA) 398.

[70] Eg, *Hall Development Company of Venezuela v B & W Inc* [1952] Ex CR 347 (federal level); *Empire-Universal Films Ltd v Rank* [1947] OR 775 and *Henderson v Newall* [1967] 1 OR 289 (Ontario); *Bank of America National Trust & Banking Association v Poyet* [1955] 1 DLR 680 (British Columbia); and *Calgary & Edmonton Corp v British American Oil Co* [1963] 41 WWR 413 (Alberta).

[71] *The Atlantic Star* [1974] AC 436 (HL).

[72] Eg, *Garseabo Nominees Pty Ltd v Taub Pty Ltd* [1979] 1 NSWLR 663 (an interstate case) and *In the Marriage of Takach (No 2)* [1980] 47 FLR 441.

[73] Eg, *Ranger Uranium Mines Pty v BTR Trading (Q) Pty Ltd* [1985] 75 FLR 422, *Yasuda Fire & Insurance Co v Nosira Lin* [1984] 1 FC 895, and *Skagway Terminal Co v Daphne* [1988] 42 DLR (4th) 200 (all at Federal level); *Rogers v Bank of Montreal* [1984] 4 DLR (4th) 507 (British Columbia); *Roger Grandmaitre Ltd v Canadian International Paper Co* [1977] 15 OR (2d) 137, *Canadian Marine Underwriters Ltd v China Union Lines Ltd* [1977] 17 OR (2d) 375, *Plibrico (Canada) Ltd v Suncor Inc* [1982] 35 OR (2d) 781, and *Pace v Synetics Inc* [1983] 41 OR (2d) 267 (all in Ontario).

[74] *McConnell Dowell Constructors Ltd v Lloyd's Syndicate 396* [1988] 2 NZLR 257. See, also, the decision in *Club Mediterranee NZ v Wendell* [1989] 1 NZLR 216, decided shortly thereafter.

in 1992,[75] where the Court of Appeal adopted the *Spiliada* doctrine as the basis for granting stays of proceedings. Moreover, as identified by Professor Fawcett,[76] the *Spiliada* doctrine was embraced in Hong Kong,[77] Ireland,[78] Brunei,[79] and Gibraltar.[80]

Scotland, too, which has been widely considered as the *forum non conveniens* doctrine's birthplace,[81] implemented the English doctrine into its laws. It is recalled from the discussion in the previous chapter that one of the most notable differences between the application of the formulation in *Spiliada*, on the one hand, and its Scottish counterpart, on the other, was the number of stages in which the tests were applied. Throughout its existence as a legal doctrine, Scottish *forum non conveniens* had been applied in one stage: the justice to the pursuers in sustaining the Scottish proceedings was considered in conjunction with all other factors – such as the law governing the dispute or the location of the evidence and witnesses – in deciding whether a foreign forum was more closely connected to the case in hand.[82] However, not long after Lord Goff's enunciation of the two-stage formula in *Spiliada*, and following the Scottish Court of Session's ruling in *Sokha v Secretary of State for the Home Department*,[83] the Scottish doctrine has been displaced by its English equivalent. As a result, courts in Scotland have thenceforth applied the *forum non conveniens* doctrine in two stages in deciding whether to exercise jurisdiction.[84]

At the same time, not all Commonwealth courts chose to evolve wholeheartedly their approaches to discretionary staying of proceedings by incorporating the *Spiliada* doctrine into their laws. In this regard, Australia and Canada are the most prominent legal systems in which the modern-day English principle has not been fully embraced. Nevertheless, as the discussion in this part seeks to illustrate, the decision in *Spiliada* has been influential in (re)shaping the law in Australia and Canada on discretionary (non-)exercise of jurisdiction. For present purposes, the focus is on private-international-law (as opposed to interstate or interprovincial) claims.

---

[75] *Brinkerhoff Maritime Drilling Corp v PT Airfast Services Indonesia* [1992] 2 SLR 776. See, also, *Eng Liat Kiang v Eng Bak Hern* [1995] 3 SLR 97, *Oriental Insurance Co Ltd v Bhavani Stores Pte Ltd* [1998] 1 SLR 253, and *PT Hutan Domas Raya v Yue Xiu Enterprise (Holdings) Ltd* [2001] 1 SLR(R) 104.

[76] JJ Fawcett, *Declining Jurisdiction in Private International Law* (Oxford, Clarendon Press, 1995) 12.

[77] *The Adhiguna Meranti* [1988] 1 Lloyd's Rep 384.

[78] In Ireland, courts continued to apply the *MacShannon* test for some time: see *Doe v Armour Pharmaceutical Co Inc* [1995] ILPr 148 and *Intermetal Group Ltd v Worslade Trading Ltd* [1997] IEHC 231. Subsequently, however, the *Spiliada* test has been applied: *Analog Devices BV v Zurich Insurance Company* [2002] IESC 1.

[79] *Syarikat Bumiputra Kimanis v Tan Kok Voon* [1988] 3 MLJ 315.

[80] *The Waylink and Brady Maria* [1998] 1 Lloyd's Rep 475.

[81] PR Beaumont and PE McEleavy, *Anton's Private International Law* 3rd edn (Edinburgh, W Green/SULI, 2011) para 8.405.

[82] See, eg, *Credit Chimique v James Scott Engineering Group Ltd* [1979] SC 406 (OH) 410 (Lord Jauncey).

[83] *Sokha v Secretary of State for the Home Department* 1992 SLT 1049 (OH).

[84] See, eg, the decisions in *PTKF Kontinent v VMPTO Progress* 1994 SLT 235 (OH) and *Royal Bank of Scotland v Davidson* 2010 SLT 92 (OH).

C. The Approach in Commonwealth Jurisdictions after *Spiliada*: Australia

As touched on earlier, for decades, courts in Australia had conceived of (and developed) their approach to discretionary (non-)exercise of jurisdiction by following outright the twists and turns in the application of the English practice. In this respect, they tended to incorporate promptly the changes in this area of English conflict of laws into Australian law. However, in two landmark rulings, rendered in quick succession in the wake of *Spiliada* – namely, *Oceanic Sun Line Special Shipping Co Inc v Fay*[85] and *Voth v Manildra Flour Mills Pty Ltd*[86] – the Australian High Court was swift to reject the opportunity to adopt the then newly-established doctrine in England. Instead, it introduced the 'clearly-inappropriate-forum test' as the basis for discretionary (non-)exercise of jurisdiction in Australia. Nevertheless, in many ways, it was the invitation to embrace the *Spiliada* test which prompted the debates that, ultimately, inspired the Australian High Court to articulate the clearly-inappropriate-forum test.

The appeal in the *Oceanic Sun Line* case came before the Australian High Court some 10 months after the decision in *Spiliada* had been handed down.[87] In doctrinal terms, the main question was whether the staying-of-proceedings practice in Australia should be revised by transplanting the *Spiliada* doctrine into Australian law. In a three-to-two majority decision, the High Court answered this question in the negative. The minority (Wilson and Toohey JJ), supported the adoption of the *Spiliada* doctrine into Australian law.[88] They considered that the Australian staying-of-proceedings practice had always mirrored the position in England.[89] Wilson and Toohey JJ noted, relying on passages in one of Professor Pryles's articles,[90] that in light of the socio-economic changes that had been happening in the latter part of the twentieth century, the Australian *forum non conveniens* doctrine was in need of becoming more outward-looking, and more balanced in its treatment of the competing rights of plaintiffs and defendants.[91] The other factor which persuaded Wilson and Toohey JJ to embrace the *Spiliada* doctrine was that they deemed that it would be 'expedient to preserve as much

---

[85] *Oceanic Sun Line Special Shipping Co Inc v Fay* (1988) 165 CLR 197.

[86] *Voth v Manildra Flour Mills Pty Ltd* (1990) 171 CLR 538.

[87] For accounts of the facts in this case see, *inter alia*, M Pryles, 'Judicial Darkness on the Oceanic Sun' (1988) 62 *Australian Law Journal* 774, FMB Reynolds, 'Forum Non Conveniens in Australia' (1989) 105 *Law Quarterly Review* 40, and A Briggs, 'Wider Still and Wider: The Bounds of Australian Exorbitant Jurisdiction' [1989] *Lloyd's Maritime and Commercial Law Quarterly* 216.

[88] *Oceanic Sun Line* (n 85) 212.

[89] In making this observation, Wilson and Toohey JJ cited pre- and post-*St Pierre* Australian authorities, as well as decisions which acknowledged the English law's change of direction after the House of Lords' decision in *The Atlantic Star*: ibid, 209–12.

[90] M Pryles, 'Liberalising the Rule on Staying Actions – Towards the Doctrine of Forum Non Conveniens' (1978) 52 *Australian Law Journal* 678, 684.

[91] *Oceanic Sun Line* (n 85) 212.

consistency as possible between the common law countries' by adopting the more-appropriate-forum test.[92]

The majority (Brennan, Deane, and Gaudron JJ), though, remained unpersuaded by the arguments in favour of the adoption of the *Spiliada* doctrine in Australia. They considered that the more-appropriate-forum test was inconsistent with the earlier case law in Australia on discretionary staying of proceedings.[93] Furthermore, Brennan, Deane, and Gaudron JJ were disinclined to embrace the *Spiliada* test as they regarded that it afforded courts too broad a discretion.[94] At the same time, the majority did not speak with one voice in outlining how the law on discretionary staying of proceedings should apply in Australia. On the one hand, Brennan J reasoned that Australian courts should rely on the vexatious-and-oppressive test.[95] But, on the other hand, the analysis of whether the more-appropriate-forum test should be adopted into Australian law drove Deane and Gaudron JJ towards favouring a more relaxed approach to staying of proceedings than the one envisaged by Brennan J. They stated that, in the context of private-international-law proceedings brought in Australia as of right, stays could be granted if, 'having regard to the circumstances of the particular case and the availability of the foreign tribunal, [the Australian court] is a clearly inappropriate forum for the determination of the dispute between the parties'.[96]

Consequently, the decision in the *Oceanic Sun Line* case created uncertainty regarding the doctrinal framework for staying of proceedings in Australia.[97] In particular, it was unclear whether the vexatious-and-oppressive test, as preferred by Brennan J, would govern the court's discretion, or the clearly-inappropriate-forum test, which was favoured by Deane and Gaudron JJ.

Just under three years later, in *Voth*, the Australian High Court was able to address the confusion generated by *Oceanic Sun Line*.[98] Except for Toohey J, whom once more insisted on adopting *Spiliada* into Australian law, the remaining Justices[99] held that it was the clearly-inappropriate-forum test which provided the basis for the application of discretionary (non-)exercise of jurisdiction in Australia.

---

[92] ibid, 212–13.

[93] ibid, 238 (Brennan J), 253 (Deane J), and 265 (Gaudron J).

[94] ibid, 238 (Brennan J), 254 (Deane J), and 265 (Gaudron J).

[95] ibid, 238–39 and 241 (Brennan J).

[96] ibid, 248 (Deane J) and 266 (Gaudron J).

[97] For criticisms of this and other aspects of the decision in *Oceanic Sun Line* see, eg, Pryles (n 87), L Collins, 'The High Court of Australia and Forum Conveniens: A Further Comment' (1989) 105 *Law Quarterly Review* 364, 364–65; and Briggs (n 87) 221–22.

[98] Noted in L Collins, 'The High Court of Australia and *Forum Conveniens*: The Last Word?' (1991) 107 *Law Quarterly Review* 182, M Pryles, 'Forum Non Conveniens – The Next Chapter' (1991) 65 *Australian Law Journal* 442, and P Brereton, '*Forum Non Conveniens* in Australia: A Case Note on *Voth v Manildra Flour Mills*' (1991) 40 *International & Comparative Law Quarterly* 895. For an in-depth study of the implications of the decision in *Voth* in the decade following the ruling, see R Garnett, 'Stay of Proceedings in Australia: A "Clearly Inappropriate" Test' (1999) 23 *Melbourne University Law Review* 30.

[99] Mason CJ, Deane, Dawson, and Gaudron JJ handed down a joint judgment. Brennan J agreed with them that the clearly-inappropriate-forum test should govern the Australian courts' exercise of jurisdiction. However, he came to a different finding on the facts.

They considered that the clearly-inappropriate-forum test, based on which courts decide to exercise (or relinquish) jurisdiction depending on whether they are (in)appropriate, offered a much better framework for the practice of discretionary (non-)exercise of jurisdiction than the test under *Spiliada*.[100] Thus, Mason CJ, Deane, Dawson, Brennan, and Gaudron JJ maintained their stance against the transplantation into Australian law of the more-appropriate-forum test.

Despite refusing to embrace the *Spiliada* doctrine, their overall attitude towards it was noticeably less hostile than the one exhibited by the majority in *Oceanic Sun Line*. Indeed, Mason CJ, Deane, Dawson, and Gaudron JJ commended the decision in *Spiliada*,[101] and were keen to stress that their new approach was not wholly dissimilar to the *Spiliada* doctrine. The following passage captures the juxtaposition of the clearly-inappropriate-forum and more-appropriate-forum tests in their eyes:

> The 'clearly inappropriate forum' test is similar and, for that reason, is likely to yield the same result as the 'more appropriate forum' test in the majority of cases. The difference between the two tests will be of critical significance only in those cases – probably rare – in which it is held that an available foreign tribunal is the natural or more appropriate forum but in which it cannot be said that the local tribunal is a clearly inappropriate one. But the question which the former test presents is slightly different in that it focuses on the advantages and disadvantages arising from a continuation of the proceedings in [Australia] rather than on the need to make a comparative judgment between the two fora.[102]

In deciding whether Australia was a clearly inappropriate forum for the litigation of the dispute, Mason CJ, Deane, Dawson, and Gaudron JJ examined broadly the same considerations as those under the *Spiliada* test.[103] What is more, they emphasised that the clearly-inappropriate-forum test applied to both the practice of discretionary staying of proceedings, *and* the related concept of permission to serve proceedings on defendants outside Australia.[104]

Without question, *Spiliada* was influential in triggering the debate which, in the end, resulted in the clearly-appropriate-forum test becoming the modern-day formulation for the application of the *forum (non) conveniens* doctrine in private-international-law cases in Australia. While Australian courts refused to adopt *Spiliada*, their preferred test was nevertheless largely inspired by (and, indeed, bears many of the hallmarks of) the English doctrine.[105] Accordingly, the role of

---

[100] *Voth* (n 86) 558–59.

[101] ibid, 557.

[102] ibid, 558.

[103] ibid, 564–65.

[104] ibid, 565. In service-out cases, the burden is on the plaintiff to obtain the permission to sue the foreign-based defendant. In as-of-right cases brought in Australia, it was the defendant who shoulders the burden of persuading the court to stay its proceedings.

[105] For an argument that, despite the narrow conceptual gap between *Voth* and *Spiliada*, the application of the two doctrines leads to *practically* similar outcomes, see A Arzandeh, 'Reconsidering the Australian *Forum (Non) Conveniens* Doctrine' (2016) 65 *International & Comparative Law Quarterly* 475.

the *Spiliada* doctrine in helping to reform its counterpart principle in Australia should not be underestimated.

D. The Approach in Commonwealth Jurisdictions after *Spiliada*: Canada

Canada is the other major Commonwealth jurisdiction which has not fully embraced the *Spiliada* doctrine. As discussed earlier, for much of the twentieth century, the Canadian courts' approach to discretionary (non-)exercise of jurisdiction had followed in the footsteps of the English practice. However, in *Amchem Products Inc v Workers Compensation Board*,[106] where the Supreme Court of Canada was presented with its first opportunity to decide on whether the *Spiliada* doctrine should be adopted in Canada, the more-appropriate-forum test was not embraced outright. Be that as it may, and in much the same way as in Australia (though to an even greater degree), the more-appropriate-forum test was influential in the articulation of the contemporary *forum (non) conveniens* doctrine in Canada.

Strictly speaking, *Amchem* was not a case in which the Canadian court had to rule on whether to exercise jurisdiction in relation to a cross-border private dispute. Rather, it concerned applications for anti-suit injunctions brought by a number of asbestos companies which sought to discontinue group-action proceedings that had been initiated against them in Texas. The main issue for the consideration of the Canadian Supreme Court concerned the principles based on which anti-suit injunctions should be granted.[107] In addressing this issue, Sopinka J, who gave the court's only reasoned judgment,[108] stated that Canadian courts should only issue anti-suit injunctions in relation to foreign proceedings where the courts there are shown to be *forum non conveniens*.[109] It was in this context where the scope and operation of the doctrine in Canada was outlined. Thus, for our purposes, this part of his judgment is especially relevant.

Sopinka J employed the *Spiliada* test as the basis for the revision of the law on discretionary (non-)exercise of jurisdiction in Canada. However, the new Canadian *forum non conveniens* doctrine was different in one important respect from its English equivalent: the new test was to be applied in one stage. In other words, the test in *Amchem* was similar to the Scottish *forum non conveniens* test, prior to it being subsumed by the more-appropriate-forum test. As a result, the question of whether staying the action caused an injustice to the plaintiff was one of a number of issues which the court had to consider when deciding whether to relinquish its (otherwise) soundly founded jurisdiction.

---

[106] *Amchem Products Inc v Workers Compensation Board* [1993] ILPr 689.
[107] ibid, 697.
[108] La Forest, Gonthier, Cory, and McLachlin JJ concurring.
[109] *Amchem* (n 106) 700.

Two reasons combine to explain Sopinka J's preference for a one-stage applica-tion of the more-appropriate-forum test in Canada. First, in outlining the history of the twentieth-century developments in England,[110] he highlighted that treat-ing (in)justice to the plaintiff as a separate requirement for granting a stay was a hangover from the days when the *St Pierre* test determined whether as-of-right proceedings should be stayed. In this regard, the following passage is particularly illustrative of Sopinka J's position:

> there is no reason in principle why the loss of juridical advantage should be treated as a separate and distinct condition rather than being weighed with the other factors which are considered in identifying the appropriate forum. The existence of two condi-tions is based on the historical development of the rule in England which started with two branches at a time when oppression to the defendant and injustice to the plain-tiff were the dual bases for granting or refusing a stay. The law in England has evolved by reworking a passage from the reasons of Scott LJ in [*St Pierre*] which contained two conditions. In its original formulation the second condition required the court to ensure that there was no injustice to the plaintiff in granting the stay. No doubt this was because the oppression test concentrated largely on the effects on the defendant of being subjected to a trial in England. When the first condition moved to an examination of all the factors that are designed to identify the natural forum, it seems to me that any juridical advantages to the plaintiff or defendant should have been considered one of the factors to be taken into account. The weight to be given to juridical advantage is very much a function of the parties' connection to the particular jurisdiction in question.[111]

In essence, therefore, Sopinka J was of the view that, given that the law had evolved in England, following the introduction of the more-appropriate-forum test in place of the earlier vexatious-and-oppressive test outlined in *St Pierre*, there was no reason why all the considerations under the new formulation could not be assessed in one stage.

The second reason why Sopinka J preferred for the test for staying of proceed-ings in Canada to be applied in one stage was that he wanted parity between its application and that of the related principle for serving proceedings on defend-ants outside Canada.[112] Based on the service-out test in Canada, courts could only allow for claims to be issued on foreign-based defendants if no other forum exists which is 'more convenient and appropriate for the pursuit of the action and for securing the ends of justice'.[113] The relevant considerations for the operation of this test are analysed in one stage. Accordingly, Sopinka J opted to adopt the same approach to the application of the more-appropriate-forum test in stay cases.

In sum, the foregoing discussion has attempted to demonstrate that the *Spiliada* doctrine's importance is very far from being confined to England alone. Rather, the decision has also been the main source of inspiration in the develop-ment of the equivalent principles across numerous Commonwealth legal systems.

---

[110] ibid, 700–01.
[111] ibid, 703–04 (citation omitted).
[112] ibid, 704.
[113] Ritchie J in *Antares Shipping Corp v Capricorn* [1976] 65 DLR (3d) 105, 123.

Many of these jurisdictions have revised their approaches to discretionary (non-)exercise of jurisdiction by fully embracing the English doctrine. But, as the discussion has sought to illustrate, even in those Commonwealth countries which have not remodelled their laws in conformity with *Spiliada* – most notably, Australian, and Canada – the *forum (non) conveniens* doctrines are nevertheless heavily influenced by the English test. This state of affairs is, in turn, noteworthy, not least because Commonwealth courts have, in modern times, tended to show reluctance in effecting legal reform by following the lead from courts in England.[114]

IV. The *Spiliada* Doctrine's Scope of Application

Having examined the *Spiliada* doctrine's modern-day operation from the perspective of its global impact, the next step in evaluating English *forum (non) conveniens* in its present form is to review the developments over the past 30 years concerning its scope of application. The review is carried out at two levels. First, the discussion enquires into whether (if at all) *Spiliada's* scope has been extended for it to become applicable in the context of other (broadly related) commercial conflict-of-laws concepts.[115] Second (and more generally), it assesses the degree to which *Spiliada's* overall operation has evolved in view of intervening changes to the law. Here, by far the most significant development has been the introduction into English law of jurisdiction rules under the Brussels regime in January 1987.

As this part proceeds to highlight, despite some attempts to rely on the test in *Spiliada* as the basis for operating other similar commercial conflict-of-laws notions – namely, the granting of anti-suit injunctions or the staying of proceedings brought in breach of foreign jurisdiction agreements – its conceptual reach has generally remained the same. However, due to the Europeanisation of private international law in England, the *forum (non) conveniens* doctrine's overall scope of operation has become markedly circumscribed. In this regard, it has been confirmed that the *Spiliada* doctrine cannot be deployed as the basis for relinquishing jurisdiction which stems from the provisions within the Brussels regime.

A. *Spiliada's* Conceptual Scope

The study of judicial doctrinal development at common law often points to a tendency on the part of the courts to apply a principle, which has become fully fledged, in resolving other similar legal problems. A very good example of this

---

[114] It is, in part, as a result of this caution that in the case of Australia, for example, it has been observed that '[t]oday, it is abundantly clear that there are separate bodies of English and Australian common law': P Finn, 'Common Law Divergences' (2013) 37 *Melbourne University Law Review* 511, 511.

[115] Accordingly, the discussion of the doctrine's effects (or otherwise) in areas such as cross-border insolvency or family disputes falls outside the book's ambit.

phenomenon is the duty of care doctrine in tort. In *Donoghue v Stevenson*,[116] the House of Lords held that a manufacturer owed the consumer of its product a non-contractual duty of care. *Donoghue* was, in a sense, a case which extracted a general principle from earlier cases. Subsequently, however, courts began to expand that decision to new areas,[117] including losses caused by negligent misstatements[118] and trespassing children.[119]

Given that the *Spiliada* ruling confirmed the grounds for discretionary (non-)exercise of jurisdiction in England, it may have been anticipated that the more-appropriate-forum test would, in due course, form the basis for the application of other sister principles within commercial conflict of laws.[120] One of the areas which could have potentially been subsumed by the *Spiliada* doctrine was anti-suit injunctions. As set out in Chapter 2, anti-suit injunctions are measures which can be utilised by English courts where they deem it inappropriate for litigants to commence (or continue with) proceedings in foreign courts. They are conceptually related to *forum (non) conveniens* – in that they both can be deployed by English courts to uphold jurisdictional values such as connectedness and party autonomy – but are ultimately different principles.

Indeed, as outlined in Chapter 3, in *Castanho v Brown & Root*,[121] the House of Lords had applied the *MacShannon* test, which was the antecedent formula to the more-appropriate-forum test, as the basis for granting anti-suit injunctions. In that case, Lord Scarman had transposed the *MacShannon* test into the context of issuing anti-suit injunctions, stating that, to obtain an injunction, the applicant had to establish:

> (a) that the English court is a forum to whose jurisdiction they are amenable in which justice can be done at substantially less inconvenience and expense, and (b) the

---

[116] *Donoghue v Stevenson* [1932] AC 562 (HL).

[117] An early such example, which may have helped to put on its way the expansion of the concept of duty of care was *Grant v Australian Knitting Mills Ltd* [1936] AC 85 (PC), where the Privy Council ruled that the duty imposed under *Donoghue* was not specific to products which manufacturers supplied in sealed and opaque containers.

[118] *Hedley Byrne & Co v Heller & Partners Ltd* [1964] AC 465 (HL).

[119] *British Railway Board v Herrington* [1972] AC 877 (HL). The expansive application of the notion of duty of care in tort reached its peak in the late 1970s, following the House of Lords' decision in *Anns v Merton London Borough Council* [1978] AC 728 (HL), and subsequent decisions such as *Junior Books Ltd v Veitchi Co Ltd* [1983] 1 AC 520 (HL). Duty of care's scope is, however, more limited now after the House of Lords in *Murphy v Brentwood District Council* [1991] 1 AC 398 (HL) overruled the *Anns* test, and devised a new formulation in *Caparo Industries plc v Dickman* [1990] 2 AC 605 (HL).

[120] It is recalled from the discussion in Chapter 2 that, for much of the period prior to the articulation of the modern practice of discretionary (non-)exercise of jurisdiction in *Spiliada*, it was generally accepted that, in the main, the same considerations governed the English courts' practice of discretionary non-exercise of jurisdiction whether (or not) concurrent proceedings involving similar (or related) parties and issues were ongoing in a foreign court. A few months after *Spiliada* was decided, Lord Goff confirmed that the more-appropriate-forum test provided the basis for the courts' decision to relinquish their jurisdiction in both stay and *lis alibi pendens* cases: *de Dampierre v de Dampierre* [1988] AC 92 (HL) 108. Thus, for our purposes, it is accepted that the English courts' approach to stay applications in cases involving concurrent proceedings elsewhere had already become subsumed by the courts' practice in *forum non conveniens* cases.

[121] *Castanho v Brown & Root* [1981] AC 557 (HL).

injunction must not deprive the plaintiff of a legitimate personal or juridical advantage which would be available to him if he invoked the [foreign] jurisdiction.[122]

Lord Scarman's liberalisation of the test for granting anti-suit injunctions effectively equated the requirements for staying of proceedings with those that had to be considered for anti-suit injunctions, thereby making it much easier than ever before to obtain anti-suit injunctions. The decision in *Castanho* was met with withering criticism.[123] Most notably, Professor Briggs observed that the ruling was erroneous because it contravened the House of Lords' intentions in *The Atlantic Star* and *MacShannon*. According to Professor Briggs,

> they were both cases in which a stay of English proceedings was sought. Nothing in the cases bears upon the criteria for granting an injunction to restrain a foreign plaintiff unless it be assumed that the same criteria apply, and it is submitted that they do not. Hardly anywhere in *The Atlantic Star* and *MacShannon* is any mention made of the need to construct guidelines that accord with the policy of non-interference with a foreign forum. Nowhere is there any suggestion that injunctions to restrain foreign plaintiffs should far more liberally be given.[124]

Put differently, Professor Briggs's point was that the House of Lords' intention in *The Atlantic Star* and *MacShannon* was to relax the approach to staying of its *own* proceedings; the liberalisation of the test for restraining proceedings in *foreign* courts was never on the agenda. Thus, Professor Briggs regarded the Privy Council's transposition in *Castanho* of the *MacShannon* test in the context of anti-suit injunctions as being liable to lead to unwarranted and excessive meddling with proceedings in foreign courts.

Despite these (well-founded) criticisms, it may have been thought that there was no turning back from the Privy Council's decision in *Castanho*, and that, before long, the test for granting anti-suit injunctions would be adapted to take account of the new test for discretionary (non-)exercise of jurisdiction under *Spiliada*. In *Spiliada* itself, Lord Goff did not make any specific pronouncements regarding whether the more-appropriate-forum test could also be extended to cases involving anti-suit injunctions. Nevertheless, certain passages in his Lordship's speech hinted at his misgivings regarding the accuracy of the position in *Castanho*.[125]

The first genuine opportunity for English courts to rule authoritatively on whether the then newly-refined test for staying of proceedings in England under *Spiliada* would subsume the principles for granting anti-suit injunctions presented itself in 1987, when the litigation in *Société Nationale Industrielle Aérospatiale v Lee Kui Jak* reached the Privy Council.[126] In this case, the facts of which are not relevant to the present discussion, the Privy Council made it clear that the

---

[122] ibid, 575.
[123] See, especially, A Briggs, 'No Interference with Foreign Court' (1982) 31 *International & Comparative Law Quarterly* 189.
[124] ibid, 193.
[125] *Spiliada* (n 1) 480.
[126] *Société Nationale Industrielle Aérospatiale v Lee Kui Jak* [1987] AC 871 (PC).

more-appropriate-forum test should not be extended to become the principle for issuing anti-suit injunctions. Lord Goff delivered the opinion of the board.[127] According to his Lordship, were the test for discretionary staying of proceedings under *Spiliada* to be adapted for issuing anti-suit injunctions, it would:

> have the effect that, where the parties are in dispute on the point whether the action should proceed in an English or a foreign court, the English court would be prepared, not merely to decline to adjudicate by granting a stay of proceedings on the ground that the English court was forum non conveniens, but, if it concluded that England was the natural forum, to restrain a party from proceeding in the foreign court on that ground alone. Their Lordships cannot think that this is right. ... [Such state of affairs] leads to the conclusion that, in a case where there is simply a difference of view between the English court and the foreign court as to which is the natural forum, the English court can arrogate to itself, by the grant of an injunction, the power to resolve that dispute.[128]

In other words, Lord Goff deemed it wrong to set the same requirements for staying of actions in England, on the one hand, as the basis for restraining litigants from commencing (or continuing with) claims before foreign courts, on the other. According to his Lordship, to apply similar principles for issuing these measures creates a situation that would 'be inconsistent with comity, and indeed [would] disregard the fundamental requirement that an injunction will only be granted where the ends of justice so require'.[129] Therefore, the *Spiliada* test was not transposed for the purposes of determining anti-suit injunction applications. What is more, the law on granting anti-suit injunctions in England was restored to its position before the *Castanho* ruling.[130]

Another broadly similar concept which might have been regarded as being susceptible for domination by the *Spiliada* formulation is the principle based on which an English court exercises jurisdiction when it is asked to hear a claim that has been brought before it in breach of a clause conferring jurisdiction on courts in a foreign forum. In these cases, the question is whether the English court should exercise its (otherwise) soundly founded jurisdiction, notwithstanding the foreign jurisdiction clause. As discussed in Chapter 2, in this type of case, the relevant principles guiding the English court's discretion whether to entertain the dispute is outlined in Brandon J's judgment in *The Eleftheria*.[131] Based on this principle, the presumption is that the proceedings in England would be stayed, unless the claimant is able to establish a 'strong cause' to the contrary. Whether a strong cause

---

[127] Lord Keith of Kinkel, Lord Griffiths, Lord Mackay of Clashfern, and Sir John Megaw concurred.

[128] *Lee Kui Jak* (n 126) 895.

[129] ibid.

[130] For a detailed outline (and analysis) of the principles for issuing anti-suit injunctions under English law see Briggs (n 3) paras 5.32–5.52.

[131] *The Eleftheria* [1970] P 94. The test was subsequently confirmed in *The El Amria* [1981] 2 Lloyd's Rep 119 (CA). For a more recent reiteration of the test in *The Eleftheria* see the House of Lords' ruling in *Donohue v Armco Inc* [2001] UKHL 64, [2002] CLC 440 (HL).

in favour of sustaining the English proceedings, notwithstanding an exclusive foreign jurisdiction clause, has been established hinges on the court's discretion.[132] In exercising the discretion, the following non-exhaustive list of factors, set out by Brandon J in *The Eleftheria*, are frequently consulted:

> (4) In exercising its discretion the court should take into account all the circumstances of the particular case. (5) In particular, but without prejudice to (4), the following matters, where they arise, may properly be regarded: (a) In what country the evidence on the issues of fact is situated, or more readily available, and the effect of that on the relative convenience and expense of trial as between the English and foreign courts. (b) Whether the law of the foreign court applies and, if so, whether it differs from English law in any material respects. (c) With what country either party is connected, and how closely. (d) Whether the defendants genuinely desire trial in the foreign country, or are only seeking procedural advantages. (e) Whether the plaintiffs would be prejudiced by having to sue in the foreign court because they would: (i) be deprived of security for their claim; (ii) be unable to enforce any judgment obtained; (iii) be faced with a time-bar not applicable in England; or (iv) for political, racial, religious or other reasons be unlikely to get a fair trial.[133]

Given the obvious similarities between Brandon J's test and Lord Goff's formula in *Spiliada*, it might have been thought that the more-appropriate-forum test would, in fullness of time, displace the test in *The Eleftheria*. *Spiliada* itself was silent on whether this development should occur. Furthermore, it is hard to imply that Lord Goff was in fact sympathetic to such a development: the contract underlying the dispute in *Spiliada* did not contain a jurisdiction clause. As such, there is nothing in *Spiliada* which warrants the doctrine's extrapolation to staying of proceedings commenced in England in contravention of a jurisdiction clause.

However, in some post-*Spiliada* decisions, courts appeared to combine the principles in *Spiliada* and *The Eleftheria* in determining whether to continue with proceedings that were brought in breach of foreign jurisdiction clauses.[134] Nevertheless, in the majority of cases over the past three decades, the test in *The Eleftheria*, and its progeny, have continued to provide the basis for the courts' treatment of applications for staying of English proceedings that had been commenced in breach of jurisdiction agreements.[135] As such, the scope of the *Spiliada* test has

---

[132] Eg, *The Eleftheria* (n 131) 99–100 and *The El Amria*, ibid 123.

[133] ibid, 99–100.

[134] In this context, arguably the most notable example is the decision in *The Nile Rhapsody* [1992] 2 Lloyd's Rep 399, a case which was brought before the English court in breach of an exclusive Egyptian jurisdiction clause. For a criticism of the decision, see A Briggs, 'Jurisdictional Clauses and Judicial Attitudes' (1993) 109 *Law Quarterly Review* 382.

[135] See, eg, *The Pioneer Container* [1994] 2 AC 324 (PC), *Citi-March v Neptune Orient Lines* [1997] 1 Lloyd's Rep 72, *The MC Pearl* [1997] 1 Lloyd's Rep 566, *Baghlaf Al Zafer Factory Co v Pakistan National Shipping Co (No 1)* [1998] CLC 716 (CA), *Konkola Copper Mines plc v Coromin Ltd (No 2)* [2006] EWHC 1093 (Comm), [2006] 2 Lloyd's Rep 446, and *Bank of New York Mellon v GV Films Ltd* [2009] EWHC 3315 (Comm), [2010] 1 Lloyd's Rep 365. See, also, *Cheshire, North & Fawcett* (n 10) 413.

not been extended for it to provide the ground for the courts' determination of whether proceedings in England should continue, despite the existence of a jurisdiction clause in favour of courts in a foreign forum.[136]

B. *Spiliada's* Scope of Application in the Face of Intervening Legal Developments

While, conceptually, the scope of *Spiliada* has remained largely unchanged, the intervening years have witnessed a major development which has affected its overall applicability. More specifically, in recent years, the number of instances in which the doctrine can be deployed have become considerably curtailed. As the discussion proceeds to illustrate, for the most part, this state of affairs has come about as a result of the Europeanisation of private international law in England.

The European influences on English private international law began to take root when jurisdiction rules under the Brussels regime were incorporated into English law in 1987, following the entry into force of the relevant provisions under the Civil Jurisdiction and Judgments Act 1982 ('CJJA'). This was a seismic development. Thereafter, courts in England were obliged to consult a new set of rules for allocating jurisdiction,[137] alongside their national rules. Additionally, and much more importantly, ever since their introduction, the jurisdiction rules under the Brussels regime have taken precedence over the provisions within the English national rules. As a result, the relevant national rules for asserting jurisdiction are only referred to if the dispute in question falls outside the material scope of the Brussels regime, or is one which is covered by Brussels Ia Regulation, Art 6(1) and Lugano II Convention, Art 4(1).

In incorporating the Brussels regime into English law, the CJJA revised certain aspects of domestic jurisdiction rules in England. In this context, one of the most significant alterations concerned the *forum non conveniens* doctrine's scope of application. Under CJJA, s 49, courts in England can only grant stays of proceedings under the doctrine if such a ruling is 'not inconsistent' with the Brussels regime. Over the years, the availability of the *forum non conveniens* doctrine has seldom been in doubt in cases which fall outside the scope of the Brussels regime.[138] Similarly, it has been widely accepted that granting a stay of proceedings

---

[136] It should be noted that 'in cases where the parties have agreed to the non-exclusive jurisdiction of the courts of another country, but there are no proceedings pending in the contractual forum, if the claimant seeks to bring proceedings in England ..., the English court will determine its jurisdiction by reference to the *Spiliada* test': J Hill and A Chong, *International Commercial Disputes: Commercial Conflict of Laws in English Courts* 4th edn (Oxford, Hart Publishing, 2010) para 9.3.4.

[137] The Brussels regime also contains provisions concerning the enforcement and recognition of judgments awarded by one Member State court in another. The discussion of these provisions falls outside the scope of this book.

[138] *Cheshire & North* (n 18) 327.

in favour of the appropriate court, which is located in a Member State, would be incompatible with the Brussels regime.[139]

By contrast, the extent to which the doctrine can apply where the English courts' jurisdiction is rooted in the Brussels regime has been considered to be a 'very thorny problem',[140] and 'one of the most controversial issues in the field of civil jurisdiction'.[141] In this area, traditionally, the most contentious debate concerned the ability of the English court to stay its proceedings in favour of the appropriate forum which is in a *non-Member State*. In relation to this issue, some commentators have proffered the view that the jurisdiction given to the English court under the Brussels regime was mandatory and, hence, could not be relinquished. Most notable among these were perhaps the editors of the eleventh edition of *Cheshire & North's Private International Law*, published in 1987. Relying in part on the Schlosser Report's stance on the matter,[142] they contended that the jurisdiction afforded under the Brussels regime was obligatory in nature and, therefore, a Member State court had 'no discretionary power to refuse to take it'.[143] As a consequence, they stated that it would be unwarranted for the English court, in those circumstances, to rely on the *forum non conveniens* doctrine to stay its proceedings.

Other commentators, though, took a diametrically opposed position, observing that, where the appropriate forum is in a non-Member State, the English court's power to stay its proceedings should not be circumscribed. For example, Professor Hartley observed that 'the case against' the applicability of the *forum non conveniens* doctrine, as made in the Schlosser Report, was not 'very strong'.[144] Likewise, Dr Kaye argued that, if the appropriate forum is located in a non-Member State, the *forum non conveniens* doctrine should 'continue to apply, notwithstanding [Brussels-rooted] jurisdiction otherwise possessed'.[145]

It was not long before the English court was presented with an opportunity to rule on this aspect of the interrelationship between the Brussels regime and English national jurisdiction rules. In the 1989 case of *S & W Berisford plc v New Hampshire Insurance Co Ltd*,[146] the English High Court favoured a more limited

---

[139] Bingham LJ (as he then was) in *Re Harrods (Buenos Aires) Ltd (No 2)* [1992] Ch 72 (CA) 101. See, also L Collins, *et al*, *Dicey & Morris on the Conflict of Laws* 12th edn (London, Sweet & Maxwell, 1993) 401, A Briggs and P Rees, *Norton Rose on Civil Jurisdiction and Judgments* 1st edn (London, LLP, 1993) 135, and P Kaye, 'The EEC Judgments Convention and the Outer World: Goodbye to Forum Non Conveniens?' [1992] *Journal of Business Law* 47, 48–49.

[140] TC Hartley, *Civil Jurisdiction and Judgments* (London, Sweet & Maxwell, 1984) 78.

[141] Hill and Chong (n 136) para 9.5.2.

[142] Report on the Convention on the Association of the Kingdom of Denmark, Ireland and the United Kingdom of Great Britain and Northern Ireland to the Convention on jurisdiction and the enforcement of judgments in civil and commercial matters and to the Protocol on its interpretation by the Court of Justice [1979] OJ C 59/71, 97.

[143] *Cheshire & North* (n 18) 328–29. See, also, S O'Malley and A Layton, *European Civil Practice* 1st edn (London, Sweet & Maxwell, 1989) 31–32.

[144] Hartley (n 140) 80.

[145] P Kaye, *Civil Jurisdiction and Enforcement of Foreign Judgments* (Oxford, Professional Books Limited, 1987) 1244–45.

[146] *S & W Berisford plc v New Hampshire Insurance Co Ltd* [1990] 2 QB 631.

scope of application for the *forum non conveniens* doctrine, consistent with the position advanced by the editors of the eleventh edition of *Cheshire & North's Private International Law*. The following passage in the judgment of Hobhouse J (as he then was) helpfully captures the reasons for the endorsement of this view:

> [i]t is clear that the [Brussels Regime] is designed (subject to [(what is now) Brussels Ia Regulation, Art 6]) to achieve uniformity and to 'harmonise' the relevant procedural and jurisdictional rules of the courts of the contracting states. The [Brussels regime] leaves no room for the application of any discretionary jurisdiction by the courts of this country; the availability of such a discretion would destroy the framework of the [Brussels regime] and create lack of uniformity in the interpretation and implementation of [it].[147]

In its immediate aftermath, this approach towards the interface between the Brussels regime and the doctrine of *forum non conveniens* – which was, subsequently, approved in *Arkwright Mutual Insurance Co v Bryanston Insurance Co Ltd*[148] – was roundly criticised by a number of leading conflict-of-laws scholars in England.[149] For instance, in a case comment, published in the *Law Quarterly Review*, Mr (now Lord) Collins observed that, the Brussels regime 'was intended to regulate jurisdiction as *between*' the Member States and, consequently, the Member States 'had no interest in requiring [the English court] to exercise a jurisdiction where the competing jurisdiction was in' a non-Member State.[150] Similarly, Professor Briggs opined, with characteristic forthrightness, that 'it may yet be proper to disregard [*Berisford* and *Arkwright*] when exercising a discretion to stay, as they have a wholly artificial smell about them'.[151]

Shortly after their publication, these criticisms proved fruitful when, in *Re Harrods (Buenos Aires) Ltd (No 2)*,[152] the Court of Appeal overturned the decisions in *Berisford* and *Arkwright*. *Harrods* concerned an action brought against a company which was domiciled in England, but practically performed all of its functions in Argentina. The plaintiff complained that the company's affairs were being conducted in a manner which was unfairly prejudicial and, hence, brought a petition under (what was then) the Companies Act 1985, s 459. The company, though, applied for a stay of proceedings under the *forum non conveniens* doctrine, pointing to Argentina as the appropriate forum. In response, the Court of Appeal concluded that, for the purpose of CJJA, s 49, it was not inconsistent with the Brussels regime for it to give up its jurisdiction – which was founded on (what is now) Brussels Ia Regulation, Art 4 – in favour of a non-Member State court

---

[147] ibid, 645.
[148] *Arkwright Mutual Insurance Co v Bryanston Insurance Co Ltd* [1990] 2 QB 649.
[149] Eg, L Collins, 'Forum Non Conveniens and the Brussels Convention' (1990) 106 *Law Quarterly Review* 535, A Briggs, 'Spiliada and the Brussels Convention' [1991] *Lloyd's Maritime and Commercial Law Quarterly* 10, and Kaye (n 139).
[150] ibid, 538–39 (emphasis in the original).
[151] Briggs (n 149) 11.
[152] *Harrods (Buenos Aires) Ltd (No 2)* (n 139).

(in Argentina). The oft-cited passage, below, in Dillon LJ's judgment, is illustrative of the court's reasoning for favouring this stance:

> [f]or the English court to refuse jurisdiction, in a case against a person domiciled in England, on the ground that the court of some [non-Member State] is the more appropriate court to decide the matters in issue does not in any way impair the object of the [Brussels regime] of establishing an expeditious, harmonious, and, I would add, certain, procedure for securing the enforcement of judgments, since ex hypothesi if the English court refuses jurisdiction there will be no judgment of the English court to be enforced in the other contracting states. Equally and for the same reason such a refusal of jurisdiction would not impair the object of the [Brussels regime] that there should, subject to the very large exception [under Brussels Ia Regulation, Art 6(1) and Lugano II Convention, Art 4(1)], be a uniform international jurisdiction for obtaining the judgments which are to be so enforced.[153]

The Court of Appeal's conception of the availability of a discretionary power to relinquish its Brussels-founded jurisdiction, which had been unanimously arrived at in *Harrods*, began to gain traction in England.[154] What is more, it was endorsed by sections of the academic community.[155] Yet, many other commentators remained doubtful about the consistency of the ruling in *Harrods* with the Brussels regime. Predictably, perhaps, the editors of the twelfth edition of *Cheshire & North's Private International Law* were the decision's most vehement critics. In this edition, published in 1992, they reiterated the mandatory nature of the jurisdiction-affording provisions within the Brussels regime. Moreover, the editors considered that the Brussels regime was not 'simply concerned with jurisdiction as *between*' Member States and, that by holding to the contrary in *Harrods*, the Court of Appeal had 'misunderstood' the Brussels regime.[156] Accordingly, they stated that 'it is hard to resist the conclusion that the decision in *Re Harrods (Buenos Aires) Ltd* [was] misguided, if not downright wrong'.[157] Indeed, even those who had spoken favourably of the decision in *Harrods* agreed that the Court of Justice's verdict on the matter was required to help to dispel ongoing doubts surrounding its soundness.[158]

In *Harrods* itself, and upon the plaintiffs' appeal to the House of Lords, a reference was made to the Court of Justice, seeking a ruling on whether it was (in)compatible with the Brussels regime for the English court to stay its proceedings, founded on (what is now) Brussels Ia Regulation, Art 4, in favour of the more

---

[153] ibid, 97.

[154] Eg, *The Po* (n 18) (stay of proceedings not granted, though the Court of Appeal emphasised that it could, in principle, have ordered it) and *Lubbe v Cape plc* [2000] 1 WLR 1545 (HL) (where stay was not granted, but *not* because it was unavailable as a result of the defendant being domiciled in England).

[155] Eg, A Briggs, 'Forum Non Conveniens and the Brussels Convention Again' (1991) 107 *Law Quarterly Review* 180 and Kaye (n 139) 75–76.

[156] *Cheshire & North* (n 40) 333.

[157] ibid, 334. See, also, J Hill, *The Law Relating to International Commercial Disputes*, 1st edn (London, LLP, 1994) paras 5.10.1.5–5.10.1.9.

[158] Briggs and Rees (n 139) 136.

appropriate forum in a non-Member State.[159] However, the case was settled before the Court of Justice could afford a judgment. It was only in *Owusu v Jackson*, in 2005, nearly 15 years after the decision in *Harrods*, that the Court of Justice was finally presented with the opportunity to make a pronouncement on this difficult legal question.

Much has been written about *Owusu*,[160] but, for the purpose of the present discussion, it suffices to say that the dispute came before the English court following an accident in Jamaica. The English claimant, who had sustained serious personal injuries, alleged that the harm suffered had been attributable to wrongful conduct on the part of the English defendant (and a number of other Jamaican entities). The defendants, in turn, applied for a stay of proceedings in England under the *forum non conveniens* doctrine, stating that Jamaica was the appropriate forum for entertaining the dispute. At first instance, the judge held that, while he was persuaded that Jamaica was the appropriate forum – as it was, factually, the dispute's centre of gravity, and capable of entertaining the case justly – it would be inconsistent with the Brussels regime for the English court to give up its jurisdiction, which had been rooted in (what is now) Brussels Ia Regulation, Art 4.

On the claimant's appeal,[161] the Court of Appeal sought a preliminary ruling from the Court of Justice. Among other things,[162] it asked the court to declare whether, in a case such as *Owusu*, it would be inconsistent with the Brussels regime for the Member State court to rely on its discretionary power and stay its proceedings in favour of a non-Member State court, which is the appropriate forum. In response, the Court of Justice stated that the Brussels regime

> precludes a court of a [Member State] from declining the jurisdiction conferred on it by [(what is now) Brussels Ia Regulation, Art 4] on the ground that a court of a [non-Member State] would be a more appropriate forum for the trial of the action, even if the jurisdiction of no other [Member State] is in issue or the proceedings have no connecting factors to any other [Member State].[163]

In delivering this ruling, the Court of Justice emphasised that (what is now) Brussels Ia Regulation, Art 4, affords jurisdiction to the Member State court in which the defendant is domiciled, regardless of the fact that the dispute involves the relationship between the court of a Member State (for example, England) and

---

[159] Case C-314/92 *Ladenimor SA v Intercomfinanz SA*.

[160] Eg, A Briggs, 'The Death of Harrods: Forum Non Conveniens and the European Court' (2005) 121 *Law Quarterly Review* 535, E Peel, '*Forum Non Conveniens* and European Ideals' [2005] *Lloyd's Maritime and Commercial Law Quarterly* 363, J Harris, 'Stay of Proceedings and the Brussels Convention' (2005) 54 *International & Comparative Law Quarterly* 933, R Fentiman, 'Civil Jurisdiction and Third States: Owusu and After' (2006) 43 *Common Market Law Review* 705, and BJ Rodger, '*Forum Non Conveniens* Post-Owusu' (2006) 2 *Journal of Private International Law* 71.

[161] *Owusu v Jackson* [2002] EWCA Civ 877, [2003] 1 CLC 246 (CA).

[162] In addition, the Court of Justice was asked to rule on whether the *forum non conveniens* doctrine could apply to afford a reflex effect to (what are now) Brussels Ia Regulation, Arts 24, 25 and 29. The court did not engage with this issue. Further discussion of this point falls outside the scope of this book.

[163] *Owusu* (n 7) [46].

its counterpart in a non-Member State (in this instance, Jamaica).[164] Additionally, and more importantly, it made it plain that (what is now) Art 4 'is mandatory in nature and that, according to its terms, there can be no derogation from the principle it lays down except in the cases expressly provided for' within the Brussels regime.[165] In sum, the Court of Justice rejected the English Court of Appeal's conception in *Harrods* of the interplay between the Brussels regime and the *forum non conveniens* doctrine.

The Court of Justice's renunciation, in *Owusu*, of the position in *Harrods* had been adumbrated by some conflict-of-laws scholars in England.[166] Nevertheless, the decision came as a major disappointment to many other leading commentators in the field whom, in turn, subjected it to stinging criticism. For instance, Professor Briggs considered, *inter alia*, that, in arriving at its interpretation of (what is now) Art 4, the Court of Justice had 'misunderstood' that 'a right given to a defendant', pursuant to the provision to be sued where he is domiciled, 'may, presumably, be given up' if *he* has sought a stay.[167] In his view, therefore, 'the court interpreted [Art 4] as though it gave rights to a claimant rather than the defendant, inverting the usual understanding'.[168] Likewise, Professor Peel opined that the decision in *Owusu* had deprived the English court from 'a valuable tool against the worst excesses of forum shopping'.[169] Finally, Professor Fentiman observed that the reasoning at the heart of the Court of Justice's pronouncement had been

> elusive, amenable to different and contradictory readings. It [was] also contentious. It is uncertain whether the Court's approach is sound in principle, or as a matter of policy. It is debateable whether the decision properly implements the objectives of the European jurisdiction regime, or correctly defines its scope.[170]

Notwithstanding these criticisms of the decision in *Owusu*, there was little doubt among *Owusu*'s detractors that there was no turning back from the decision. Pointedly, in this regard, the editors of *Dicey, Morris & Collins*, in its fourteenth edition published in 2006, noted that 'the width of the language chosen by the [Court of Justice] to express its rejection of the principle of *forum non conveniens* makes it impossible to argue that *Re Harrods (Buenos Aires) Ltd* has not been comprehensively overruled'.[171]

Indeed, the Court of Justice's ruling in *Owusu* has, for the most part,[172] been adhered to by English courts in cases that have been brought before it in

---

[164] ibid, [35].
[165] ibid, [37].
[166] Eg, W Kennett, '*Forum Non Conveniens* in Europe' (2005) 54 *Cambridge Law Journal* 552.
[167] Briggs (n 160) 538.
[168] ibid. See, similarly, Harris (n 160) 937.
[169] Peel (n 160) 372.
[170] Fentiman (n 160) 713.
[171] L Collins, *et al, Dicey, Morris & Collins on the Conflict of Laws* 14th edn (London, Sweet & Maxwell, 2006) [12-020].
[172] Perhaps the most notable examples of where English courts have hinted at sidestepping the ruling in *Owusu* (but ultimately did not do so because the defendants were unable to establish that

subsequent years. For instance, in *Gomez v Gomez-Monche Vives*,[173] a case in which the English court's jurisdiction was based on (what was then) Brussels I Regulation, Art 5(6), Morgan J (as he then was) held that, due to the *Owusu* ruling, he was unable to order a stay of proceedings in favour of the court in Liechtenstein.[174] Likewise, in *Equitas Ltd v Allstate Insurance Co*,[175] where the court's competence to hear the dispute was based on (what is now) Brussels Ia Regulation, Art 25, Beatson J (as he then was) rejected a stay-of-proceedings application. He noted that, to have held otherwise, notwithstanding the English jurisdiction clause, would have 'subvert[ed] the principle in *Owusu*'s case'.[176]

As a consequence, the overall scope of operation for the *forum non conveniens* doctrine in England has become limited to those cases falling within (what are now) Brussels Ia Regulation, Art 6(1)[177] and Lugano II Convention, Art 4(1),[178] or, indeed, altogether outside the Brussels regime. However, it should be noted that, recently, in *Cook v Virgin Media Ltd*,[179] the Court of Appeal has ruled that the English court could give up its Brussels-based jurisdiction, based on the doctrine, in a case in which Scotland was shown to be the more closely connected forum to the dispute. According to this ruling, the scope of the *forum non conveniens* doctrine has remained unaffected in the context of what it labelled as 'purely domestic' cases.[180]

As can be seen, over the course of its existence, the *Spiliada* doctrine's scope of application has become progressively limited. Before the coming into force of the Brussels-based jurisdiction rules in English law on 1 January 1987, and for just over a month, the *Spiliada* doctrine's scope of application in England was in no way conditioned. Thereafter, however, and except for a short period between 1987 and 1991, English courts took the stance that it was entirely consistent with

England was *forum non conveniens*) were *Antec International Ltd v Biosafety USA Inc* [2006] EWHC 47 (Comm), *HIT Entertainment Ltd v Gaffney International Licensing Pty Ltd* [2007] EWHC 1282 (Ch), and *Bankhaus Wolbern & Co v China Construction Bank Corp* [2012] EWHC 3285 (Comm).

[173] *Gomez v Gomez-Monche Vives* [2008] EWHC 259 (Ch), [2008] 3 WLR 309.

[174] ibid, [105]–[116]. The decision was reversed upon appeal, though this aspect of Morgan J's ruling remained unchanged: [2008] EWCA Civ 1065, [2009] Ch 245.

[175] *Equitas Ltd v Allstate Insurance Co* [2008] EWHC 1671 (Comm), [2009] 1 All ER (Comm) 1137.

[176] ibid, [72]. For other examples of the English courts' upholding of the ruling in *Owusu*, see, eg, *Skype Technologies SA v Joltid Ltd* [2009] EWHC 2783 (Ch), [2011] ILPr 8; *Blue Tropic Ltd v Chkhartishvili* [2014] EWHC 2243 (Ch), [2014] ILPr 33; *AAA v Unilever plc* [2017] EWHC 371 (QB) (affirmed by the Court of Appeal: [2018] EWCA Civ 1532); and *Lungowe v Vedanta Resources plc* [2016] EWHC 975 (TCC), [2016] BCC 774 (affirmed by the Court of Appeal: [2017] EWCA Civ 1528, [2017] BCC 787 (CA)).

[177] Under Art 6(1) 'if the defendant is not domiciled in a Member State, the jurisdiction of the courts of each Member State shall, subject to Article 18(1), Article 21(2) and Articles 24 and 25 [of the Brussels Ia Regulation], be determined by the law of that Member State'.

[178] According to Art 4(1) 'If the defendant is not domiciled in a State bound by this Convention, the jurisdiction of the courts of each State bound by this Convention shall, subject to the provisions of Articles 22 and 23 [of the Lugano II Convention], be determined by the law of that State'.

[179] *Cook v Virgin Media Ltd* (Joined with *McNeil v Tesco plc*) [2015] EWCA Civ 1287, [2016] 1 WLR 1672 (CA).

[180] For a critical assessment of this decision, see M Hemsworth, 'Forum Non Conveniens, Jurisdiction and Civil Disputes within the UK' (2016) 35 *Civil Justice Quarterly* 299.

the Brussels regime for them to apply the *forum non conveniens* doctrine and give up their Brussels-based jurisdiction in favour of a more appropriate forum in a non-Member State. However, the Court of Justice's ruling in *Owusu*, in 2005, made it clear that Brussels-based jurisdiction rules were mandatory in nature, and that the *Spiliada* doctrine could not be resorted to as the basis for relinquishing this jurisdiction in favour of a more appropriate foreign forum.

More significantly, and even in its more circumscribed post-*Owusu* form, existential doubts about the *forum non conveniens* doctrine were raised during the process of revising the Brussels I Regulation. In its report for the review of Brussels I, published in December 2010,[181] the European Commission had proposed for (what was then) Brussels I Regulation, Art 4 – which, subject to certain provisions within the Regulation, allowed courts of Member States to apply their own jurisdiction rules to disputes in cases where the defendant is not domiciled in a Member State – to be erased. The adoption of this proposal would have led to national jurisdiction rules of the Member States to be discarded and replaced by the jurisdictional provisions under the Brussels regime. In the case of England, the plans would have spelt the end of its national conflict-of-laws rules, including the *forum (non) conveniens* doctrine. In the end, the European Commission's preferred approach was abandoned, with Brussels I Regulation, Art 4 and its contents surviving.[182] In turn, and where appropriate, Member State courts have maintained the right to resort to their national rules.

Thus, from the throes of near-death, the *Spiliada* doctrine has continued to live on and remains significant in the context of the allocation of jurisdiction in England. In fact, the English *forum (non) conveniens* doctrine may well be about to witness an upturn in fortunes. The UK voters' decision in the referendum in June 2016 to leave the European Union ('Brexit') is likely to bring about wholesale changes to the private-international-law landscape in England. Inevitably, it will take some time before the dust settles and the precise nature and format of these changes become clear. Nevertheless, it is conceivable that the *Spiliada* doctrine's application will be restored to the position prior to the *Owusu* ruling, thus enabling it to play a greater role in the post-Brexit English private international law.

V. Conclusion

The principal aim of this chapter has been to take stock of the evolution of the *forum (non) conveniens* doctrine in the three or so decades after it was eventually recognised by the House of Lords in England in the *Spiliada* case. In this context,

---

[181] The document's full title is 'Proposal for a Regulation of the European Parliament and of the Council on jurisdiction and the recognition and enforcement of judgments in civil and commercial matters', Brussels, COM (2010) 748 final.

[182] The latest incarnation of Brussels I Regulation, Art 4 is Brussels Ia Regulation, Art 6.

the doctrine's contemporary operation and ambit was analysed from three main perspectives. The first perspective, outlined in Part II, focused on the *doctrinal* developments, concerning the more-appropriate-forum test, in the post-*Spiliada* era. In this context, the key question for consideration was whether, in doctrinal terms, there have been any changes to the more-appropriate-forum test in the years following its articulation in *Spiliada*. In order to answer this question, the English courts' application of the test in cases concerning staying of as-of-right proceedings, and those relating to the granting of permission to sue foreign-based defendants, were analysed separately. The assessment of the case law and related commentary on the application of the more-appropriate-forum test in stay cases showed that, except for a short-lived expansion of the meaning of availability, it has been applied in the same manner as when it was outlined in *Spiliada*. Similarly, and in spite of opposing observations, made predominantly by Professor Briggs, the current application of the test in service-out cases is not doctrinally different from that set out in *Spiliada* back in 1986.

The second perspective from which the contemporary English *forum (non) conveniens* doctrine was explored related to its global influence, especially in (re)shaping the evolution of the equivalent principles concerning discretionary (non-)exercise of jurisdiction across the Commonwealth. The analysis of this aspect of the *Spiliada* doctrine, presented in Part III, has illustrated that its importance has not been limited to England. The more-appropriate-forum test has also been the main source of inspiration in the development of the equivalent measures across numerous Commonwealth legal systems. Many of these jurisdictions have revised their approaches to discretionary (non-)exercise of jurisdiction by fully embracing the English doctrine. But, as the discussion went on to show, even in those Commonwealth countries which have not remodelled their laws in complete compliance with *Spiliada* – chiefly, Australia and Canada – the *forum (non) conveniens* doctrines are still heavily influenced by it.

Finally, the English *forum (non) conveniens* doctrine was evaluated from the perspective of its scope of application over the past 30 years. The analysis here, which was carried out in Part IV, focused on the evolution of both the doctrine's *conceptual* and *overall* scope. It was stated that, while conceptually the scope of *Spiliada* has remained largely unaltered, the intervening years have witnessed a major development in its overall ambit. More specifically, and following the Court of Justice's judgment in the *Owusu* case, it has been confirmed that the *Spiliada* doctrine is unavailable to English courts, as a tool for granting stays of their proceedings in favour of foreign forums,[183] in those instances where their jurisdiction is rooted in the provisions within the Brussels regime. Be that as it may, it was acknowledged that this might ultimately prove to be a short-lived limitation on *Spiliada*'s overall operation. The Brexit vote is likely to have given the doctrine

---

[183] In this respect, courts within the other UK countries are not regarded as being foreign courts: *Cook* (n 179).

a new lease of life. Of course, the future shape of English private international law, and within it the overall ambit of the *Spiliada* doctrine, depend on the outcome of the Brexit negotiations concerning the litigation of civil and commercial matters. But, at any rate, it seems likely that the *Spiliada* doctrine will play a greater role in the post-Brexit English private international law. The analysis in Chapter 5 concludes the book's examination of the English *forum (non) conveniens* doctrine by focusing on its future. In particular, the chapter assesses whether there is any case for the revision of the *Spiliada* test, in view of its current application, and (if so) it explores the most prudent manner in which that revision should be brought about.

5

Forum (Non) Conveniens – The Future

I. Introduction

The previous three chapters in this book have served to locate the place of the *forum (non) conveniens* doctrine within the English national jurisdiction rules (Chapter 2), re-examine (and refine) our understanding of the historical developments which preceded the articulation of the modern-day doctrine in England in *Spiliada Maritime Corporation v Cansulex Ltd*[1] (Chapter 3), and closely inspect its contemporary application (Chapter 4). Building on the discussions in these chapters, the focus at this juncture turns to the future of the English *forum (non) conveniens* doctrine. In this context, the main issues for consideration are whether the basis for the doctrine's application – namely, the more-appropriate-forum test – should be refined further – and, if so, what form should that revision take.

When compared with the volume of academic commentary on the historical development of the English *forum (non) conveniens* doctrine, or indeed those accounts that are concerned with its modern-day application, much less has been written about whether the *Spiliada* test should be subjected to further modification. This state of affairs is likely to be due to the generally positive way in which the House of Lords' decision in *Spiliada* has been received within academic and judicial circles, both in its immediate aftermath and the decades following it. For example, in a case note, published in the *Cambridge Law Journal* in 1987, Collier welcomed the *Spiliada* ruling, observing that it had addressed a number of previously unresolved questions concerning how the test for discretionary (non-)exercise of jurisdiction was to be applied.[2] Similarly, in an article in a law journal, which was representative of the spirit in which the *Spiliada* ruling was received, Professor Pryles expressed the view that the more-appropriate-forum test had rendered the English approach to the *forum (non) conveniens* doctrine much more consistent with the interdependent world of the latter part of the twentieth century, and respectful of the comity of nations.[3] What is more, in his concurring speech in *Spiliada*, Lord Templeman held out the prospect that the test

---

[1] *Spiliada Maritime Corporation v Cansulex Ltd* [1987] AC 460 (HL).
[2] JG Collier, 'Staying of Actions and Forum Non Conveniens. English Law Goes Scotch' (1987) 46 *Cambridge Law Journal* 33. See, also, A Briggs, 'Forum Non Conveniens – The Last Word? (*Spiliada Maritime Corporation v Cansulex Ltd*)' [1987] *Lloyd's Maritime and Commercial Law Quarterly* 1.
[3] M Pryles, 'Judicial Darkness on the Oceanic Sun' (1988) 62 *Australian Law Journal* 774.

formulated by Lord Goff of Chieveley in that case would enable judges to decide whether the court should exercise jurisdiction over the dispute swiftly and with minimum cost to the litigants.[4]

The *Spiliada* test's favourable reception was not just limited to the period immediately after its articulation. Indeed, an assessment of some of the more contemporary accounts of the *forum (non) conveniens* doctrine in England points to an overall satisfaction with the doctrine (and its application) over the past three or so decades. In this context, in *Private International Law in English Courts*, published in 2014, Professor Briggs has considered *Spiliada* as having been (and continuing to be) effective in giving 'the court an overall discretion which is capable of responding to the interests of justice in the individual case'.[5] Elsewhere, and more tellingly, in the latest edition of *Civil Jurisdiction and Judgments*, published in 2015, Professor Briggs has observed that:

> [t]he law as finally put in place by *Spiliada*, striking the balance as it now stands, is the brilliant product of true judicial creativity. As Lord Goff of Chieveley put it, the principle of *forum non conveniens* is 'one of the most civilised of legal principles'. Further comment would be impertinent.[6]

In many ways, these and similar remarks that have been made repeatedly in the past,[7] are typical of the wider perception of the *Spiliada* test. Based on this understanding, the law on the practice of discretionary (non-)exercise of jurisdiction in England reached its final destination following the enunciation of the more-appropriate-forum test in *Spiliada*. As a result, there has been limited appetite among scholars and judges to explore whether the English *forum (non) conveniens* doctrine could (or, in fact, should) be improved on through additional reform.

Be that as it may, the *Spiliada* test has not been without its critics. In an article published in the *Law Quarterly Review* in 1987, Professor Robertson claimed that, following the decision in *Spiliada*, the staying-of-proceedings practice in England had become subjected to a 'judicial discretion so broad and so vaguely circumscribed as to amount to "an instinctive process"'.[8] Similarly, in his critique of the adoption of the more-appropriate-forum test, as the basis for the English courts' (non-)exercise of jurisdiction, Slater observed that:

> [l]itigants and their advisors do not always see things in the same light as judges who enunciate principles or jurists who analyse them. The more reflective litigant may have

---

[4] *Spiliada* (n 1) 465.

[5] A Briggs, *Private International Law in English Courts* (Oxford, Oxford University Press, 2014) para 4.413.

[6] A Briggs, *Civil Jurisdiction and Judgments* 6th edn (Abingdon, Informa Law from Routledge, 2015) para 4.39.

[7] See, eg, A Briggs and P Rees, *Civil Jurisdiction and Judgments* 4th edn (London, Informa Law, 2005) para 4.20 and A Briggs and P Rees, *Civil Jurisdiction and Judgments* 5th edn (London, Informa Law, 2009) para 4.34.

[8] DW Robertson, '*Forum Non Conveniens* in America and England: "A Rather Fantastic Fiction"' (1987) 103 *Law Quarterly Review* 398, 414, citing Lord Wilberforce in *The Atlantic Star* [1974] AC 436 (HL) 468.

wondered whether it was really necessary to have a 'code' to regulate the question of where a trial should take place. He may have felt that on such a question simple rules of thumb are preferable to flexible and sensitive provisions [at the heart of the more-appropriate-forum test] whose application tends to produce time-consuming and expensive disputes. Certainly, in this area of the law, it is likely that considerations of cost and convenience will be in the forefront of his mind and the concepts of 'judicial comity' and rules which are 'suitable to the twentieth century' will scarcely enter into his thinking.[9]

As touched on in Chapter 4, this perception of the *Spiliada* doctrine – as one which affords courts an unduly broad discretionary power – was instrumental in the refusal of the High Court of Australia to embrace it in *Oceanic Sun Line Special Shipping Co Inc v Fay*.[10] In that case, Brennan J, who was perhaps the most vehement opponent of the adoption of the more-appropriate-forum test in Australia, levelled the charge that 'the English law [had] moved from a discretion confined by a tolerably precise principle [under *St Pierre v South American Stones (Gath & Chaves) Ltd*[11]] to a broad discretion'.[12]

For the most part, these criticisms of the *Spiliada* test have been downplayed by its proponents.[13] However, as this chapter seeks to demonstrate, there is in fact a body of precedent which bears out the misgivings foreshadowed by the doctrine's critics, particularly in relation to its unpredictable application. Moreover, the evaluation of these authorities highlights that, contrary to the views expressed by Lord Templeman and Professor Pryles, the application of the *Spiliada* doctrine has had the propensity to lead to protracted and wasteful litigation, as well as judicial chauvinism.

As this chapter proceeds to argue, the main source of these problems with the application of the *Spiliada* test is the disproportionately broad discretion afforded to English courts under its second limb. It is argued that, for both theoretical and pragmatic reasons, the law in this area should be reformed. The analysis sets out to show that it would be unwarranted to discard completely the English courts' discretion under the doctrine's second limb. Instead, it is contended that legal reform in this area should steer a middle course. Accordingly, a doctrinal framework should be adopted which would curtail the courts' room to manoeuvre at the second stage of the *Spiliada* test, but fall short of completely scrapping it. In this respect, it is argued that, a fruitful doctrinal avenue resides in the context of the protection of a person's right to a fair trial under the European Convention on

---

[9] AG Slater, 'Forum Non Conveniens: A View From the Shop Floor' (1988) 104 *Law Quarterly Review* 554, 554.

[10] *Oceanic Sun Line Special Shipping Co Inc v Fay* (1988) 165 CLR 197 (Brennan, Deane and Gaudron JJ, Wilson and Toohey JJ dissenting).

[11] *St Pierre v South American Stones (Gath & Chaves) Ltd* [1936] 1 KB 382 (CA).

[12] *Oceanic Sun Line* (n 10) 238. Deane J shared a similar reservation about the *Spiliada* doctrine: 254.

[13] See, especially, AS Bell, *Forum Shopping and Venue in Transnational Litigation* (Oxford, Oxford University Press, 2002) paras 3.149–3.169. See, also, Briggs (n 6) para 4.39.

Human Rights ('ECHR'),[14] Art 6(1), as applied in expulsion proceedings. Thus, the chief contention is that, in cases concerning service-out applications or staying of proceedings brought as of right, as a starting position, English courts should not exercise jurisdiction over a dispute which has been shown to be more closely connected to another available foreign forum. That position should be only departed from where the claimant can establish that sending the matter to its centre of gravity would render the United Kingdom in breach of its ECHR obligations, by virtue of the violation in that forum of the claimant's Art 6(1) rights (as defined in expulsion cases).

The discussion in the main body of this chapter is presented in five parts. Part II contains a (very short) summary of how the *Spiliada* test in its current form is applied. Part III, then, identifies and advances the main reasons behind the positive reception of the more-appropriate-forum test as the basis for the English courts' discretionary (non-)exercise of jurisdiction in the past 30 or so years. Thereafter, Part IV, proceeds to submit that, notwithstanding the doctrine's virtues, its application leads to problematic outcomes. In particular, it critically evaluates key authorities in this area which illustrate the breadth of the court's discretion under *Spiliada*'s second limb. Part V puts forth the theoretical and pragmatic arguments for reforming the *Spiliada* test. Finally, Part VI examines the possible options for revising the law, and attempts to offer a novel approach for perfecting the test for the application of the *forum (non) conveniens* doctrine in England.

II. A Brief Outline of the *Spiliada* Test

The grounds for the modern-day application of the *Spiliada* test were stated in detail in the previous two chapters. Nevertheless, and for the benefit of readers who might prefer a brief reminder of the grounds for the operation of the test, it will be helpful to recite them once more. As outlined in Chapters 3 and 4, the premise for the English courts' (non-)exercise of jurisdiction under the test is set out in the passage below in Lord Goff's speech in *Spiliada*:

> … a stay will only be granted on the ground of forum non conveniens where the court is satisfied that there is some other available forum, having competent jurisdiction, which is the appropriate forum for the trial of the action, i.e. in which the case may be tried more suitably for the interests of all the parties and the ends of justice.[15]

There are two limbs to the doctrine. Under the first limb, and in cases where defendants seek to obtain stays of proceedings brought against them during their presence in the forum, they bear the burden of persuading the court to relinquish

---

[14] European Convention for the Protection of Human Rights and Fundamental Freedoms, Rome, 4 November 1950, 213 UNTS 221.

[15] *Spiliada* (n 1) 476.

its (otherwise) properly established jurisdiction in favour of another foreign court which would both entertain the dispute, and is more closely connected to the claim than England.[16] The type of considerations which are in play in relation to this limb include the degree to which the parties, and the events giving rise to their dispute, are connected with a particular country and also the governing law of the litigants' dispute. Additionally, where relevant, the court takes into account the fact that the parties before it are involved in related proceedings in another foreign forum.[17] It should be noted that none of these factors is, by itself, conclusive in determining whether the English proceedings should be stayed. The question is whether, on balance, the dispute belongs to England or the forum elsewhere which would hear the case.

In the event that the defendant is unsuccessful in convincing the English court that a more closely connected foreign forum exists that would assert jurisdiction over the case, then the stay application would fail and the proceedings in England would be sustained. Otherwise, it becomes necessary to examine the second limb of the *Spiliada* test. At this juncture, the claimant can seek to resist a stay on the basis that substantial justice would not be obtained in the foreign forum.[18] The claimant must adduce 'cogent evidence' in support of his contention which signifies examples of injustice being caused at virtually any stage in the civil litigation process in the more closely connected forum.[19] They can include (but are in no way confined to):

> risk that justice will not be obtained by a foreign litigant in particular kinds of suits whether for ideological or political reasons, … inexperience or inefficiency of the judiciary, … excessive delay in the conduct of the business of the courts or the unavailability of appropriate remedies.[20]

The *Spiliada* ruling made it plain that the more-appropriate-forum test applied to both the practice of discretionary staying of proceedings, *and* the related concept of permission to serve claims on foreign-based defendants.[21] Thus, the same set of considerations, as those underpinning decisions concerning stay applications, are consulted by courts in England in deciding whether to exercise their jurisdiction in as-of-right and service-out cases. In applying the more-appropriate-forum test in a service-out case, though, the claimant shoulders the burden of convincing the court that England is the more appropriate forum for the litigation.[22] This burden

---

[16] For the sake of simplicity, the forum which is identified by the first stage of the *Spiliada* test is referred to as 'the more closely connected forum'.

[17] For a more detailed account of the considerations under the *Spiliada* doctrine's first limb, and how the courts apply them when hearing stay applications, see Briggs (n 6) paras 4.19–4.29, and P Torremans, *et al*, *Cheshire, North & Fawcett's Private International Law* 15th edn (Oxford, Oxford University Press, 2017) 365–69 and 395–400.

[18] *Spiliada* (n 1) 478.

[19] ibid, citing Lord Diplock's statement in *The Abidin Daver* [1984] 1 AC 398 (HL) 411.

[20] *The Abidin Daver*, ibid (Lord Diplock).

[21] *Spiliada* (n 1) 478–82.

[22] ibid, 480.

is typically discharged where the English court finds, on balance, that England is the dispute's centre of gravity,[23] or the 'proper forum in which to bring the claim'.[24] Even when England is not the proper forum, the English court may nevertheless rule that it is *forum conveniens*, if it concludes that the foreign forum cannot justly dispose of the parties' litigation.[25]

III. The *Spiliada* Test's Positive Reception

As set out in the introduction to this chapter, the *Spiliada* ruling, with its reliance on the more-appropriate-forum test as the basis for the discretionary (non-)exercise of jurisdiction in stay and service-out cases, has been widely admired within the academic and judicial circles. When considered against the backdrop of the historical developments which preceded the modern-day doctrine's articulation, at least three reasons as to why it is so positively received can be identified.

First, the *Spiliada* doctrine allows for a much more even-handed treatment of the competing rights of claimants and defendants who clash over whether their dispute should be litigated in England (or another foreign forum). As Chapter 3 sought to argue, for nearly 30 years at the start of the twentieth century, English courts were generally balanced in their application of the vexatious-and-oppressive test in stay cases. During this period, defendants were often successful in their stay applications in England.[26] However, from the late 1920s until the mid-1970s, English courts hardly ever relinquished their jurisdiction where the defendant had been sued while present in England.[27] In almost all stay or *lis alibi pendens* cases in that era, the courts' main priority appeared to be the protection of the plaintiffs' right to commence proceedings in England. Such was the level of prominence afforded to the plaintiffs' entitlement to sue the defendants in England that it was effectively impossible for defendants to obtain stays of proceedings. It was only after the vexatious-and-oppressive test was liberalised in *The Atlantic Star*,[28] and subsequently reformulated in *MacShannon v Rockware Glass Ltd*,[29]

---

[23] L Collins, *et al, Dicey, Morris & Collins on the Conflict of Laws* 15th edn (London, Sweet & Maxwell, 2012) para 11-143.

[24] Briggs (n 6) para 4.88.

[25] *Dicey, Morris & Collins* (n 23) para 11-144. See, eg, *Oppenheimer v Louis Rosenthal & Co AG* [1937] 1 All ER 23 (CA), *Roneleigh Ltd v MII Exports Inc* [1989] 1 WLR 619 (CA), *Islamic Arab Insurance Co v Saudi Egyptian American Reinsurance Co* [1987] 1 Lloyd's Rep 315, *Cherney v Deripaska* [2008] EWHC 1530 (Comm), [2009] 1 All ER (Comm) 333 – affirmed by the Court of Appeal [2009] EWCA Civ 849, [2009] 2 CLC 408 (CA), and *Altimo Holdings and Investment Ltd v Kyrgyz Mobil Tel Ltd* (also known as, *AK Investment CJSC v Kyrgyz Mobil Tel Ltd*) [2011] UKPC 7, [2012] 1 WLR 1804 (PC).

[26] See, eg, the English courts' decisions in *Logan v Bank of Scotland (No 2)* [1906] 1 KB 141 (CA), *Egbert v Short* [1907] 2 Ch 205, and *In re Norton's Settlement* [1908] 1 Ch 471 (CA).

[27] For the only reported case in this period in which the English court stayed its proceedings on a discretionary basis see *The Marinero* [1955] P 68 (a *lis alibi pendens* case).

[28] *The Atlantic Star* (n 8).

[29] *MacShannon v Rockware Glass Ltd* [1978] AC 795 (HL).

that the English courts' approach to discretionary (non-)exercise of jurisdiction began to become less one-sided in the plaintiffs' favour. In many ways, the introduction of the more-appropriate-forum test in *Spiliada* underscored the more even-handed attitude on the part of the English courts towards the parties' conflicting interests regarding where the claim should be heard.

Second, and in the same vein as the first reason why *Spiliada* enjoys such a broad support, the more-appropriate-forum test affords English courts a much more effective means of controlling forum shopping than they previously had at their disposal. According to Dr Bell, the test provides

> a neutral and objective solution to clashes between parties relating to the venue for the resolution of a transnational dispute – something of a tie-breaker in cases of contested jurisdiction and at the same time a corrective to the phenomenon of forum shopping.[30]

The discussion in Chapter 2 illustrated that forum shopping arises where a litigant by-passes the dispute's 'home' and, instead, initiates his claim in a venue which he regards would afford him the most favourable judgment, notwithstanding that the forum has very little (or no) connection with the dispute.[31] It was pointed out in Chapter 3 that, by the mid-twentieth century, it had become commonplace for English courts to entertain cross-border private disputes that merely had tangential connection with England. The English courts' mostly plaintiff-friendly application of the vexatious-and-oppressive test, in the middle third of the twentieth century, was the main reason behind this development. Perhaps the most telling evidence of the English courts' relaxed attitude in that era to forum shopping is the following oft-cited passage in Lord Denning MR's judgment in *The Atlantic Star* in 1972:

> No one who comes to these courts asking for justice should come in vain. … This right to come here is not confined to Englishmen. It extends to any friendly foreigner. He can seek the aid of our courts if he desires to do so. You may call this 'forum-shopping' if you please, but if the forum is England, it is a good place to shop in, both for the quality of the goods and the speed of service.[32]

It was attitudes of this kind, prior to the House of Lords' liberalisation and reform of the law on staying of proceedings in England from the mid-1970s onwards, which prompted some commentators to remark that the law in that era had acted as 'something of an inducement towards forum shopping, or at least provided no effective bar [to it], even in blatant cases'.[33] The English courts' views on forum shopping began to change, once the process of departing from the vexatious-and-oppressive test began in earnest. The adoption of the more-appropriate-forum test in *Spiliada* represented the English courts' arrival at a settled position which was against forum shopping. By being more balanced in its treatment of the litigants'

---

[30] Bell (n 13) para 3.89.
[31] *Boys v Chaplin* [1971] AC 356 (HL) 401 (Lord Pearson).
[32] *The Atlantic Star* [1973] QB 364 (CA) 381G and 382C.
[33] Bell (n 13) para 3.78.

competing rights to have the dispute heard in England or elsewhere, the *Spiliada* doctrine makes important strides towards ensuring that disputes that do not really belong to England are not litigated in the forum, and thereby reduces the instances of forum shopping in England.

The third (and final) main reason why the *Spiliada* test has been so widely admired is that its introduction has rendered the law on discretionary (non-)exercise of jurisdiction much more in tune with the wider socio-economic developments which had been unfolding in the latter part of the twentieth century, and, as a result, showed greater respect to other legal system. In this context, in an article which lamented the Australian High Court's decision in the *Oceanic Sun Line* case not to adopt the more-appropriate-forum test as the basis for the application of the Australian *forum (non) conveniens* doctrine, Professor Pryles observed that *Spiliada* was a more desirable formulation in view of the changing world in the latter part of the twentieth century:

> Teachers of Conflict of Laws or Private International Law often refer to the homeward bound trend of judges. Judges feel most comfortable with their own law and formerly there was a view that the local courts dispensed superior justice to that of foreign courts. But in an interdependent world such as exists in the latter part of the twentieth century there must be a degree of international respect and comity. Local parochialism in the legal sphere can be as disruptive to the international system as political or economic parochialism. In an international legal dispute it does not follow that a court which has jurisdiction, sometimes under exorbitant bases should, and must, exercise that jurisdiction. Countervailing considerations such as the lack of any significant connection between the litigation and the forum may dictate that the litigation should be determined in a different venue. It is not an answer to this simply to assert that local justice is superior for this will be disruptive to the international system and will, in the end, harm all countries, including the forum. We have to co-exist in an interdependent world and part of that co-existence requires a tolerance towards foreign legal systems and courts and an ability to recognise that some actions which may be litigated in the local forum do not properly belong there.[34]

In other words, the *Spiliada* test has been lauded because it makes provision for disputes that, to all intents and purposes, belong to another available foreign forum to be litigated there. The test has created a much more outward-looking regime for discretionary (non-)exercise of jurisdiction than had been in existence in England from the late 1920s until the mid-1970s – which tended to prioritise the plaintiffs' right to commence their claims in England over the defendants' right to have the disputes litigated in the appropriate foreign venues.

Undoubtedly, the *Spiliada* test has helped to enhance the English conflict-of-laws rules, by addressing many of the shortcomings which arose from the application of the earlier regime for discretionary (non-)exercise of jurisdiction. Moreover, the law's transformation – from the House of Lords' relaxation of the vexatious-and-oppressive test in *The Atlantic Star* in 1973 to the enunciation of the

---

[34] Pryles (n 3) 786–87.

more-appropriate-forum test in *Spiliada* in 1986 – happened at a relatively rapid pace. In these circumstances, it may be deemed to be imprudent to subject the *Spiliada* test to further modification, as it is liable to cause uncertainty for litigants in cross-border private disputes. All these factors combine to explain (and perhaps justify) why there have been no attempts towards exploring ways in which the doctrine could evolve beyond its present form.

At any rate, and despite its many virtues, the more-appropriate-forum test is not without its own shortcomings. As the analysis, below, of the case law over the past three decades or so seeks to demonstrate, the application of the *Spiliada* test has given rise to a number of problems. For the most part, these problematic implications are due to the disproportionately broad discretion afforded to the courts under the doctrine's second limb.

IV. Problems with the Application of the *Spiliada* Test

In the introduction to this chapter, it was pointed out that, amidst all the praise for the *Spiliada* doctrine in some quarters, it also faced robust criticisms in others. The main basis for these criticisms was that, in the eyes of the doctrine's critics, *Spiliada* afforded English courts an unduly broad discretionary power when deciding whether to exercise jurisdiction in international private disputes. In order to assess whether it has been fair to level this charge against the doctrine, it is necessary to consider how the more-appropriate-forum test has been applied in practice.

As the brief outline, in Part II, of the application of the modern-day *forum (non) conveniens* doctrine in England illustrates, the courts' inquiries under the two limbs of the *Spiliada* test are different in focus and nature. Under the first limb, courts are effectively engaged in a fact-finding exercise which pursues two main objectives. The first is to avoid situations in which cross-border commercial litigation that is scarcely connected with England is brought in the forum. Second, in the context of *lis alibi pendens* cases, the first limb enables English court to stay its proceedings, if it considers that the existence of concurrent litigation abroad among other factors, makes the foreign court better placed to resolve the dispute. An examination of the post-*Spiliada* case law suggests that the first instance judges' findings under the doctrine's first limb have not been generally subjected to appeals. Furthermore, there have been few academic discussions which have highlighted problems arising from the application of the court's discretion under the doctrine's first limb.[35] Accordingly, it is argued that, barring relatively few exceptions,[36] the courts have applied their discretion under the *Spiliada*'s first

---

[35] See, eg, A Briggs, 'Forum Non Conveniens and Unavailable Courts' (1996) 67 *British Yearbook of International Law* 587, L Merrett, 'The Meaning of an "Available" Forum' (2004) *Cambridge Law Journal* 309, and L Merrett, 'Uncertainties in the First Limb of the *Spiliada* Test' (2005) 54 *International and Comparative Law Quarterly* 211.

[36] One such instance was the recent Supreme Court decision in *VTB Capital plc v Nutritek International Corp* [2013] UKSC 5, [2013] 2 WLR 398 (SC).

limb fairly consistently. This consistency in approach, in turn, indicates that, in the main, the court's discretion under this part of the doctrine has not been so extensive as to render its application problematic.

The position is different with regard to *Spiliada*'s second limb. At this stage, the doctrine aims to ensure that any potential injustice to the claimant in sending his claim to the more closely connected forum is avoided. In this respect, the court can consider almost any factor to do with the civil-litigation processes in the relevant foreign forum. Not all courts value, or give equal weight to, the same factors. Therefore, in its own right, the court's discretion is much wider under *Spiliada*'s second limb than under its first limb. The finding of injustice in the more closely connected forum under the doctrine's second limb can surpass the finding under its first limb. Thus, any potential for uncertainty in the application of the court's discretion under *Spiliada*'s second limb affects the predictability of the doctrine as a whole.

In these circumstances, it is worth exploring whether the scope of the court's discretion under *Spiliada*'s second limb is, in fact, so broad as to justify the criticisms raised by the doctrine's critics. Due to limitations in both time and space, it is not possible to consider every case in which the doctrine's second limb was applied. Hence, the analysis concerns only authorities of doctrinal import.

A. Recent Decisions

In the past few years, numerous cases concerning the *forum (non) conveniens* doctrine have been brought before the courts in England. Most of these decisions have simply reiterated Lord Goff's formulation in *Spiliada*. However, there have been at least four cases which stand out: *Cherney v Deripaska;*[37] *OJSC Oil Company Yugraneft (in liquidation) v Abramovich;*[38] *Pacific International Sports Clubs Ltd v Soccer Marketing International Ltd;*[39] and, *Altimo Holdings and Investment Ltd v Kyrgyz Mobil Tel Ltd.*[40] These cases are important as they exemplify some serious problems with the application of the courts' discretion under the *Spiliada* doctrine, particularly in the course of exercising discretion under the doctrine's second limb.

Although the facts of these cases are highly complex, they are not essential for our purposes, and are only briefly restated. In many respects, these cases were broadly similar: put simply, they concerned allegations of large-scale fraud by the

---

[37] *Cherney v Deripaska* (n 25).
[38] *OJSC Oil Company Yugraneft (in liquidation) v Abramovich* [2008] EWHC 2613 (Comm).
[39] *Pacific International Sports Clubs Ltd v Soccer Marketing International Ltd* [2009] EWHC 1839 (Ch) – affirmed by the Court of Appeal [2010] EWCA Civ 753 (CA).
[40] *Altimo Holdings* (n 25).

claimants against the defendants. In *Cherney*, the claimant, a businessman with substantial personal and business connection with Russia, sought the English court's permission to serve the proceedings on the foreign-based defendant, a Russian resident. The claimant argued that, due to the defendant's wrongdoing, he had been deprived of his interest in a Russian aluminium company. *OJSC* was also a service-out case in which the claimant complained that it had been defrauded of its interest in a large oil company by defendants who had no presence in England. The substance of the dispute in *Pacific International* concerned the ownership of Dynamo Kiev Football Club. In proceedings brought in England against the defendants as of right, the claimants contended that the defendants had diluted their ownership in the football club. Lastly, in *Altimo Holdings*, a Manx case which had reached the Privy Council, the claimants sought to serve proceedings outside the Isle of Man. In that case, the ownership of a Kyrgyz mobile telephone company was at the heart of the parties' long-running dispute. In each of these cases, it was abundantly clear that England had virtually no connection to the parties' dispute. Rather, the more closely connected forum in each case was in a former Soviet state: Russia in *Cherney* and *OJSC*; Ukraine in *Pacific International*; and, Kyrgyzstan in *Altimo Holdings*. Hence, the outcome in each case hinged entirely on the application of *Spiliada*'s second limb.

In each of these cases, the claimants advanced copious evidence in seeking to persuade the English court that the more closely connected forum would not be able to justly entertain their claims. In *Cherney*, the claimant argued that, if he went to Russia, his life would be in danger, he would face trumped-up charges, and he would be denied a fair hearing.[41] In *OJSC*, the claimant accused the Russian courts of 'incompetence or corruption or both'.[42] In *Pacific International*, the claimants alleged that Ukrainian courts were 'susceptible to political pressure'.[43] Moreover, they stated that their poor relationship with the Ukrainian establishment, and the way the Ukrainian court had decided their claim over the ownership of the football club in recent proceedings, meant that their claim would not be justly disposed of in Ukraine.[44] Finally, in *Altimo Holdings*, the claimants pointed to their history of litigation in Kyrgyzstan in relation to the case in hand, contending that judgments against them in those proceedings had been obtained by fraud. What is more, they argued that there was a risk that their claim would not receive a fair hearing were it to be brought in Kyrgyzstan.[45] In *Cherney* and *Altimo Holdings*, the court was persuaded by the claimants' arguments regarding *Spiliada*'s second limb, while in *OJSC* and *Pacific International* it was not.

---

[41] *Cherney v Deripaska* [2008] EWHC 1530 (Comm) [198].
[42] *OJSC* (n 38) [491].
[43] *Pacific International Sports Clubs Ltd v Soccer Marketing International Ltd* [2010] EWCA Civ 753 (CA) [43].
[44] ibid.
[45] *Altimo Holdings* (n 25) 1810 and 1816.

B. Problems Exposed in the Recent Decisions

As discussed in Chapter 4, Professor Briggs has been particularly critical of the decision in these cases.[46] His critique is specifically directed at the judgments in *Cherney* and *Altimo Holdings*. At one level, Professor Briggs criticised the readiness with which the courts accepted the claimants' disparaging submissions about the quality of justice provided in Russia and Kyrgyzstan. He noted that it was 'unprecedented' that, in a case where England was not the dispute's centre of gravity, 'concerns about a foreign court doing real injustice' led to the proceedings being served on foreign-based defendants.[47] In relation to *Cherney*, Professor Briggs opined that, while Russia's legal system may not be without fault, the rule of law had not failed in Russia. He, therefore, questioned the English court's assumption of jurisdiction over a dispute which was effectively Russian.[48] As for the decision in *Altimo Holdings*, Professor Briggs considered it 'surprising' that the Privy Council had allowed for doubts about the ability of the Kyrgyz courts to justly entertain the claimants' disputes to '*drive* the entire application for permission to serve out'.[49]

At another level, and more generally, Professor Briggs has expressed misgivings about the future implications of the decisions in *Cherney* and *Altimo Holdings* for the operation of the *Spiliada* doctrine. In his opinion, these decisions would invite claimants, whether in cases concerning service-out applications or staying of proceedings brought as of right, to make submissions that question the ability of the courts in the forum more closely connected to the dispute to do justice to the parties when hearing their claims.[50]

As argued in Chapter 4, while the courts' rulings in *Cherney* and *Altimo Holdings* might be the first examples of their kind, where claimants were able to serve proceedings on foreign-based defendants, they should not be seen as signifying an evolution in the application of the *Spiliada* doctrine. After all, the courts' approach to its (non-)exercise of jurisdiction in these authorities was, in broad terms, consistent with how the more-appropriate-forum test has always been applied in service-out applications. Thus, it is unlikely that Professor Briggs's predictions about the likely consequence of the judgments in *Cherney* and *Altimo Holdings* will come to pass. But, at any rate, the study of these decisions exposes at least three broader (and more pressing) problems with the application of the second limb of the *Spiliada* test.

---

[46] See A Briggs, 'Russian Oligarchs and the Conflict of Laws' (2008) 79 *British Yearbook of International Law* 543; A Briggs, '*Forum Non Satis*: Finding Fault with a Foreign Court' (2009) 80 *British Yearbook of International Law* 575; A Briggs, 'Forum Non Satis: *Spiliada* and an Inconvenient Truth' [2011] *Lloyd's Maritime and Commercial Law Quarterly* 329; and Briggs (n 6) para 4.91.
[47] Briggs, 'Forum Non Satis: *Spiliada* and an Inconvenient Truth' (n 46) 331.
[48] Briggs, 'Russian Oligarchs and the Conflict of Laws' (n 46) 547.
[49] Briggs, 'Forum Non Satis: *Spiliada* and an Inconvenient Truth' (n 46) 330 (emphasis in the original, citation omitted).
[50] See Briggs (n 6) para 4.91 and Briggs, 'Forum Non Satis: *Spiliada* and an Inconvenient Truth' (n 46) 333.

The first problem is that the *Spiliada* doctrine is open to the charge that it leads to unpredictable outcomes. In any given case, it is very difficult to know, with reasonable certainty, in whose favour the second limb of the *Spiliada* test is likely to be applied. As stated earlier, the issues for consideration in each of the four cases considered in this section were not wildly different from one another: the claimants' basic argument was that the defendants had unjustifiably interfered with their proprietary interests. It was, therefore, reasonable to anticipate that the application of *Spiliada*'s second limb in each of these cases would lead to the same result. Yet, that did not happen. Take, for example, the decisions in *Pacific International* and *Altimo Holdings*. In both cases, the claimants in the English proceedings argued that in earlier court hearings, concerning similar issues as those before the English courts, the Ukrainian and Kyrgyz courts' judgments against them had been obtained fraudulently. A submission of a similar nature was dismissed by the court in *Pacific International*, while it provided one of the main grounds for the Privy Council's ruling in *Altimo Holdings* that England was *forum conveniens*. This can hardly be an appealing position to be in. It gives credence to Professor Robertson's claim that, under a doctrine like *Spiliada*, 'seemingly indistinguishable cases have far too often yielded diametrically opposite results'.[51]

The second problem associated with the application of the *Spiliada* doctrine is linked to the first: the doctrine's application is resource-inefficient. As pointed out in part II, the application of the *Spiliada* test is fact specific. Additionally, when the court is applying the test's second limb, almost any factor germane to the process of civil litigation in the more closely connected foreign forum can be taken into account. Consequently, the court has to contend with a sizeable volume of evidence. In turn, this evidential burden further complicates and lengthens the hearing on where the dispute should be litigated. In *OJSC*, for example, nearly half of an eight-day trial period involved submissions about whether the Russian court could justly dispose of the parties' dispute. In *Pacific International*, more than half of a six-day hearing, at first instance, and the whole of a two-day hearing, before the Court of Appeal, were devoted to the discussion of whether the claimant could receive justice if the English proceedings were to be stayed. Additionally, in these cases, the courts' decision whether to exercise its jurisdiction was dominated by a very extensive process of evidential assessment. For example, the first instance judges in *Cherney*[52] and *Pacific International*,[53] spent over 60 paragraphs examining the (in)ability of the courts in the more closely connected forums to subject the parties' dispute to a fair hearing. The following passage in Lord Collins of Mapesbury's judgment in *Altimo Holdings*, is also telling:

> this case has been excessively complicated by any standards. The hearings before the deemster and the Staff of Government Division each lasted for four days or more. The hearing before the Board lasted four days. The written cases of the parties exceeded

---

[51] Robertson (n 8) 415.
[52] *Cherney* (n 41) [197]–[263] (Christopher Clark J).
[53] *Pacific International* [2009] EWHC 1839 (Ch), [35]–[99] (Blackbourne J).

200 pages, and more than 30 volumes of documents were placed before the Board, containing almost 14,000 pages, as well as 170 authorities in 12 volumes. The core bundle alone consisted of six volumes. The list of 'essential' pre-reading for the Board listed documents totalling some 700 pages. All of this was wholly disproportionate to the issues of law and fact raised by the parties.[54]

Similarly, in the course of his judgment in the *VTB Capital* case, Lord Neuberger of Abbotsbury PSC observed that:

> [82] The first point is that hearings concerning the issue of appropriate forum should not involve masses of documents, long witness statements, detailed analysis of the issues, and long argument. It is self-defeating if, in order to determine whether an action should proceed to trial in this jurisdiction, the parties prepare for and conduct a hearing which approaches the putative trial itself, in terms of effort, time and cost. There is also a real danger that, if the hearing is an expensive and time-consuming exercise, it will be used by a richer party to wear down a poorer party, or by a party with a weak case to prevent, or at least to discourage, a party with a strong case from enforcing its rights.
>
> [83] Quite apart from this, it is simply disproportionate for parties to incur costs, often running to hundreds of thousands of pounds each, and to spend many days in court, on such a hearing. The essentially relevant factors should, in the main at any rate, be capable of being identified relatively simply and, in many respects, uncontroversially. There is little point in going into much detail: when determining such applications, the court can only form preliminary views on most of the relevant legal issues and cannot be anything like certain about which issues and what evidence will eventuate if the matter proceeds to trial.[55]

This state of affairs is clearly lucrative for the English legal profession. And, in any event, English courts have rarely shown displeasure in allocating time and resources to the litigation of disputes that have at best tangential connection with England.[56] Nevertheless, it is hardly appropriate that the current doctrinal framework for *Spiliada*, particularly in relation to its second limb, lends itself to being the source for wasteful litigation in England. When *Spiliada* was decided, Lord Templeman had hoped that a judge would be able to apply Lord Goff's basic principle in *Spiliada* to the case before him 'in the quiet of his room without expense to the parties ... and that submissions [would] be measured in hours and not days'.[57] This statement may have been made more in hope rather than in expectation.[58] Nevertheless, in practice, the modern-day *Spiliada* doctrine has

---

[54] *Altimo Holdings* (n 25) 1808.

[55] *VTB* (n 36) [82]–[83].

[56] Contrast the position in the United States (particularly courts in New York), where the problem of court dockets congested with 'alien disputes' was a catalyst in the development of the practice of discretionary staying of proceedings: see, eg, P Blair, 'The Doctrine of Forum Non Conveniens in Anglo-American Law' (1929) 29 *Columbia Law Review* 1.

[57] *Spiliada* (n 1) 465.

[58] Indeed, as noted by Lord Neuberger, what Lord Templeman had hoped would happen 'was a rather optimistic aspiration, not least when one bears in mind the understandable desire of lawyers to do, and to be seen by their clients to be doing, everything they can to advance their clients' case, especially where the dispute over jurisdiction may well be determinative of the outcome': *VTB* (n 36) [88].

not proved to make it any easier to realise Lord Templeman's expectation (or aspiration).

The third problem with the existing *Spiliada* test is that it can lead to judicial chauvinism. As touched on in Part III of this chapter, the fact that the *St Pierre* test encouraged English courts to consider themselves better placed in addressing international commercial disputes, than courts of foreign countries, was one of the main reasons for the law's gradual refinement and the ultimate adoption of the *Spiliada* doctrine. The following passage in Lord Diplock's speech in *The Abidin Daver*, stated not long before the *Spiliada* test was formulated, emphasises that, in the eyes of the English court, the departure from the *St Pierre* formula had marked the end of judicial chauvinism in this area of the law

> the essential change in the attitude of the English courts to pending or prospective litiga-
> tion in foreign jurisdictions that has been achieved step-by-step during the last 10 years
> as a result of the successive decisions of this House in *The Atlantic Star, MacShannon
> v Rockware Glass Ltd* and *Amin Rasheed Shipping Corporation v Kuwait Insurance Co* is
> that judicial chauvinism has been replaced by judicial comity.[59]

It is true that the law on discretionary (non-)exercise of jurisdiction under *Spiliada* is much more respectful of the comity of nations than the vexatious-and-oppressive test, as applied in the middle third of the twentieth century. However, an assessment of the recent case law casts doubt on the idea that the *Spiliada* doctrine has immunised the English law to the accusation of being chauvinistic. The potentially wide range of factors that can be considered under the doctrine's second limb means that, inescapably, the English court may become engaged in what is akin to a forensic examination of the (in)ability of the court in the dispute's centre of gravity to dispose justly of the claimant's action. In other words, the second limb of *Spiliada* effectively allows it to be used as a conduit for the English court to call into question the quality of justice likely to be delivered by a foreign legal system. This problem was particularly evident in the four cases under consideration, where the parties advanced large volumes of evidence to establish that the Russian, Ukrainian, and Kyrgyz courts were (un)able to resolve the disputes involved in their interests and the interests of justice. The fact that the doctrine's second limb draws the English court into such an inquiry is undesirable in as much as it encourages judicial chauvinism.[60]

C. Similar Problems in Earlier Decisions

Significantly, the shortcomings arising from the broad-brush discretion afforded to the English court under the second limb of the *Spiliada* doctrine are not novel developments and have existed ever since its formulation. Moreover, they are

---

[59] *The Abidin Daver* (n 19) 411 (citations omitted).
[60] See, eg, Briggs, 'Forum Non Satis: *Spiliada* and an Inconvenient Truth' (n 46) 331.

not confined to cases where the claimant has sought to cast doubt on the integrity of a foreign legal system which is closely connected to the parties' dispute. Indeed, these problems may be detected in a wider range of cases decided since the *Spiliada* test was outlined.[61]

For present purposes, it will suffice to consider examples in one other category of cases. This category involves actions in which the allegation is that the venue more closely connected to the dispute lacks the necessary resources or expertise to entertain the matter. In this context, one noteworthy example is *Lubbe v Cape*.[62] Here, a number of miners brought group litigation against their employers' parent companies, which were domiciled in England,[63] seeking compensation for contracting terminal illnesses as a result of exposure to toxic material while working at their mines in South Africa. There was little doubt that South Africa was the dispute's centre of gravity. Therefore, the principal issue for consideration in *Lubbe* concerned the application of *Spiliada*'s second limb. The plaintiffs argued that they would not receive justice if their claim were sent to South Africa because, due to lack of legal-aid provision there, they could not afford to bring their claim. Additionally, the plaintiffs stated that the South African legal system was not experienced enough to entertain a large-scale dispute like the one in that case – which had involved claims by more than 3,000 litigants. The litigation in *Lubbe* was appealed all the way to the House of Lords, which unanimously admitted the plaintiffs' submissions and rejected the defendants' stay applications.

The same problems with the application of the doctrine's second limb as those identified in some of the recent decisions can be detected in *Lubbe*. In the first place, the way in which the *Lubbe* litigation unfolded best exemplifies how unpredictable the application of the doctrine's second limb can be. In that case, the court had entertained the dispute in two rounds of litigation. In the first round, the court of first instance had ordered for the English proceedings to be stayed, but that decision was reversed on the plaintiff's appeal.[64] Thereafter, a second round of litigation was commenced, supplanting the first-round hearing. In the second set of proceedings, the plaintiffs' arguments had been rejected both at first instance[65] and the Court of Appeal.[66] A unanimous House of Lords, however, hearing the claims on broadly the same body of evidence, admitted the plaintiffs' submissions and ruled that the English proceedings should not be stayed. Moreover, the decision in *Lubbe* emphasises the tendency in the doctrine's application to result

---

[61] For a discussion about the same problems as those identified in this section (and a few others), see J Hill, 'Jurisdiction in Civil and Commercial Matters: Is There a Third Way?' [2001] *Current Legal Problems* 439, 449–54.

[62] *Lubbe v Cape* [2000] 1 WLR 1545 (HL). See, also, the decision in *Connelly v RTZ Corporation* [1998] AC 854 (HL) which highlights broadly similar problems with the *Spiliada* doctrine's application.

[63] It should be noted that, the decision in Case C-281/02 *Owusu v Jackson* [2005] ECR I-1383; [2005] QB 801 means that, in a case like *Lubbe* (and *Connelly*), there would have been no question the English court could not stay its proceedings on the grounds that it was *forum non conveniens*.

[64] *Lubbe* [1998] CLC 1559 (CA).

[65] *Lubbe*, Judgment of 30 July 1999 (unreported).

[66] *Lubbe* [2000] CLC 45.

in drawn-out and resource-inefficient litigation.[67] Even a casual glance at the submissions and the speeches in this case would suffice for one to appreciate the extensiveness of materials presented at all stages of the litigation.[68] Finally, the House of Lords' reasoning in *Lubbe* was, in effect, a lengthy and forensic appraisal of the (in)capabilities of the courts and processes in the legal system of a friendly foreign state, with the ultimate conclusion that the South African legal system could not cope with the complicated nature of the claims involved. This state of affairs illustrates that, even after the articulation of the *Spiliada* test, the English *forum (non) conveniens* doctrine has continued to allow for decisions to be made that can be regarded as being judicially chauvinistic.

In the *MacShannon* case, not long after the law's transformation from the *St Pierre* test to the modern-day *forum (non) conveniens* doctrine had begun, Lord Diplock observed that the approach to the discretionary staying of proceedings in England 'must manifest a reasonable consistency as between one case and another' and that its exercise 'ought to be predictable, so that lawyers may know broadly what advice to give to their clients'.[69] However, as this part has sought to illustrate, the position under the *Spiliada* test falls far short of Lord Diplock's desired position. Furthermore, the doctrine's application has led to lengthy and expensive proceedings and judicial chauvinism. In sum, despite the *Spiliada* doctrine's virtues, its application has given rise to problematic implications. These shortcomings, in turn, signify that the courts' discretion under *Spiliada*'s second limb is indeed disproportionately broad. Consequently, the recent developments in the case law justify much of the criticism levelled by Professor Robertson and the majority in the *Oceanic Sun Line* case about the ambit of the discretion afforded to the English courts under the *Spiliada* doctrine.

V. The Case for Revising *Spiliada*'s Second Limb

Notwithstanding these problems arising from the courts' broad discretion under *Spiliada*'s second limb, it might nevertheless be argued that the case for its revision is less than pressing. As set out towards the end of Chapter 4, following the Court of Justice's decision in *Owusu v Jackson*,[70] there are more limited occasions where the *Spiliada* doctrine could be applied, because English courts cannot rely on their national law provisions to relinquish their Brussels-rooted jurisdiction. Hence, currently, the problems highlighted in a case like *Lubbe* do not arise, because the English courts' Brussels-based jurisdiction is mandatory.[71] However,

---

[67] See Hill (n 61) 449–50.
[68] The abundance of the evidence before the courts did not go unnoticed by Lord Bingham of Cornhill: *Lubbe* (n 62) 1557.
[69] *MacShannon* (n 29) 813.
[70] *Owusu* (n 63).
[71] This observation would similarly apply in so far as the *Connelly* case is concerned. However, it should be noted that, recently, in *Cook v Virgin Media Ltd* (Joined with *McNeil v Tesco plc*) [2015]

in view of the UK voters' decision to leave the European Union, this position could well change in the near future. Of course, until the outcome of the Brexit negotiations concerning litigation of civil and commercial matters becomes clear, the future shape of English private international law – and, within it, the overall scope of *Spiliada* – will remain open to speculation. Nevertheless, it is plausible that, in the post-Brexit era, English courts would no longer face the limitations they presently face in applying the doctrine. In other words, it is likely that the *forum (non) conveniens* doctrine would have a wider scope of application after Brexit, perhaps even akin to the position in the intermediate years between the decisions in *Re Harrods (Buenos Aires) Ltd (No 2)*[72] and *Owusu*. In such circumstances, there could well be a corresponding increase in the instances where the doctrine's application proves problematic.

But, even supposing that the scope of the *Spiliada* doctrine remains unchanged following the completion of the Brexit process, there are still other theoretical and pragmatic arguments in favour of revisiting the current doctrinal basis for the operation of *Spiliada*'s second limb. At a theoretical level, the common law jurisdiction rules are not without their own problems. To begin with, they can enable English courts to assume jurisdiction over a cross-border private dispute which has only the slightest of connections with England. Additionally, they can afford English courts adjudicatory competence in the context of *lis alibi pendens* cases, thereby increasing the risk of irreconcilable judgments in the English and foreign forums. *Spiliada*'s first limb seeks to address these potential shortcomings with the common law jurisdiction rules. At the same time, pursuant to *Spiliada*'s second limb, the avoidance of these problems is subject to the claimants not being deprived of the right to have a just disposal of their claims. If it is accepted that the scope of the courts' discretion under *Spiliada*'s second limb is disproportionately broad, then it is questionable whether the right balance between the competing aims under the doctrine's first and second limbs can be struck. More significantly, and given that the courts' finding, following the application of *Spiliada*'s second limb, can trump their conclusion arising from their enquiry under the doctrine's first limb, there is a real risk that the important role played by the doctrine's first limb can be undermined. In these circumstances, the problems which the first limb is supposed to tackle would remain unresolved.

Aside from the abovementioned theoretical reasons for revisiting the current doctrinal basis for the operation of *Spiliada*'s second limb, the case for legal reform can also be made at a pragmatic level. In this context, at least two reasons can be advanced. First, the problems highlighted in decisions like *Lubbe* could still arise in the context of service-out cases. As the decisions in *Cherney* and *Altimo Holdings* underscored, the alleged inability of the courts of the more closely

EWCA Civ 1287, [2016] 1 WLR 1672 (CA) the Court of Appeal has ruled that the English court could give up its Brussels-based jurisdiction, based on the doctrine, in a case in which Scotland was shown to be the more closely connected forum to the dispute.

[72] *Re Harrods (Buenos Aires) Ltd (No 2)* [1992] Ch 72 (CA).

connected forum to entertain the claim justly can be sufficient to persuade English courts to give permission for service of process outside England, notwithstanding that England is not the dispute's centre of gravity. In other words, although since *Owusu* the likelihood of problems arising with the application of *Spiliada*'s second limb has become more curtailed in proceedings that have been brought against an English domiciliary in England as of right, there is much scope for these problems to arise in service-out cases.

The second (and arguably more pressing) pragmatic reason for reforming the law in this area arises mainly as a result of the changing nature of international commercial litigation. Over the past two decades, there has been a sharp increase in global trade with countries that are often collectively labelled as the 'emerging-market economies'.[73] One of the main forces for this development has been the general liberalisation of economic policies in those countries. This move has, in turn, opened them to greater levels of international trade and investment. In this context, a useful example is the de-nationalisation of industries after the collapse of the Soviet Union which generated wide-ranging business opportunities. As the number of large and complex international business transactions with close links to emerging-market economies has increased, so has the likelihood of legal disputes arising from them. Given London's global reputation as a centre for international commercial litigation, its courts have attracted (and are likely to continue to attract) a considerable proportion of claims that have stronger connections with the emerging-market economies than with England. Many of these nations have only just begun the arduous process of social, political and economic modernisation. Their legal systems are also undergoing a process of development. When judged against the standards of the so-called 'developed nations', these legal systems may not be as independent, resourceful, and experienced in resolving international commercial disputes. It is, therefore, conceivable that in many of those cases, the claimants in the English proceedings would be predominantly reliant on *Spiliada*'s second limb, by citing inadequacies or limitations in the legal systems within the emerging markets as the sole basis for keeping (or commencing) the proceedings in England. For all these reasons, it is argued that *Spiliada*'s second limb should be revised.

VI. The Way Forward

The discussions in Parts IV and V of this chapter have sought to argue that, the discretion afforded to English courts in applying *Spiliada*'s second limb has in fact been disproportionately broad, leading to problematic implications arising from

---

[73] It appears that this term does not characterise a specific group of countries. Nevertheless, it is widely (and loosely) regarded as defining the economies in those countries that are undergoing rapid social and economic modernisation.

the operation of the doctrine. At this juncture, the analysis proceeds to examine potential ways in which the law in this area could be refined.

One obvious way of circumventing the shortcomings arising from the application of the *Spiliada* doctrine (along with other potential imperfections) is to embark on an outright overhaul of the common law jurisdiction rules.[74] As touched on in Chapter 2, these rules could allow courts to assume jurisdiction over disputes which have no (or hardly any) connection with the forum. Any limitation of the grounds for the English courts' assumption of jurisdiction over an international commercial dispute would, in turn, result in a much more reduced need for a doctrine like *forum (non) conveniens*. In practice, though, it is ambitious (if not unrealistic) to think that the prospect for such a wholesale change is even achievable. Instead, a more fruitful line of inquiry would be to focus on redefining the *Spiliada* doctrine's second limb by limiting the scope of the court's discretion. In this respect, the main task here is to identify the doctrinal avenue through which to make this change.

A. Should *Spiliada*'s Second Limb Be Completely Abolished?

One (and perhaps the most extreme) way of confining the English court's discretion under the doctrine's second limb would be to discard it completely. Based on this approach, all that would have to be shown is that a foreign forum has a closer connection with the parties' dispute than the English court and that the forum is competent to entertain the dispute. This model broadly resembles the *forum non conveniens* doctrine in Scotland, before the formulation of the *Spiliada* test in 1986.[75]

As highlighted in Chapter 4, shortly after the enunciation of the *Spiliada* doctrine, a clutch of commentators suggested that Lord Goff had simply replaced the existing approach in England with the Scottish doctrine.[76] This view is not entirely accurate, however. It is widely known that Scotland is the birthplace of the *forum non conveniens* doctrine. As such, Lord Goff's articulation of the *Spiliada* test was very much inspired by Scottish case law and commentary on the doctrine.[77]

---

[74] For an argument along these lines see Hill (n 61).

[75] As noted in chapter four, after its adoption in England, the *Spiliada* doctrine has supplanted the pre-existing position in Scotland: see, eg, the Scottish courts' decisions in *Sokha v Secretary of State for the Home Department* 1992 SLT 1049 (OH), *PTKF Kontinent v VMPTO Progress* 1994 SLT 235 (OH), and *Royal Bank of Scotland v Davidson* [2009] CSOH 134, 2010 SLT 92 (OH). See, also, PR Beaumont and PE McEleavy, *Anton's Private International Law* 3rd edn (Edinburgh, W Green & Son Ltd, 2011) 363.

[76] See, eg, Collier (n 2), E Blackburn, 'Lis Alibi Pendens and Forum Non Conveniens in Collision Actions After the Civil Jurisdiction and Judgments Act 1982' [1988] *Lloyd's Maritime and Commercial Law Quarterly* 91, and M Pryles, 'Forum Non Conveniens – The Next Chapter' (1991) 65 *Australian Law Journal* 442.

[77] Most notably, his Lordship relied on the Scottish decisions in *Sim v Robinow* (1892) 19 R 665 (IH) and *Société de Gaz de Paris v Société Anonyme de Navigation 'Les Armateurs Français'* 1926 SC (HL) 13,

Notwithstanding this influence, there were important differences between the two jurisdictions' approaches to the discretionary staying of proceedings.

The study of Scottish case law indicates that, from before the House of Lords' endorsement of the doctrine in Scotland in *Société de Gaz de Paris v Société Anonyme de Navigation 'Les Armateurs Français'* in 1925,[78] until the decision in *Spiliada*,[79] the Scottish *forum non conveniens* doctrine had been applied as a one-stage test.[80] Under the Scottish test, courts in Scotland stayed their proceedings once persuaded that it was 'in the interests of all the parties and the ends of justice' to do so.[81] In this context, a considerably different meaning had been afforded to the term 'ends of justice' in Scotland than the one ascribed to the equivalent aspect under the *Spiliada* doctrine. There have been no reported cases in which, after enquiring and concluding that a foreign forum is the one more closely connected to the dispute, the Scottish court has proceeded to assess whether justice would be done in that forum. The analysis within the leading private-international-law treatise in Scotland also reflects this understanding of the Scottish case law.[82] In summary, the Scots' approach provided that, if a foreign forum was the dispute's centre of gravity, then it followed that it could justly dispose of the parties' dispute.

There are obvious advantages to discarding *Spiliada*'s second limb in line with the classic position in Scotland. It would greatly simplify the doctrine's

but also the analysis in AE Anton, *Private International Law* 1st edn (Edinburgh, W Green & Son Ltd, 1967) 148–54.

[78] ibid. See, eg, *David Fairweather and Others (Adamson's Trustees) v Mactagart* (1893) 1 SLT 41 (IH), *Hine v MacDowall* (1897) 5 SLT 12 (OH), *M'Lachlin v London and North-Western Railway Co* (1899) 7 SLT 244 (OH), *Powell v Mackenzie & Co* (1900) 8 SLT 182 (OH), *Lane v Foulds* (1903) 11 SLT 118 (OH), *Gemmell v Emery* (1905) 13 SLT 490 (OH), *Anderson, Tulloch & Co v JC & J Field* 1910 1 SLT 401 (OH), *James Howden & Co Ltd v Powell Duffryn Steam Coal Co Ltd* 1912 1 SLT 114 (OH), *Rothfield v Cohen* 1919 1 SLT 138 (OH), and *French v Hohback* 1921 2 SLT 53 (OH).

[79] See, eg, *Lawford v Lawford's Trustees* 1927 SC 360 (IH), *Robinson v Robinson's Trustees* 1929 SC 360 (IH) – overturned in *Robinson v Robinson's Trustees* 1930 SC (HL) 20, *Owners of SS 'Sheaf Lance' v Owners of SS 'Barcelo'* 1930 SLT 445 (IH), *Woodbury v Sutherland's Trustees* 1938 SLT 371 (OH), *Woodbury v Sutherland's Trustees* 1938 SC 689 (IH), *McLean v McLean* 1947 SC 79 (IH), *Jubert v Church Commissioners for England* 1952 SC 160 (OH), *Babington v Babington* 1955 SC 115 (IH), *Argyllshire Weavers Ltd v A Macaulay (Tweeds) Ltd* 1962 SC 388 (IH), *Balshaw v Kelly (otherwise Balshaw)* 1966 SLT 297 (OH), *Balshaw v Balshaw* 1967 SC 63 (IH), and *Credit Chimique v James Scott Engineering Group Ltd* 1979 SC 406 (OH). As set out in chapter four, after the decision in *Spiliada* the more-appropriate-forum test displaced the pre-*Spiliada* approach to discretionary staying of proceedings in Scotland.

[80] See Lord Jauncey's statement in the *Credit Chimique* case, where his Lordship summarised the position under Scottish law regarding the application of the *forum non conveniens* doctrine: '(1) … the burden of satisfying the tribunal that the case submitted to it for decision should not be allowed to proceed lie[d] upon the defender who table[d] the plea; (2) … this burden [could] only be discharged where weighty reasons [have been advanced] why an admitted jurisdiction should not be exercised, mere balance of inconvenience being insufficient; (3) … there [was] another court of competent jurisdiction in which the matter in question [could] be litigated; and (4) … considerations of these reasons [led] to the conclusion that the interests of the parties [could] more appropriately be served and the ends of justice [could] more appropriately be secured in that other court': ibid, 410.

[81] Lord Kinnear in *Sim* (n 77) 668. See, similarly, Lord Sumner in *Les Armateurs Français* (n 77) 22.

[82] See, eg, Anton (n 77) 148–54, and AE Anton and PR Beaumont, *Private International Law* 2nd edn (Edinburgh, W Green & Son Ltd, 1990) 212–18.

application: establishing that the forum is the 'home' of the litigation would become the courts' sole preoccupation. As a result, the problems arising from the courts' broad discretion under *Spiliada*'s second limb would be avoided. Indeed, in so far as service-out cases are concerned, Professor Briggs seems to favour an interpretation of the *Spiliada* test which focuses only on finding the dispute's centre of gravity.[83]

Nevertheless, it is argued that the abolition of *Spiliada*'s second limb would be a disproportionate response to the existing problems. In the overwhelming majority of the Scottish *forum non conveniens* cases, Scottish courts hardly ever had to address a situation in which the ability of the more closely connected forum to do justice to the parties was even doubted. Instead, virtually all the arguments focused on identifying the venue with which the dispute was connected – which in most instances happened to be England. It is perfectly conceivable that, if the Scottish court had routinely encountered submissions that the more closely connected forum could not justly deal with the parties' dispute, Scottish courts may have been forced to develop a more nuanced conception of the 'ends of justice' in the *forum non conveniens* context.

More significantly, without its second limb, the English court would have to relinquish jurisdiction in favour of the more closely connected forum (or refuse the service-out application), notwithstanding the fact that doing so could subject the claimant to the gravest forms of injustice in the dispute's centre of gravity. Such extreme instances of injustice to the claimant could include cases where the legal system of the claim's centre of gravity would discriminate against the claimant on racial,[84] religious,[85] or political[86] grounds, or where there has been a complete breakdown in the rule of law in that forum.[87] For these reasons, there is little merit in discarding completely *Spiliada*'s second limb.

---

[83] According to Professor Briggs 'if England is not [the more closely connected forum], ... , service out of the jurisdiction will not be authorised, even if the foreign court is not much good': Briggs, 'Forum Non Satis: *Spiliada* and an Inconvenient Truth' (n 46) 333. See, also, Briggs, '*Forum Non Satis*: Finding Fault with a Foreign Court' (n 46) 575, 578.

[84] An example could be where, during the rule of the Apartheid regime in South Africa, the English court would have had to send there a Black South African's case (that was more closely connected to South Africa).

[85] See, eg, *Oppenheimer* (n 25). As illustrated in Chapter 4, this was a service-out case involving a German plaintiff of the Jewish faith who sought to sue his German employer in England. Despite the overwhelming connection between the claim and Germany, the plaintiff was granted permission to serve proceedings on the defendant. It was almost certain that the plaintiff would not receive a fair hearing if the matter was remitted to Nazi-ruled Germany, where he could well have been arrested and persecuted. Another similar example, albeit in a different context, is *Ellinger v Guinness, Mahon & Co* [1939] 4 All ER 16. In this case, despite the existence of an exclusive jurisdiction clause in favour of the German court, the Jewish plaintiff sought to pursue his claim in England, fearing persecution by the Nazi regime.

[86] See, eg, *Carvalho v Hull Blyth (Angola) Ltd* [1979] 1 WLR 1228 (CA), where the Portuguese plaintiff brought an action in England notwithstanding the Angolan exclusive jurisdiction clause. He argued that, in light of the Angolan revolution against the Portuguese rule, his claim would not be entertained justly).

[87] See, eg, *889457 Alberta Inc v Katanga Mining Ltd* [2008] EWHC 2679, [2009] 1 BCLC 189.

A more prudent course of action would be to refine the *Spiliada* doctrine with a view to limiting (rather than completely abolishing) the court's room to manoeuvre at the second stage. One point needs to be made at this stage. In redefining the scope of the discretion accorded to English courts under *Spiliada*'s second limb, the objective is not to remove their discretion in its entirety, and thereby to effectively codify this aspect of the doctrine. Instead, the aim is to afford courts a more narrowly circumscribed discretion which would help to reduce the scope for problems arising with the application of the doctrine's second limb.

B. ECHR, Art 6(1) (as Applied in Expulsion Cases) as the Basis for Refining *Spiliada*'s Second Limb

In searching for a way to curtail the scope of the courts' discretion under *Spiliada*'s second limb, a potentially fruitful doctrinal avenue is that which underpins the protection of persons' right to fair trial under ECHR, Art 6(1), when they are being subjected to expulsion proceedings. Art 6(1) provides that, '[i]n the determination of his civil rights and obligations or of any criminal charge against him, everyone is entitled to a fair and public hearing within a reasonable time by an independent and impartial tribunal established by law'. An ECHR Contracting State is obliged to protect the Art 6(1) rights of those within its jurisdiction in two broad classes of case.[88] The first concerns the so-called 'domestic cases', where the state party must ensure that its conduct within its own territory does not infringe the rights enshrined under Art 6(1) of those present within its jurisdiction.[89] The second class of cases in which an ECHR Contracting State has to protect individuals' Convention rights relates to deportation or extradition proceedings. In these cases, the Contracting State has to ensure that the expulsion of the individual in question to the other state – which may (or may not) be a Contracting State – would not lead to the violation in the receiving state of the individual's Art 6(1) rights.[90] In other words, the state party would fall foul of its ECHR obligations if the relevant individual's Art 6(1) rights were breached in the event of his deportation to the receiving state. It is the application of Art 6(1) rights in the context of expulsion cases which is of interest for our purposes.

Of course, there are differences between expulsion and *forum (non) conveniens* cases. For instance, in the former group, the question is whether an English court

---

[88] It is notable that these obligations on the part of a signatory state apply in relation to all other rights within the ECHR.

[89] Lord Bingham in *R (Ullah) v Special Adjudicator* [2004] UKHL 26, [2004] 2 AC 323 (HL) 340.

[90] This aspect of a Contracting State's ECHR obligations also applies in relation to other Convention rights: see, eg, *Ullah*, ibid (concerning the prospective deportee's Art 3 rights), *EM (Lebanon) v Secretary of State for the Home Department* [2008] UKHL 64, [2009] 1 AC 1198 (HL) (concerning the prospective deportee's Art 8 rights). For more discussion about the state party's obligations arising in the context of expulsion cases see, *inter alia*, *Soering v United Kingdom* (Application No 14038/88) (1989) 11 EHRR 439, *Drozd v France* (Application No 12747/87) (1992) 14 EHRR 745, and *Mamatkulov and Askarov v Turkey* (Applications Nos 46827/99 and 46951/99) (2005) 41 EHRR 494.

should expel a *person* to another forum. In the latter group, however, the main issue is whether the *dispute* should be remitted to a foreign forum. Nevertheless, it is argued that these categories of case are analogous.[91] In both instances, courts are effectively concerned with whether the person would be subjected to injustice if he (in expulsion cases) or his claim (in *forum (non) conveniens* cases) is removed to a foreign state. In view of this analogy, it is useful to identify the doctrinal avenue through which the court ensures that the individuals' Art 6(1) rights are protected in expulsion cases. This examination sheds light on how (in)justice in the receiving state is defined in the context of those cases and whether this conception could be transplanted as the doctrinal basis for applying *Spiliada's* second limb.

In expulsion cases, deporting an individual from a Contracting State would only amount to a breach of his Art 6(1) rights if there is a real risk of 'a flagrant denial of justice' in the receiving country of the deportee's right to fair trial.[92] Neither the case law nor the associated literature contains a conclusive definition of what amounts to a real risk of a flagrant denial of justice. Nevertheless, there have been various pronouncements that have tried to explain the meaning of this term. For example, in *Mamatkulov and Askarov v Turkey*, the Strasbourg Court[93] observed that

> the use of the adjective [flagrant] is clearly intended to impose a stringent test of unfairness going beyond mere irregularities or lack of safeguards in the trial procedures such as might result in a breach of article 6 if occurring within the contracting state itself … what the word 'flagrant' is intended to convey is a breach of the principles of fair trial guaranteed by article 6 which is so fundamental as to amount to a nullification, or destruction of the very essence, of the right guaranteed by that article.[94]

Similarly, in *Devaseelan v Secretary of State for the Home Department*, the United Kingdom Immigration and Appeals Tribunal considered that the removal of an individual would lead to a flagrant denial of justice in the receiving state where Art 6(1) rights

> will be completely denied or nullified in the destination country – that it can be said that removal will breach the treaty obligations of the signatory State however those

---

[91] For a similar argument, see JJ Fawcett, 'The Impact of Article 6(1) of the ECHR on Private International Law' (2007) 56 *International & Comparative Law Quarterly* 1, 4.

[92] *Soering* (n 90) [113], *Einhorn v France* Reports of Judgments and Decisions 2001-XI, [32]–[33], *Tomic v United Kingdom* (Application No 17837/03) Judgment of 14 October 2003 (unreported), [3], *Mamatkulov and Askarov* (n 90) [90], *Al-Saadoon v United Kingdom* (Application no 61498/08) (2010) 51 EHRR 9, [149], and *Othman v United Kingdom* (Application No 8139/09) (2012) 55 EHRR 1, [258]. If it is concluded that there is a real risk of a flagrant denial of justice in the receiving state, then the individual's deportation would amount to a breach of the contracting state's ECHR obligations, unless the deporting country is given sufficient diplomatic assurances that the individual would not be subjected to such injustice.

[93] The 'Strasbourg Court' is used as shorthand when referring to the European Court of Human Rights.

[94] *Mamatkulov and Askarov v Turkey* (n 90) [90]. This wording has subsequently been used in other cases: see, eg, *Brown v Government of Rwanda* [2009] EWHC 770 (Admin), [24]–[25], and *Othman* (n 92) [260].

obligations might be interpreted or whatever might be said by or on behalf of the destination State.[95]

These passages indicate that the test for establishing a flagrant denial of justice in the receiving state is a rigorous one, and that courts have limited discretion when deciding whether expelling the individual to the receiving state would violate his rights under Art 6(1). Put another way, in these cases the conception of (in) justice in the receiving state is very narrowly defined. Indeed, there appears to have been only one reported case where an individual's deportation from a signatory state to a receiving state would have led to the signatory state being in breach of its Art 6(1) obligations. That case was *Othman v United Kingdom*.[96] *Othman* concerned the deportation of Abu Qatada, a controversial Muslim cleric, from the United Kingdom to Jordan. The Strasbourg Court held that Abu Qatada's removal to Jordan for trial in that country would breach his Art 6(1) rights because some of the evidence that was likely to be used in a prosecution against him had been extracted through the torture of third parties in Jordan. In *Othman*, the Strasbourg Court also outlined a number of examples from the case law which highlighted the narrow scope of 'flagrant denial of justice'.[97] These examples included

> conviction *in absentia* with no possibility subsequently to obtain a fresh determination of the merits of the charge;[98] a trial which is summary in nature and conducted with a total disregard for the rights of the defence;[99] detention without any access to an independent and impartial tribunal to have the legality of the detention reviewed;[100] and deliberate and systematic refusal of access to a lawyer, especially for an individual detained in a foreign country.[101]

This list of examples is not exhaustive. Yet, it shows that, in expulsion cases, what amounts to injustice in the receiving state has a much narrower scope than is the case under *Spiliada*'s second limb – or, indeed, in so far as the way in which injustice has been defined in domestic cases. In the context of expulsion cases, injustice in the receiving state means very serious procedural unfairness which would almost completely deny the individual's Art 6(1) rights in that forum. However,

---

[95] *Devaseelan v Secretary of State for the Home Department* [2002] UKIAT 702, [2003] Imm AR 1, [111]. This conception of flagrant denial of justice has been adopted in subsequent decisions: see, eg, *Ullah* (n 89), *R (Razgar) v Secretary of State for the Home Department (No 2)* [2004] UKHL 27, [2004] 2 AC 368 (HL), and *EM (Lebanon)* (n 90).

[96] *Othman v United Kingdom* (n 92). For examples of where the applicants' claims that remitting them to the receiving state would amount to a breach in that territory of their Art 6(1) rights proved to be unsuccessful, see, eg, *Drew v Poland* [2012] EWHC 3073 (Admin), *Elombah v Germany* [2013] EWHC 2233 (Admin), *AT v Luxembourg* [2013] EWHC 4010 (Admin).

[97] ibid, [259]. Abu Qatada was finally deported from the United Kingdom to Jordan on 7 July 2013, following an agreement between the two governments. Based on the agreement, the Jordanian government undertook that evidence obtained against Abu Qatada through torture would not be used in any future hearing that he would be subjected to in Jordan.

[98] *Einhorn* (n 92) [33] and *Stoichkov v Bulgaria* (2007) 44 EHRR 14, [56].

[99] *Bader v Sweden* (2008) 46 EHRR 13, [47].

[100] *Al-Moayad v Germany* (Application No 35865/03) (2007) 44 EHRR SE22, [101].

[101] ibid.

in relation to *Spiliada*'s second limb, as discussed in Part II of this chapter, injustice covers a far wider range of potential shortcomings in the more closely connected forum.[102] What is more, this conception of (in)justice is almost identical to the way in which (in)justice is defined in the context of the protection of Art 6(1) rights in domestic cases.

The more limited conception of (in)justice in expulsion cases is rationalised 'against the background of the general principle of international law that states have the right to control the entry, residence and expulsion of aliens'.[103] While, no doubt, it would be problematic to replace this notion of (in)justice with that underpinning the application of *Spiliada*'s second limb, there is no reason in principle or policy as to why the reverse of this transplantation would be illegitimate. Indeed, the disproportionately broad conception of (in)justice for the purposes of *Spiliada*'s second limb suggests that the English court is more protective of a claimant's *action* (in a *forum (non) conveniens* case) than it is of an *individual* (in an expulsion case). If a foreign legal system is good enough to receive an individual, then it is surely good enough to entertain an individual's case. Accordingly, it is argued that it would be appropriate for the notion of (in)justice under *Spiliada*'s second limb to be remodelled on the basis of what amounts to a flagrant denial of justice in the receiving state, as set out in Art 6 expulsion cases.

C. The Refined *Spiliada* Test and its Application

The foregoing argument has attempted to posit that the *Spiliada* doctrine should continue to be applied in two stages, but that the reformulated second stage should take as its inspiration the test from ECHR, Art 6(1), as applied in expulsion cases. Such reform would lead to the following position: to obtain a stay of proceedings commenced in England as of right, first, the burden is on the defendant to show – relying on the factors that are currently consulted under the first limb of *Spiliada* – that another foreign state is the dispute's centre of gravity and its courts have jurisdiction to entertain it. If this burden is not discharged, then the stay application would be rejected and the case would be heard by the English court. If, however, the English court is satisfied that there is an available forum which is more closely connected with the dispute than England, it should stay the proceedings, unless the claimant can show that sending the dispute to that forum would lead to a violation of his Art 6(1) rights in that forum (as defined in expulsion cases). In relation to service-out cases, the English court should only give permission for service out if England is the proper forum for the dispute or, failing that, if the claimant can show that he would suffer a breach of his Art 6(1) rights (as defined in the expulsion cases) in the event that the dispute were to be tried in the more closely connected forum. In short, in both service-out and as-of-right

---

[102] See, also, Fawcett (n 91) 38–39.
[103] Lord Hope of Craighead in *EM (Lebanon)* (n 90) 1208.

proceedings, in the event that, to all intents and purposes, the action belongs to another available foreign forum, the English court should only exercise jurisdiction over it if the United Kingdom would otherwise be in breach of its ECHR obligations, by virtue of the violation in the dispute's centre of gravity of the claimant's Art 6(1) rights (as defined in expulsion cases).

This new doctrinal framework, it is argued, represents the more appropriate middle ground that can be realistically achieved between the polarised options of completely discarding the courts' discretion under *Spiliada*'s second limb, on the one hand, and persevering with the current (problematic) status quo, on the other. At one level, the new doctrinal model would prevent a situation from arising where staying the proceedings in England (or rejecting a service-out application) would lead to the claimant being subjected to the most extreme forms of injustice in the more closely connected forum. As stated earlier, in the absence of the discretionary power under *Spiliada*'s second limb, disputes like the ones in *Oppenheimer v Louis Rosenthal, Ellinger v Guinness, Mahon & Co, Carvalho v Hull Blyth (Angola) Ltd*, and *Alberta Inc v Katanga Mining Ltd* would not be decided the same way – because none of those disputes had any connection with England. It is, however, patently clear that, in such cases, the claimant would be subjected to profound injustice if he had to litigate his claim in the dispute's centre of gravity. Indeed, had any of these been an expulsion case, deporting the individual to the receiving forum would have clearly put the UK Government in breach of its Art 6(1) obligations. Accordingly, the application of the new test would allow the English court to assume jurisdiction over the dispute, in the sort of factual contexts exemplified in these cases, even though the connection between England and the parties' claims was tenuous (or, indeed, non-existent).

At another level, though, the new doctrinal basis would clearly provide a more tightly-defined scope for the application of the courts' discretion under *Spiliada*'s second limb than at present. In the context of deportation proceedings, the conception of (in)justice in the receiving state to an individual involved in those proceedings has a narrow ambit. If that notion of (in)justice replaces the one currently under *Spiliada*'s second limb, it would become more difficult for a claimant to convince the court to depart from the provisional conclusion reached under the doctrine's first limb. Indeed, it is unlikely whether any of the cases mentioned above in which the court had decided to exercise jurisdiction over the claim despite the lack of any meaningful connection with England – namely, *Cherney, Altimo Holdings,* and *Lubbe* – would be decided the same way. *Cherney* was certainly not a case like *Carvalho*, for instance, where it was virtually clear that, because of the political upheaval following the Angolan independence, the plaintiff had become 'the sort of person who would be anathema to the present government in Angola'.[104] In *Cherney*, the claimant's extensive submissions essentially listed out various problems that would arise if his case were to be litigated in Russia. They did not, however, establish that his Art 6(1) rights would be completely

---

[104] Geoffrey Lane LJ in *Carvalho* (n 86) 1241.

nullified (as defined in expulsion cases) if his claim were not to be litigated in England.[105] In other words, had *Cherney* been an expulsion case, and had the court ruled in favour of deporting Mr Cherney to Russia, it is highly unlikely that the UK Government would have been found to be in breach of its ECHR, Art 6(1) obligations. Likewise, in *Altimo Holdings*, despite all its assertions, the claimant did not establish that it was the type of litigant so disliked and prejudiced against by the relevant Kyrgyz authorities that the very essence of its Art 6(1) rights would have been violated if its dispute were to be litigated in Kyrgyzstan. Indeed, in that case, the claimant's attack at the Kyrgyz court's integrity came before that court had even had the opportunity to consider the case.[106] It is, therefore, highly unlikely that, in a case like *Altimo Holdings*, the trial in Kyrgyzstan would have amounted to a violation of the claimants' Art 6(1) rights (as defined in expulsion cases). It is also improbable that arguments about the lack of resources and experience in the more closely connected forum, in cases like *Lubbe* (and *Connelly*), would be sufficient to satisfy the proposed discretionary basis under *Spiliada*'s second limb. It was not conceded in either of these cases that no financial assistance would be available in Namibia (in *Connelly*) or in South Africa (in *Lubbe*) to allow the plaintiffs to bring their claims and that the only route available to them was for them to litigate their complicated case in person.[107] Instead, in each case there were strong arguments highlighting the availability of financial resources and legal expertise in Namibia and South Africa. The fact that such expertise or means existed in those forums (albeit contested by the plaintiffs) meant that it was not a case where sending the plaintiffs to the dispute's centre of gravity would lead to a breach of their Art 6(1) rights (as defined in expulsion cases).

In the long run, this proposed change in the law could mitigate the problems identified with the application of the existing English *forum (non) conveniens* doctrine. As indicated in Part II, broadly, English courts have been consistent in applying their discretion under *Spiliada*'s first limb. By limiting the court's room for manoeuvre under *Spiliada*'s second limb, there would be fewer instances where English courts would depart from their finding under the doctrine's first limb. Consequently, the proposed remodelling of *Spiliada* would render the English *forum (non) conveniens* doctrine more predictable. One other by-product of circumscribing the scope of justice under *Spiliada*'s second limb is that it would make legal proceedings more efficient. It would no longer be possible for claimants to rely on a virtually endless list of factors in challenging the ability of the more closely connected forum to the dispute to do justice to their claims. Indeed, having a more narrowly-focused framework for applying the discretion could at least in certain (if not most) cases discourage claimants from seeking to overturn

---

[105] Professor Briggs was also sceptical about the persuasiveness of the claimant's arguments concerning the integrity of the Russian legal system: Briggs, '*Forum Non Satis*: Finding Fault with a Foreign Court' (n 46) 578.

[106] See, in this context, Briggs, '*Forum Non Satis: Spiliada* and an Inconvenient Truth' (n 46) 332.

[107] See *Airey v Ireland* (Series A, No 32) (1979–80) 2 EHRR 305, where the Irish Government conceded that legal aid was not available to a woman who was involved in divorce proceedings.

the finding under the doctrine's first limb. The focus of the court and the parties would be on finding the forum which is more closely connected to the dispute. While there is no denying the fact that identifying that forum could require detailed evidential assessment, it would clearly be less resource-intensive than is presently the case. Lastly, the refinement of *Spiliada* in a manner consistent with the proposed framework in this chapter would make it a doctrine which is less chauvinistic and more tolerant of the natural (and, indeed, inevitable) differences of approach in different legal systems to the litigation of cross-border private disputes. In short, therefore, the proposed formulation would represent an improvement on the existing staying-of-proceedings and service-out regimes in England.

It might be observed that there is no guarantee that the courts would not apply the revised *Spiliada* test so flexibly as to, in effect, render its operation similar to the current test. Nevertheless, it can be reasonably expected that the existence of a considerable body of expulsion cases – in which the courts have ascribed consistently a very narrow conception to the potential injustices in the receiving state – would go a long way to limit the court's discretion in applying the revised doctrine. In this respect, the reform in the law would be a step in the right direction in mitigating the problems that have emerged from the application of the second limb of the existing *Spiliada* principle. This development would, in turn, help the doctrine to remain consonant with the changing nature of international commercial litigation.

VII. Conclusion

This chapter has attempted to build on the analysis advanced in Chapters 2 to 4, by exploring the possible future direction of travel for the English *forum (non) conveniens* doctrine. As mentioned at the start, the questions of whether (and, if so, how) the doctrine, as it is applied today, could be further refined have been generally under-examined in the existing literature. This state of affairs has had much to do with the generally positive way in which the House of Lords' decision in *Spiliada* has been received within the academic and judicial circles in the subsequent decades. After a short summary, in Part II, of how the English doctrine operates, Part III set out the main reasons behind the widespread goodwill towards the *Spiliada* test. It was argued that the articulation of the test has unquestionably helped to enhance the law in England on discretionary (non-)exercise of jurisdiction, by addressing many of the shortcomings which arose from the application of the earlier principles in this area. The fact that this encouraging change in the law had been made at a rather rapid pace – the House of Lords adopted a relaxed interpretation of the vexatious-and-oppressive test in *The Atlantic Star* in 1973, and embraced the more-appropriate-forum test in *Spiliada* in 1986 – may have also played a part in the reduced appetite for further reform, perhaps for fear that it would cause litigants increased uncertainty. These considerations have contributed to the understanding that Lord Goff's enunciation of the more-appropriate-forum test in *Spiliada* marked the final destination for the development of the practice of discretionary (non-)exercise of jurisdiction in England. Thus, the prevalent view in the contemporary literature is that there is no need for the law to undergo additional revision.

Be that as it may, as the examination of the relevant authorities in Part IV has shown, the application of the current *forum (non) conveniens* doctrine in England has given rise to shortcomings which it would be unwise to overlook. They included a propensity for the doctrine's operation in England to give rise to unpredictable, protracted, and wasteful litigation, and to exhibit elements of judicial chauvinism. It was argued that, in the main, these problems have been occasioned because of the disproportionately broad discretion afforded to the courts under the second limb of the *Spiliada* test.

The discussion in Part V proceeded to argue that, both theoretically and pragmatically, there is a genuine need to revise the law. Accordingly, Part VI assessed the possible way(s) in which the doctrine's future might be shaped. It was contended that a doctrinal framework should be adopted which would limit the courts' scope of discretion at the second stage of the *Spiliada* test, but fall short of discarding it altogether. In this respect, the chief contention has been that the *Spiliada* doctrine should continue to be applied in two stages, but that the new second stage should be modelled on the test from ECHR, Art 6(1), as applied in expulsion cases. Accordingly, to obtain a stay of proceedings commenced in England as of right, the defendant has to establish – relying on the factors that are currently used under the first limb of *Spiliada* – that another foreign forum that would assume jurisdiction over the claim is its centre of gravity. If this burden is successfully discharged, then the court should stay the proceedings, unless the claimant can show that sending the dispute to its centre of gravity would lead to a violation of his Art 6(1) rights in that forum (as defined in the expulsion cases). In service-out cases, the English court should only give permission for the claim form to be served outside the jurisdiction if England is the dispute's proper forum or, failing that, if the claimant can demonstrate that he would suffer a breach of his Art 6(1) rights (as defined in expulsion cases) if the dispute were to be brought in its proper forum. In short, in both groups of case, if the action essentially belongs to another available foreign forum, the English court should only exercise jurisdiction over it if the United Kingdom would otherwise be in breach of its ECHR obligations, by virtue of the violation in the dispute's centre of gravity of the claimant's Art 6(1) rights (as defined in expulsion cases). It is submitted that reforming the law in this manner would help to respond to many of the existing shortcomings in the law's application and, in turn, enhance the doctrine's effectiveness as a device through which the question of where the case should be heard is answered.

6

Conclusions

The principal objective of this book has been to examine the *forum (non) conveniens* doctrine's past, present, and future from the perspective of the law in England. London's reputation worldwide as a centre for the litigation of international commercial disputes means that the doctrine has been routinely in contention before its courts, specifically in situations where parties disagree over the venue in which the case should be heard. These occasions arise both in cases where courts are asked to stay the proceedings brought before them as of right (based on the *forum non conveniens* doctrine), and in cases in which permission is sought to serve claim forms on defendants outside England (through the operation of the *forum conveniens* doctrine).

This has been the first book-length study of its kind which has devoted its entire attention to the assessment of the *forum (non) conveniens* doctrine in England. Through a critical analysis of relevant historical and contemporary sources in England (and elsewhere), the book has sought to fill gaps in relevant knowledge of the English doctrine, and challenge certain views concerning its operation that have come to be regarded as representing the orthodoxy. In this respect, the aim has been to refine our understanding of the doctrine's historical development, assess its application in the years following its formal recognition in England in *Spiliada Maritime Corporation v Cansulex Ltd*,[1] and, ultimately, explore the case for its revision, in view of the evolving nature of cross-border private disputes.

The substantive discussion was presented in four chapters. It began in Chapter 2, which set out to identify the place of the *forum (non) conveniens* doctrine within the English national rules of jurisdiction. There, it was highlighted that addressing the 'jurisdiction questions' is one of the key tasks for a court which is faced with a cross-border private dispute. In this respect, the court must decide if it has jurisdiction to entertain the claim, and (in the event that it does) whether it will actually exercise that jurisdiction. It was shown that, in trying to resolve the jurisdiction question, the most prudent course of action for legal systems is to articulate and apply rules which, in the process of allocating jurisdiction, uphold a number of 'jurisdictional values'. Chief among these values are party autonomy, connectedness, and the avoidance of parallel or related proceedings.[2] Not all

---

[1] *Spiliada Maritime Corporation v Cansulex Ltd* [1987] AC 460 (HL).
[2] These values have been identified and outlined in J Hill, 'Jurisdiction in Civil and Commercial Matters: Is There a Third Way?' (2001) *Current Legal Problems* 439, 458–59.

aspects of English national jurisdiction rules promote these values. Consequently, and over the centuries, English courts have taken steps, through devising different legal doctrines, to protect, and (where necessary) prioritise the values. The application of these doctrines, in turn, help to increase the likelihood for private-international-law disputes to be heard in courts to which they really belong. *Forum (non) conveniens* is an important part of this family of principles.

Having located *forum (non) conveniens* within English national jurisdiction rules, and demarcated its sphere of operation from its doctrinal siblings, the discussion in Chapter 3 proceeded to outline the background to the emergence of the modern-day practice of discretionary (non-)exercise of jurisdiction in England. In broad terms, the main objective of the analysis in that chapter was to provide a more extensive (and nuanced) account of the historical developments which predated the articulation of the more-appropriate-forum test in *Spiliada*. More specifically, though, the intention was to shed light on those aspects concerning the earlier origins of the practice of discretionary (non-)exercise of jurisdiction in England which, in relative terms, have been largely overlooked in the literature. Put simply, the chapter sought to map out the law's evolution in this area from its embryonic form up to the House of Lords' formal recognition of the *forum (non) conveniens* doctrine in *Spiliada*. Additionally, and through a close inspection of the relevant case law and associated academic commentary, the analysis revisited some of the prevailing views regarding the English *forum (non) conveniens* doctrine's past.

As was demonstrated in Chapter 3, the existing practice of discretionary (non-)exercise of jurisdiction in England is almost entirely English in pedigree and is traceable to the tests applied in two separate bodies of nineteenth-century precedent in England: (i) cases concerning the service of proceedings on foreign-based defendants – so-called service-out cases; and (ii) cases where English courts had been asked to relinquish their (otherwise) soundly founded jurisdiction where the defendants had been sued while present in England – so-called stay-of-proceedings cases. In relation to stay-of-proceedings cases, it was towards the latter part of the nineteenth century when courts began to acknowledge clearly that they could, if persuaded by the defendants, decide not to exercise their jurisdiction. In its earliest form, this acknowledgement happened in *McHenry v Lewis* in 1882,[3] a *lis alibi pendens* case. In this case, and through what might be described as a process of analogical reasoning, the court relied on the vexatious-and-oppressive test – which itself had been used by courts in England for centuries for the purpose of issuing common injunctions and (later on) anti-suit injunctions. The next major development in the law on staying of proceedings in England came at the start of the twentieth century when courts granted stays, regardless of whether parallel proceedings were pending elsewhere. In three cases decided

---

[3] *McHenry v Lewis* (1882) 22 Ch D 397 (CA).

between 1906 and 1908 – namely, *Logan v Bank of Scotland (No 2)*,[4] *Egbert v Short*,[5] and *In re Norton's Settlement*[6] – the vexatious-and-oppressive test was relied on as providing the foundation for the courts' (non-)exercise of jurisdiction in actions commenced in England as of right. The examination of these cases (and related academic commentary), in turn, illustrated that the law on discretionary staying of proceedings in England in the first few years of the twentieth century was, in fact, applied in much the same way as its Scottish counterpart under the *forum non conveniens* doctrine.[7] Indeed, because of the similarities between the two approaches, it may have been anticipated that English courts would soon proceed to import (and adopt) the Scottish doctrine for the purpose of staying of proceedings. Therefore, contrary to the view that before the mid-1970s English staying-of-proceedings practice was overly favourable towards plaintiffs,[8] the analysis of the relevant case law at the start of the twentieth century has demonstrated that, when faced with stay applications, English courts were broadly even-handed in their treatment of the parties' competing interests. What is more, and in so far as the courts' discretion in service-out cases was concerned, the discussion in the chapter showed that, from the 1920s onwards, the English courts' approach was broadly akin to the one in Scotland under the *forum non conveniens* doctrine. Indeed, it was in a number of service-out cases in that period that courts began to use the phrase '*forum conveniens* considerations' to refer to the factors which affected their decision whether to allow for claim forms to be served on defendants outside of England.[9] In sum, and in practical terms, by the mid-1920s, a similar set of factors were central to the application of the courts' discretion in stay and service-out cases in England, on the one hand, and *forum non conveniens* cases in Scotland, on the other.

It was, in fact, between the late 1920s and the mid-1970s that the English courts' treatment of stay applications in England became noticeably pro-plaintiff. Somewhat curiously, the Court of Appeal's ruling in *St Pierre v South American Stones (Gath & Chaves) Ltd*[10] appears to be the main turning point in the law's development. Curiously, because, to all outward appearances, the judgment in *St Pierre* – particularly, Scott LJ's *dictum*, which came to be seen as the standard

---

[4] *Logan v Bank of Scotland (No 2)* [1906] 1 KB 141 (CA).

[5] *Egbert v Short* [1907] 2 Ch 205.

[6] *In re Norton's Settlement* [1908] 1 Ch 471 (CA).

[7] See, eg, AD Gibb, *The International Law of Jurisdiction in England and Scotland* (Edinburgh, William Hodge & Co, 1926) 212–13 and P Blair, 'The Doctrine of Forum Non Conveniens in Anglo-American Law' (1929) 29 *Columbia Law Review* 1 who appeared to regard the English and Scottish staying-of-proceedings practices as being similar.

[8] A Briggs, *Civil Jurisdiction and Judgments* 6th edn (Abingdon, Informa Law from Routledge, 2015) para 1.01.

[9] See, *Rosler v Hilbery* [1925] Ch 250 (CA), *In re Schintz* [1926] Ch 710 (CA), *Ocean Steamship Company Ltd v Queensland State Wheat Board* [1941] 1 KB 402 (CA), and *Vitkovice Horni A Hutni Tezirstvo v Korner* [1951] AC 869 (HL).

[10] *St Pierre v South American Stones (Gath & Chaves) Ltd* [1936] 1 KB 382 (CA).

test for non-exercise of jurisdiction in stay or *lis alibi pendens* cases – was founded on the same authorities – among others, *Logan*, *Egbert*, and *Norton* – where English courts had actually treated the plaintiffs' and defendants' competing rights even-handedly. Nevertheless, in almost all post-*St Pierre* stay or *lis alibi pendens* cases, it became the courts' chief concern to protect the plaintiffs' right to commence proceedings in England. Consequently, hardly any stay applications were success-ful between the late 1920s and the mid-1970s. This state of affairs was explained in the chapter as being one of the unique features of development at common law. At common law, how a judge's *dictum* is received and applied in subsequent authorities and/or academic discussions can sometimes be more important in characterising the decision than what was actually stated in the ruling itself.

The restrictive application of the vexatious-and-oppressive test after the *St Pierre* ruling led to the creation of a number of negative side-effects. In particular, the law's application had encouraged forum shopping in England, and meant that the English staying-of-proceedings practice was out of step with the wider socio-economic changes that were unfolding in the mid- to late twentieth century. This state of affairs prompted the beginning of a gradual depar-ture from a strict application of the vexatious-and-oppressive test in the House of Lords' ruling in *The Atlantic Star* in 1973. In a 13-year period, the law underwent a step-by-step modification which, finally, led to the formal recognition of the *forum (non) conveniens* doctrine in England in the *Spiliada* case in 1986, and the articulation of the more-appropriate-forum test.

After outlining the historical developments which preceded the emergence of the more-appropriate-forum test in *Spiliada*, Chapter 4 went on to examine the present-day application and scope of the English *forum (non) conveniens* doctrine. Fundamentally, the chapter's aim was to facilitate a more comprehen-sive understanding of the law's development in the post-*Spiliada* era. To realise this objective, the law was revisited from three different perspectives. The first perspective concentrated on *Spiliada*'s development over the past three decades as a doctrine. It was seen that, in so far as the English courts' application of the *forum non conveniens* doctrine in stay cases is concerned, except for a short-lived expansion of the meaning of availability in the mid-1990s, it has been applied in the same manner as when it was articulated in *Spiliada*. In the same vein, and notwithstanding opposing observations, put forth most prominently by Professor Briggs,[11] the current application of the *forum conveniens* test in service-out cases is not doctrinally different from that outlined in *Spiliada* back in 1986.

The second perspective focused on the present-day *forum (non) conveniens* doctrine's global reach especially in influencing, the evolution of the equivalent principles concerning discretionary (non-)exercise of jurisdiction across the Commonwealth. The assessment of this aspect of the *Spiliada* doctrine illustrated

---

[11] Briggs (n 8) para 4.91.

that its contemporary significance has not been limited only to England. Indeed, the more-appropriate-forum test has been the main source of inspiration for the development of the equivalent principles across numerous Commonwealth legal systems. Many of these jurisdictions have revised their approaches to discretionary (non-)exercise of jurisdiction by fully embracing the English doctrine. Even in those Commonwealth countries – most notably, Australia and Canada – which have not remodelled their laws in conformity with *Spiliada*, their *forum (non) conveniens* doctrines have nevertheless been heavily influenced by it.

The final perspective concerned the *Spiliada* doctrine's application. The focus of this aspect of the analysis was on both the contemporary evolution of the doctrine's *conceptual* and *overall* scope. It was stated that, while conceptually the scope of *Spiliada* has remained mostly unaltered, the intervening years have witnessed a major limitation on its overall applicability. More specifically, following the Court of Justice's judgment in *Owusu v Jackson*,[12] it has been confirmed that the *Spiliada* doctrine is unavailable to English courts in those instances where their jurisdiction is rooted in the provisions within the Brussels regime.[13] Nevertheless, this could well prove to be a short-lived limitation on *Spiliada's* overall operation. The Brexit vote has given the doctrine a new lease of life, making it conceivable for its application to be restored to the position prior to the *Owusu* ruling after the completion of the Brexit process.

In comparison to the discussions regarding the historical development of the English *forum (non) conveniens* doctrine or, indeed, its contemporary application, which were central to the coverage in Chapters 3 and 4 of this book, the questions of whether the modern-day doctrine could be refined further (and, if so, how) have not received the same level of attention in the literature. Consideration of these questions was at the heart of the analysis in Chapter 5. There, it was highlighted that the introduction of the more-appropriate-forum test in *Spiliada* addressed many of the shortcomings which existed under the earlier regime for discretionary (non-)exercise of jurisdiction in England. To begin with, the *Spiliada* doctrine has allowed for a much more balanced treatment of the competing rights of claimants and defendants who clash over whether their disputes should be litigated in England (or foreign forums elsewhere). Additionally, the more-appropriate-forum test has provided English courts with a much more potent tool in thwarting the litigants' attempts at forum shopping. Lastly, the *Spiliada* test has rendered the law on discretionary (non-)exercise of jurisdiction in England much more consonant with the wider socio-economic developments which had been in train in the latter part of the twentieth century. Owing, primarily, to these

---

[12] Case C-281/02 *Owusu v Jackson* [2005] ECR I-1383, [2005] QB 801.
[13] However, it has been stated recently that, in the context of the case in which the English court's jurisdiction is based on the provisions within the Brussels regime but the more appropriate forum for hearing the dispute is the court in another country within the United Kingdom, the court in England can rely on the *forum non conveniens* doctrine to relinquish its jurisdiction: *Cook v Virgin Media Ltd* (joint with *McNeil v Tesco plc*) [2015] EWCA Civ 1287, [2016] 1 WLR 1672 (CA).

positive developments, which have occurred following the articulation of the more-appropriate-forum test, the *Spiliada* ruling has widely been seen as representing the final word on this aspect of English conflict of laws. Thus, the received view in the contemporary literature is that there is no need for any additional revision of the law.[14]

However, as the assessment of post-*Spiliada* case law illustrated, the application of the current *forum (non) conveniens* doctrine in England has given rise to problems which it would be ill-advised to ignore. These shortcomings include a tendency for the doctrine's application to lead to unpredictable, protracted, and wasteful litigation. Additionally, and contrary to beliefs in the build-up to (and the immediate aftermath of) the enunciation of the more-appropriate-forum test, *Spiliada's* application has exhibited elements of judicial chauvinism. It was argued that, predominantly, these problems are generated due to the disproportionately broad discretion afforded to the courts under *Spiliada's* second limb. As the chapter contended, both theoretical and practical considerations can be presented in favour of refining the law. Having assessed the different ways in which legal reform can be achieved, it was stated that a doctrinal framework should be adopted which limits the courts' scope of discretion at the second stage of the *Spiliada* test, but falls short of jettisoning it altogether. In this respect, the chief contention was that the *Spiliada* doctrine should continue to be applied in two stages, but that the new second stage should be modelled on the test under the European Convention on Human Rights ('ECHR'),[15] Art 6(1) (as applied in expulsion cases). Accordingly, to obtain a stay of proceedings commenced in England as of right, the defendant would need to establish – relying on the factors that are currently used under the first limb of *Spiliada* – that another foreign forum that would assume jurisdiction over the claim is its centre of gravity. If this burden is successfully discharged, then the court should stay the proceedings, unless the claimant can show that sending the dispute to its centre of gravity would lead to a violation of his Art 6(1) rights in that forum (as defined in the expulsion cases). By the same token, in service-out cases, the English court should only give permission for the claim form to be served outside the jurisdiction if England is the dispute's proper forum or, failing that, if the claimant can demonstrate that he would suffer a breach of his Art 6(1) rights (as defined in expulsion cases) if the dispute were to be brought in its proper forum. In short, in both categories of case, if the action essentially belongs to another available foreign forum, the English court should only exercise jurisdiction over it if the United Kingdom would otherwise be in breach of its ECHR obligations, by virtue of the violation in the dispute's centre of gravity of the claimant's Art 6(1) rights (as defined in expulsion cases). It is submitted that reforming the law in this manner would help to respond to many

---

[14] See, eg, Briggs (n 8) para 4.39.
[15] European Convention for the Protection of Human Rights and Fundamental Freedoms, Rome, 4 November 1950, 213 UNTS 221.

of the existing shortcomings in the law's application, and enhance the doctrine's effectiveness as a device through which the question of where the case should be heard is answered.

In bringing the discussion in this book to a close, a more general (but salient) lesson can be deduced: the law's pursuit of incremental modification is relentless. The survey of the English *forum (non) conveniens* doctrine, particularly its historical development, illustrated the ebb and flow in the English courts' approach to discretionary (non-)exercise of jurisdiction in private-international-law disputes. A myriad of considerations was identified as having been influential in shaping (and reshaping) the law in this area for over a century. In this respect, perhaps the most powerful forces, which ultimately led to the articulation of the *Spiliada* doctrine, were the desire for the law to treat the parties' competing claims regarding where the case should be heard even-handedly, and for it to be congruous with the wider contemporaneous socio-economic developments. Unquestionably, the *Spiliada* doctrine represents much improvement on the law which it replaced. The temptation, therefore, might be to think that it need not be refined further. Nevertheless, *Spiliada*'s modern-day application has exposed certain significant shortcomings. What is more, the environment within which the test operates and the nature of international commercial litigation have evolved since 1986. In these circumstances, the question of whether the *Spiliada* test should undergo additional revision deserves greater attention. Indeed, if, as it seems plausible, *Spiliada*'s overall scope of application is restored to its pre-*Owusu* days at the end of the Brexit process, then it will become all the more apposite to engage with the question – as there could well be a corresponding rise in the instances where the doctrine's application proves problematic. It is hoped that this book's attempt at exploring the case for (and the possible means of) modifying the *forum (non) conveniens* doctrine in England, against the backdrop of its re-evaluation of the doctrine's historical development and current application, will provide the impetus for a wider debate regarding its future.

SELECTED BIBLIOGRAPHY

Books

Anton AE, *Private International Law* 1st edn (Edinburgh, W Green & Son Ltd, 1967).
Anton AE and Beaumont PR, *Private International Law* 2nd edn (Edinburgh, W Green & Son Ltd, 1990).
Baker JH, *An Introduction to English Legal History* 3rd edn (London, Butterworths, 1990).
Beaumont PR and McEleavy PE, *Anton's Private International Law* 3rd edn (Edinburgh, W Green, 2011).
Bell AS, *Forum Shopping and Venue in Transnational Litigation* (Oxford, Oxford University Press, 2002).
Brand RA and Jablonski SR, *Forum Non Conveniens: History, Global Practice, and Future Under the Hague Convention on Choice of Court Agreements* (New York, Oxford University Press, 2007).
Briggs A, *Private International Law in English Courts* (Oxford, Oxford University Press, 2014).
——, *Civil Jurisdiction and Judgments* 6th edn (Abingdon, Informa Law from Routledge, 2015).
Briggs A and P Rees, *Norton Rose on Civil Jurisdiction and Judgments* 1st edn (London, LLP, 1993).
——, *Civil Jurisdiction and Judgments* 4th edn (London, Informa Law, 2005).
——, *Civil Jurisdiction and Judgments* 5th edn (London, Informa Law, 2009).
Cheshire GC, *Private International Law* 2nd edn (Oxford, Clarendon Press, 1938).
——, *Private International Law* 5th edn (Oxford, Clarendon Press, 1957).
Cheshire GC and North PM, *Cheshire's Private International Law* 8th edn (London, Butterworths, 1970).
Collins L, *et al*, *Dicey & Morris on the Conflict of Laws* 12th edn (London, Sweet & Maxwell, 1993).
——, *Dicey & Morris on the Conflict of Laws* 13th edn (London, Sweet & Maxwell, 2000).
——, *Dicey, Morris & Collins on the Conflict of Laws* 14th edn (London, Sweet & Maxwell, 2006).
——, *Dicey, Morris & Collins on the Conflict of Laws* 15th edn (London, Sweet & Maxwell, 2012).
Dicey AV, *Conflict of Laws* 1st edn (London, Stevens & Sons, 1896).
——, *Conflict of Laws* 2nd edn (London, Stevens & Sons, 1908).
Dicey AV and Keith AB, *Conflict of Laws* 3rd edn (London, Stevens & Sons, 1922).
Eden RH, *A Treaties on the Law of Injunctions* (London, J Butterworth and J Cooke, 1821).
Fawcett JJ, *Declining Jurisdiction in Private International Law* (Oxford, Clarendon Press, 1995).
Gibb AD, *The International Law of Jurisdiction in England and Scotland* (Edinburgh, William Hodge & Co, 1926).
Hill J, *The Law Relating to International Commercial Disputes* 1st edn (London, Lloyd's of London Press, 1994).
Hill J and Chong A, *International Commercial Disputes: Commercial Conflict of Laws in English Courts* 4th edn (Oxford, Hart Publishing, 2010).
Kaye P, *Civil Jurisdiction and Enforcement of Foreign Judgments* (Oxford, Professional Books Limited, 1987).
Kerr WW, *A Treaties on the Law and Practice of Injunctions* 2nd edn (London, William Maxwell & Son, 1878).
Morris JHC, *Cases on Private International Law* 1st edn (Oxford, Clarendon Press, 1939).
Morris JHC, *et al*, *Dicey's Conflict of Laws* 6th edn (London, Stevens & Sons Ltd, 1949).
——, *Dicey's Conflict of Laws* 7th edn (London, Stevens & Sons Ltd, 1958).

——, *Dicey and Morris on the Conflict of Laws* 8th edn (London, Stevens & Sons Ltd, 1967).
North PM, *Cheshire's Private International Law* 9th edn (London, Butterworths, 1974).
——, *Cheshire and North's Private International Law* 10th edn (London, Butterworths, 1979).
North PM and Fawcett JJ, *Cheshire & North's Private International Law* 11th edn (London, Butterworths, 1987).
——, *Cheshire and North's Private International Law* 12th edn (London, Butterworths, 1992).
——, *Cheshire and North's Private International Law* 13th edn (London, Butterworths, 1999).
O'Malley S and A Layton, *European Civil Practice* 1st edn (London, Sweet & Maxwell, 1989).
Torremans P, *et al*, *Cheshire, North & Fawcett's Private International Law* 15th edn (Oxford, Oxford University Press, 2017).
Weinreb LL, *Legal Reason: The Use of Analogy in Legal Argument* (New York, Cambridge University Press, 2005).

Articles, Chapters and Casenotes

Arzandeh A, 'Reconsidering the Australian *Forum (Non) Conveniens* Doctrine' (2016) 65 *International & Comparative Law Quarterly* 475.
——, 'The Origins of the Scottish *Forum Non Conveniens* Doctrine' (2017) 13 *Journal of Private International Law* 130.
Blackburn E, 'Lis Alibi Pendens and Forum Non Conveniens in Collision Actions After the Civil Jurisdiction and Judgments Act 1982' [1988] *Lloyd's Maritime and Commercial Law Quarterly* 91.
Blair P, 'The Doctrine of Forum Non Conveniens in Anglo-American Law' (1929) 29 *Columbia Law Review* 1.
Brereton P, '*Forum Non Conveniens* in Australia: A Case Note on *Voth v Manildra Flour Mills*' (1991) 40 *International & Comparative Law Quarterly* 895.
Briggs A, 'No Interference with Foreign Court' (1982) 31 *International & Comparative Law Quarterly* 189.
——, 'Forum Non Conveniens – Now We Are Ten?' (1983) 3 *Legal Studies* 74.
——, 'The Staying of Actions on the Ground of "Forum Non Conveniens" in England Today' [1984] *Lloyd's Maritime and Commercial Law Quarterly* 227.
——, 'Forum Non Conveniens – The Last Word? (*Spiliada Maritime Corporation v Cansulex Ltd*)' [1987] *Lloyd's Maritime and Commercial Law Quarterly* 1.
——, 'Wider Still and Wider: The Bounds of Australian Exorbitant Jurisdiction' [1989] *Lloyd's Maritime and Commercial Law Quarterly* 216.
——, 'Spiliada and the Brussels Convention' [1991] *Lloyd's Maritime and Commercial Law Quarterly* 10.
——, 'Forum Non Conveniens and the Brussels Convention Again' (1991) 107 *Law Quarterly Review* 180.
——, 'Jurisdictional Clauses and Judicial Attitudes' (1993) 109 *Law Quarterly Review* 382.
——, 'Forum Non Conveniens and Unavailable Courts' (1996) 67 *British Yearbook of International Law* 587.
——, '*Forum Non Conveniens* and the Cost of Litigation' (1997) 68 *British Yearbook of International Law* 357.
——, 'The Availability of the Natural Forum and the Definition of the Issue' (1999) 70 *British Yearbook of International Law* 319.
——, 'The Death of Harrods: Forum Non Conveniens and the European Court' (2005) 121 *Law Quarterly Review* 535.
——, 'Russian Oligarchs and the Conflict of Laws' (2008) 79 *British Yearbook of International Law* 543.
——, '*Forum Non Satis*: Finding Fault with a Foreign Court' (2009) 80 *British Yearbook of International Law* 575.
——, 'Forum Non Satis: *Spiliada* and an Inconvenient Truth' [2011] *Lloyd's Maritime and Commercial Law Quarterly* 329.

Carter PB, 'Staying of Actions and the Doctrine of Forum Non Conveniens' (1972–1973) 46 *British Yearbook of International Law* 428.

——, 'Jurisdiction: The Propriety of an English Forum' (1978) 49 *British Yearbook of International Law* 291.

Collier JG, 'Staying of Actions and Forum Non Conveniens. English Law Goes Scotch' (1987) 46 *Cambridge Law Journal* 33.

Collins L, 'The High Court of Australia and Forum Conveniens: A Further Comment' (1989) 105 *Law Quarterly Review* 364.

——, 'Forum Non Conveniens and the Brussels Convention' (1990) 106 *Law Quarterly Review* 535.

——, 'The High Court of Australia and *Forum Conveniens*: The Last Word?' (1991) 107 *Law Quarterly Review* 182.

Dickinson A, 'Keeping Up Appearances: The Development of Adjudicatory Jurisdiction in the English Courts' (2016) 86 *British Yearbook of International Law* 6.

Fawcett JJ, 'Lis Alibi Pendens and the Discretion to Stay' (1984) 47 *Modern Law Review* 481.

——, 'The Impact of Article 6(1) of the ECHR on Private International Law' (2007) 56 *International & Comparative Law Quarterly* 1.

Fentiman R, 'Civil Jurisdiction and Third States: *Owusu* and After' (2006) 43 *Common Market Law Review* 705.

Finn P, 'Common Law Divergences' (2013) 37 *Melbourne University Law Review* 511.

Garnett R, 'Stay of Proceedings in Australia: A "Clearly Inappropriate" Test?' (1999) 23 *Melbourne University Law Review* 30.

Harris J, 'Stay of Proceedings and the Brussels Convention' (2005) 54 *International & Comparative Law Quarterly* 933.

Hemsworth M, 'Forum Non Conveniens, Jurisdiction and Civil Disputes within the UK' (2016) 35 *Civil Justice Quarterly* 299.

Hill J, 'Jurisdiction in Civil and Commercial Matters: Is There a Third Way?' (2001) *Current Legal Problems* 439.

Inglis BD, 'Forum Conveniens – Basis of Jurisdiction in the Commonwealth' (1964) 13 *American Journal of Comparative Law* 583.

——, 'Jurisdiction, the Doctrine of *Forum Conveniens*, and Choice of Law in Conflict of Laws' (1965) 81 *Law Quarterly Review* 380.

Kaye P, 'The EEC Judgments Convention and the Outer World: Goodbye to Forum Non Conveniens?' [1992] *Journal of Business Law* 47.

Kennett W, '*Forum Non Conveniens* in Europe' (2005) 54 *Cambridge Law Journal* 552.

Maclean A, 'Foreign Collisions and *Forum Conveniens*' (1973) 22 *International & Comparative Law Quarterly* 748.

McClean JD, 'Jurisdiction and Judicial Discretion' (1969) 18 *International & Comparative Law Quarterly* 931.

Merrett L, 'The Meaning of an "Available" Forum' (2004) *Cambridge Law Journal* 309.

——, 'Uncertainties in the First Limb of the *Spiliada* Test' (2005) 54 *International & Comparative Law Quarterly* 211.

Peel E, 'Forum Non Conveniens and the Impecunious Plaintiff – Legal Aid and Conditional Fees' (1997) 113 *Law Quarterly Review* 43.

——, 'Forum Non Conveniens and European Ideals' [2005] *Lloyd's Maritime and Commercial Law Quarterly* 363.

Pryles M, 'The Basis of Adjudicatory Competence in Private International Law' (1972) 21 *International & Comparative Law Quarterly* 61.

——, 'Liberalising the Rule on Staying Actions – Towards the Doctrine of Forum Non Conveniens' (1978) 52 *Australian Law Journal* 678.

——, 'Judicial Darkness on the Oceanic Sun' (1988) 62 *Australian Law Journal* 774.

——, 'Forum Non Conveniens – The Next Chapter' (1991) 65 *Australian Law Journal* 442.

Reynolds FMB, 'Forum Non Conveniens in Australia' (1989) 105 *Law Quarterly Review* 40.

Robertson DW, '*Forum Non Conveniens* in America and England: "A Rather Fantastic Fiction"' (1987) 103 *Law Quarterly Review* 398.

Rodger B, '*Forum Non Conveniens* Post-*Owusu*' (2006) 2 *Journal of Private International Law* 71.

Rudden B, 'Courts and Codes in England, France and Soviet Russia' (1973–1974) 48 *Tulane Law Review* 1010.

Schuz R, 'Controlling Forum-Shopping: The Impact of *MacShannon v. Rockware Glass Ltd*.' (1986) 35 *International & Comparative Law Quarterly* 374.

Slater AG, 'Forum Non Conveniens: A View From the Shop Floor' (1988) 104 *Law Quarterly Review* 554.

INDEX

www.ingramcontent.com/pod-product-compliance
Lightning Source LLC
Chambersburg PA
CBHW061312220326
41599CB00026B/4845